Highrise – Common Ground
Art and the Amsterdam Zuidas Area

Editor:
Jeroen Boomgaard

Contributors:
BAVO
Jeroen Boomgaard
Gerard Drosterij
Renée Kool
Stan Majoor
Chantal Mouffe
Orgacom/Quintus Masius
Roemer van Toorn
Paul Toornend/Jelle Post
Daniel van der Velden
Barbara Visser
Henk de Vroom
Joost Zonneveld

Valiz Publishers, Amsterdam
Research Group Art and Public Space /
Gerrit Rietveld Academie, Amsterdam

HIGHRISE

—

Jeroen Boomgaard (ed.)

COMMON GROUND

Art and the Amsterdam Zuidas Area

BAVO
Gerard Drosterij
Renée Kool
Stan Majoor
Chantal Mouffe
Orgacom/Quintus Masius
Roemer van Toorn
Paul Toornend/Jelle Post
Daniel van der Velden
Barbara Visser
Henk de Vroom
Joost Zonneveld

Highrise – Common Ground

Contents

Contents

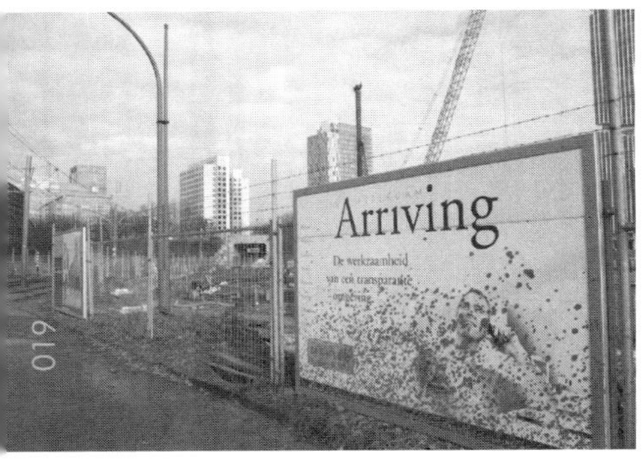
Arriving
De werkzaamheid
van een transparante
omgeving

Jeroen Boomgaard

Foreword

The construction of the Zuidas (South Axis) in Amsterdam has entered a crucial phase. The near future will make clear whether the area is genuinely likely to become a success and what it will look like. It will also become clear what role art is to play at the Zuidas. It is an appropriate moment, therefore, to take stock.

In this book, this stock taking takes the form of articles and art projects produced over the last four years, commissioned by the Research Group Art and Public Space of the Gerrit Rietveld Academie. This Research Group was set up in 2002 as a partnership between the Gerrit Rietveld Academie, the Sandberg Institute, the Universiteit van Amsterdam, the Virtual Museum Zuidas (VMZ) and the Foundation Art and Public Space (SKOR) with a mandate to provide critical reflection on the role of art in public space in general and at the Zuidas in particular. The Research Group has fulfilled this mandate by organizing symposia and expert meetings, lectures and publications and assigning research commissions to artists. The result of a portion of these activities is reflected in this volume (for a complete overview, see www.lkpr.nl).

A great many people have been involved in the activities of the Research Group. I would therefore like to thank, in addition to the insti-

Jeroen Boomgaard

tutions that make the Research Group possible and the writers/artists who have contributed to this book, the following people. The organization of the Research Group: Esther Deen, Alexandra Landré and Henk de Vroom. The advisory committee: Mariska van den Berg, Jelle Bouwhuis, Gijs Frieling, Anneloes van der Leun, Dees Linders, Siebe Thissen, Roemer van Toorn, Daniel van der Velden and Huib Haye van der Werf. The members of the Research Group: Lucy Cotter, Ellert Haijtema, Saskia Janssen, Wim Kok, Renée Kool, Sophie Krier, Frank Mandersloot, Sabine Mooibroek, Holger Nickisch, Rianne Petter, René Put, Bert Taken, Raoul Teulings and Willem van Weelden. And finally the makers of this book: Marieke van Giersbergen, Anette Tibud and Astrid Vorstermans.

The Research Group Art and Public Space pledges to continue critically and constructively monitoring the development of the Zuidas – including during this new, crucial phase.

Jeroen Boomgaard
Gerrit Rietveld Academie
Febuary 2008

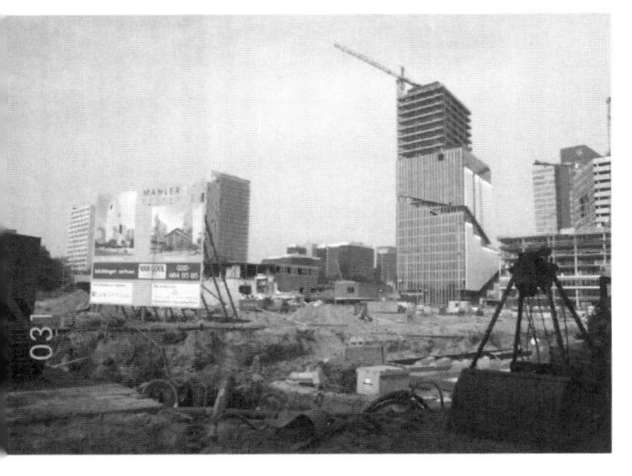
MAHLER

Jeroen Boomgaard

Highrise *and* Common Ground

The Zuidas is not alone. The relatively narrow strip of land south of Amsterdam intended to house a bustling urban centre by 2030 has numerous counterparts. Throughout Europe, conglomerations are being built that plainly express, by means of large-scale projects, an ambition to convert stagnation into movement and breathe new life into somnolent cities. It is no secret that this impulse is primarily economic. Properly channelled flows of capital will lead the right people to the desired location, but this influx of cash can only be initiated if the new domain exudes quality. This makes the design of the area a concern of the utmost importance. Experience has shown that a business district alone is not enough. Wealthy visitors/residents/entrepreneurs want more: they want high-quality entertainment and leisure facilities, and therefore culture is often high on the developers' agenda. What counts as culture in these cases is not always clear, but at the very least, a podium should be created where flexible expats, captains of industry and members of the creative class can meet unhindered, in order that the machinery of growth may spin even faster.

Jeroen Boomgaard

The Zuidas will be unique – that is what the plans repeatedly emphasize. The exceptional nature of the project, however, also serves to proclaim an exceptional situation, a state of emergency in which normal procedures and decision-making processes are replaced by opaque and fragile coalitions of government and market parties. And as with other states of emergency, its proclamation is accompanied by a certain level of aggression. Anyone who doubts its necessity doesn't get it; anyone who resists it has missed the boat forever. Yet this rhetoric of exception is in danger of being defeated by a lack of support. The stakes are too great, the parties they represent too small. The sky-high ambitions are unstable; they are not securely grounded.[1]

Exception is often a condition for creating good art. Works of art are not the product of the time-consuming consultation structures that typify democracy, but of the determined effort of the passionate loner. Suspending the rules, as is being done at the Zuidas, therefore seems the ideal condition for creating an environment in which the visual arts can fully function. The appointment of a separate visual art supervisor and the establishment of the Virtual Museum Zuidas showed that everyone was cognizant of the opportunities presented here. The ambitions that had developed in terms of art in the last several years were in fact almost as high as the ambitions for the area as a whole, but the implementation of the projects has run into frequent obstacles.[2] This troublesome state of affairs, incidentally, is not limited to art. It is a logical consequence of the mistrust that marks all negotiations. The huge investments on the one hand and the vagueness of the procedure to be followed, the lack of clear rules, on the other has resulted in stagnations that are at odds with the decisiveness suggested by the bottom-up ideology of the development of areas like the Zuidas. Art that is supposed to participate in the construction of the city cannot avoid the squabbles associated with the construction of exceptional projects. For art, however, this mistrust is particularly detrimental. The return on investment that exceptional art can deliver cannot be calculated. Investing in it cannot, therefore, be the subject of a negotiations process; it must be based on the willingness to provide room for the unexpected and the unknown. To achieve interesting art in the area, it is necessary to make an exception to the exception. Only when the role of art in the public domain of the Zuidas is defined in such a way that its unique character is clear and accepted by all parties can the sky-high ambition that pervades the plans be made reality.

Jeroen Boomgaard

Domain

On the Mahlerplein at the Zuidas, at one of the entrances to the main offices of ABN-Amro, sits a bronze puppy made by Tom Claassen. At first glance it is unclear what it is doing there. In so carefully designed an area, this statue must surely be part of a well-considered plan. The Virtual Museum Zuidas, however, has had no hand in it. The statue is a literal and figurative watchdog for the bank. It signals that this portion of the plaza is private property and that the bank decides what to do with it. And in this the puppy demonstrates precisely the specific character of public space at the Zuidas.

The privatization of public space seems an irreversible process. And the public space of the Zuidas, where design as well as management and security must meet the demands of investors, can surely not escape this trend.[3] It remains to be seen, however, what consequences this privatization has for public space and for the role that works of art play in it. The bronze watchdog has been erected as proof of the occupation of a place by a private enterprise, but in this the artwork is no different from much of the art erected by the government in public space. The diverse objects of stone or metal that have popped up across the Netherlands in the past few decades, at spots that apparently needed emphasis or beautification for one reason or another, are more than innocent or superfluous decoration. The placement of a work of art 'defines' a spot that was hitherto nondescript, an undefined area, which only then becomes genuinely 'public'. In this the word 'public' implies the opposite of what it suggests. An undefined, openly accessible place, when explicitly labelled public domain, is taken out of its undefined state and absorbed within the domain of authority. The predominant characteristic of this strategy is, in the words of Michel de Certeau, a victory of place over time. An area is withdrawn from a process of chance and occupied forever.[4] The artwork ultimately serves as the flag that signals this occupation, and that artwork is there to stay.

The master plan drawn up by the initial supervisor, Pi de Bruijn, was predicated on an urban public space in which the streets and plazas between the iconic buildings would form an empty stage for the convergence of capital and creativity. The undefined quality of the public domain on this site demonstrates an optimism about the safe and monocultural meeting zone that would be created. Experience has shown, however, that this open space is primarily a meeting place for conflicting interests. What has been built up to now mainly represents the private interest. In addition to the bank's puppy logo, a museum display of

Jeroen Boomgaard

sculptures from the collections of the corporations located in the area has been set up. By contrast, the creation of works that are supposed to represent an indescribable public interest and that should underscore the exceptional character of the area through their exceptional qualities has repeatedly run into insurmountable obstacles. The designs commissioned by the Virtual Museum Zuidas for the Gershwinplein, for example, have been rejected time and time again because the various participating parties feel that the work should satisfy the tastes of the group each represents. Art, therefore, is not only demonstrating the ongoing and acute privatization of the public space by its presence, but also, by its absence, the lack of a guiding government and therefore of a public domain, that is to say a place established by the government, claimed in the name of the public interest. What seems to be emerging is an area in which only the emptiness of corporate culture reigns and in which art that seeks to develop the specific quality of the place is actually not welcome.[5]

Identity

The fragmentation of interests the Zuidas is in danger of exuding demands a solution, because even administrators and investors know that only an area that manages to suggest more than business and capital is genuinely viable. The appointment of a new supervisor, in the person of Belgian architect bOb Van Reeth, can thus be seen as an attempt to break the impasse. Van Reeth has chosen a radically different approach. He is trying to replace the fragmentary character of the place with a coherent image with a clear identity. The emphasis on design must be jettisoned in favour of sustainability, and the disparate public space must be fused together into a simple and clear concept that visually connects to Amsterdam's historic city centre. His objective is to create a genuine public space, where a democratic exchange of ideas can take place.[6]

However well-intentioned this principle of Van Reeth's may be, it does raise certain objections. He seems to forget that the public space he is creating is to be commissioned by the recently established NV Zuidas and that its democratic quotient will probably still be a reflection of how the project's development has unfolded. The image of coherence that Van Reeth wants to apply to the public domain thus seems more intended to get

Jeroen Boomgaard

developers and investors on the same page so that the process can be implemented faster. The openness and the room to experiment that should be the hallmarks of a free exchange of ideas seems to be more advised against than encouraged. One indication of this is Van Reeth's rejection of Jennifer Tee's most recent design for an artwork for the Gershwinplein. This rejection is based on the fact that Tee's plan is supposedly too self-contained and would not succeed in ensuring the desired unity in the area. Van Reeth seems to have a predilection for a cohesive public space to which an artwork can ultimately be added as a finishing touch. In the process, however, he is repeating on a large scale what ABN-Amro has done on a small scale. The identity that Van Reeth wants to create is a corporate identity, and it is more about recognizability than confrontation.

Van Reeth is not alone in his quest for a clear identity. The disintegration of the consensus society of the Netherlands is leading to a nostalgic longing for unity and a sense of belonging, and a great deal of policy is aimed at reinforcing, if not creating, specific identities. Much is now expected of art in this production of identity.[7] This represents a radical shift in the role of art in public space. As outlined above, art used to demarcate a place in the public domain, usually in the name of an institution of authority that sought to establish itself there. Within this framework, the artwork, depending on the place and on the ideology that was being represented, could be an example of purely individual expression or a fully adapted complement to the architecture, as well as everything in between these two extremes, but the point was always the effect of the work on the surrounding area. If a target audience was mentioned, it was not described in detail and the work usually served mankind in general.[8] Now, however, a work of art in public is expected to serve a particular group, to represent a certain interest. The work of art can no longer focus exclusively on the place; it must also relate to the identity or the outlook of the people who live or work there. This shifts preferences toward art that creates recognizability and affirmation, or that allows for an active, or interactive, form of appropriation. The void left behind by the gradual retrenchment of the government is being filled, at the instigation of this same government, with strategies of identification and parochialization. In other words, artists are expected to do more to satisfy the tastes of a particular target audience, not just to serve the interests of this group, but primarily to create a cohesive identity associated with a particular domain.[9] The new visual quality plan being developed for the Zuidas is in fact not so much aimed at countering the fragmentation of public space under the influence of commer-

Jeroen Boomgaard

cial interests as it is designed to create an identity associated with space that serves, a priori, as a home for a fairly clearly identified group of future residents.

On its Own

The central question in this book is what position art can adopt under such conditions. Highly divergent angles are examined, but no unequivocal answer is provided. Is it possible, for instance, to have a work of art play an 'agonistic' role in an area like the Zuidas, have it be a disruptive factor that sharply points out the hypocritical and concealing nature of its image of unity and consensus and that stimulates dissent in order to reveal the radical oppositions among different segments of the population? Or should the work of art strenuously avoid such politicization of the public domain and instead, through the opportunity for personal experience, open up a genuinely public area?[10] The answer must lie somewhere between the sharply defined interest of the group and the tolerance inherent in the public interest, between the unbridgeable difference and the fragile tolerance of the other.

To find this answer, not only does this book examine various theoretical positions, but also explores the area culturally through the eye of the artist/designer. The identity of the Zuidas, after all, is defined not just by its buildings and public space, but by the images and the stories that are associated with the place. From the beginning, the area has been defined by idealized visions and words of fantasy that attempt to conjure up a future that contrasts sharply with the somewhat colourless reality attached to the place at the moment. The initial plans for the area, for instance, were accompanied by a rhetoric that can be deemed characteristic of the way in which project developers use branding today to sell a project to those directly involved. The future was painted in comparisons that are almost comical: the Zuidas was supposed to become something akin to the Rive Gauche in Paris, and the Parnassusweg (the street that transects the Zuidas area) would show similarities to the Ramblas in Barcelona.[11]

We can, of course, puncture this imagined future based on an idealized past and reveal it as the collection of slogans it really is. But perhaps we could also take these literally, implement them in a way that was probably not intended. If the Zuidas starts to display the rather dark side of Barcelona's cultural thoroughfare, and if the area starts to resemble the neighbourhood in which the Situationists wandered without ever wanting to do any work, a new piece of city will really have been created. To achieve this, however, the art will have to have an effect, one that is the reverse of the effect on deprived urban areas that is

Jeroen Boomgaard

attributed to it. This book provides an advance preview of this de-gentrification by criss-crossing the area with images, cultural interventions, that reveal an entirely different aspect. The projects by Barbara Visser, Orgacom, Logoparc, Paul Toornend/Jelle Post and Renée Kool provide the images that disrupt the developers' dreams. In the process, this book offers not only an analysis of the possibilities and impossibilities for art at the Zuidas, but also a concrete preview of the inappropriate and maladjusted things the area needs in order to wake up.

If we subscribe to Jacques Rancière's philosophy that art is politics in that it makes visible things that remain out of sight within the allocation of space,[12] then art at the Zuidas can thwart the major interests of the small groups that are in charge by showing the individual dream that does not aim to serve any interest at all. Jennifer Tee's design for the Gershwinplein is entitled *Oeverloos Verlangen*, 'boundless desire'. This work, which as previously noted has come under fire in recent planning, fits its setting because it underscores its ostentatious ambitions and at the same time seems to create the meeting place that plays such a significant role in considerations of public space at the Zuidas. But the work goes further: the desire it attests to is boundless. And it is precisely through this unattainability that it creates the utopian dimension the Zuidas so

badly lacks. Until now, everything in the area
has been attuned to use, adapted to the interests of particular parties; there is no room for
the disruptive element, the individual factor.
The autonomy that underpins Tee's customized
design, however, creates an individualizing
moment; it represents an interest that can
never be served, an identity that wants to
remain undefined, and it claims an area
without boundaries. It is works like this that
can lend the Zuidas a dose of reality, make it
real by making the public interest of individual
presence visible. And that is exactly the down-
grading that the area needs in order to achieve
genuine quality.

Jennifer Tee, in collaboration with Richard Niessen and
Joost Vermeulen, *Oeverloos verlangen* 2007, design
Gershwinplein (montage)

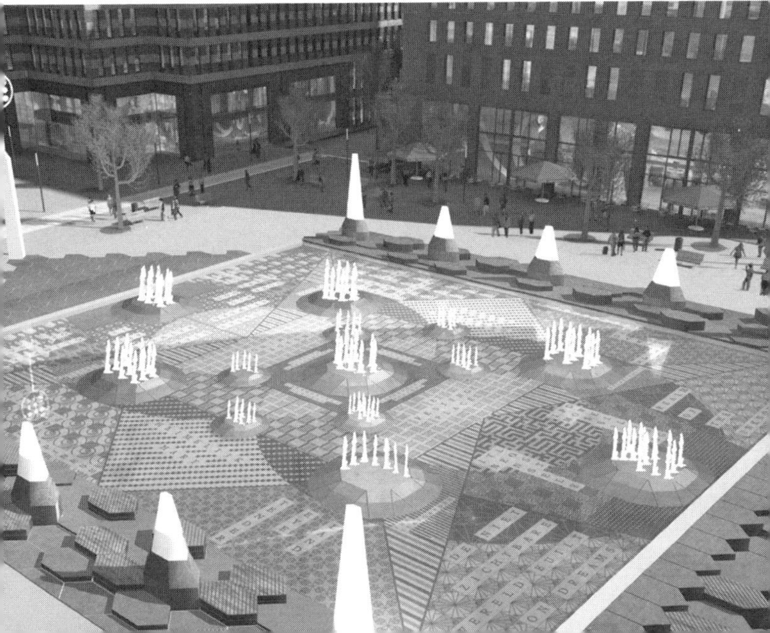

Jeroen Boomgaard

Notes
1. The specific character of this kind of project is very
clearly explicated in E. Swyngedouw, 'A New Urbanity?
The ambiguous politics of large-scale urban development
projects in European cities', in Willem Salet and Stan
Majoor (eds.), *Amsterdam Zuidas. European Space*
(Rotterdam: 010 Publishers, 2005), pp. 61-79. The
consequences of this state of affairs for the Zuidas are
further examined in the present volume in the contributions by Joost Zonneveld, Stan Majoor and BAVO.
2. For the ambitions of the Virtual Museum Zuidas and its
setbacks, see the article by Henk de Vroom in this volume.
3. This problem has been thoroughly analyzed from
various viewpoints over the last several years. See for
example Maarten Hajer and Arnold Reijndorp, *In Search
of New Public Domain* (Rotterdam: NAi Publishers, 2001);
Lieven de Cauter, *The Capsular Civilization* (Rotterdam:
NAi Publishers, 2005); René Boomkens, *Een drempelwereld. Moderne ervaring en stedelijke openbaarheid*
(Rotterdam: NAi Publishers, 1998).
4. Michel de Certeau, *The Practice of Everyday Life* (Los
Angeles/Berkeley/London: University of California Press,
1984), pp. 34-37. De Certeau shows that authority not
only withdraws a place from the process of change in
order to appropriate it forever, but that a central spot is
occupied as well, in panoptic fashion, to keep an eye on
the surroundings, while a specific form of knowledge
about the place is also applied, one not accessible to
others. All of these elements play a role in the placement
of a work of art on a site that thereby falls entirely, as
public space, under the purview of authority. This also
explains why in some instances the placement of a work of
art elicits so much aggression among area residents, who
recognize that the arrival of the artwork means something

is being taken from them.

5. For a further elaboration of this viewpoint, see the articles in this volume by Daniel van der Velden and by Roemer van Toorn, on Paul Toornend and Jelle Post's *Untitled_Spaces*.

6. Marina de Vries, '5 vragen aan bOb Van Reeth', *Krant no. 3* (September 2007), published by the Virtual Museum Zuidas.

7. This obsession with identity is also demonstrated by the prevailing predilection for community art among all sorts of national and local administrators. It is the hallmark of a retrenching government that no longer claims an area as public space, but that still wants to keep social processes under control and wants to suggest consensus by means of temporary artworks and events. On this see also J. Boomgaard, *Radical Autonomy*, in this volume.

8. A good example of this is the work of the Arnhem School in the 1970s. The designs for public space of this movement were no longer about individual expression, but about a form of direction or serviceability to the spectator who was posited in the most general of terms. On this, see Camiel van Winkel, *Moderne leegte. Over kunst en openbaarheid* (Nijmegen: SUN, 1999).

9. There was a prelude to this very popular form of community art in the 1970s, when artists' collectives, working with local residents, decorated the crumbling walls of deprived neighbourhoods with cheerful and accessible murals. A comparison between the current boom in community projects that serve to visually appropriate a domain and this prelude has yet to be written, but it is clear that in the 1970s, these collabora-tive projects applied a much more generalized view of humanity than today's projects aimed at focus groups. In *One Place after Another* (Cambridge (Mass.)/London:

Jeroen Boomgaard

The MIT Press, 2002) Miwon Kwon provides an excellent analysis of the shift from place to discourse undergone by art in the public domain. She pays insufficient attention, however, to the fusion of domain and target audience.
10. On these positions, see the articles by Chantal Mouffe and Gerard Drosterij in this volume.
11. Willem Salet, 'The Creation of European Space. An Interview with Klaas de Boer and Pi de Bruijn', in: Salet and Majoor (eds.), op. cit. pp. 42-60 (see note 1).
12. 'Politics is the conflict about which things belong in its space and which do not, which subjects take part in it and which do not. Art can only be called political when the space and time it subdivides and the forms it selects to occupy this space and time, overlaps the division of space and time, of subjects and objects, of the private and the public, of possibilities and impossibilities through which the political community defines itself.' Jacques Rancière, 'Die Politik der Kunst und ihre Paradoxien', in: Jacques Rancière, *Die Aufteilung des Sinnlichen*, (Berlin: b-books Verlag, 2006), p. 77.

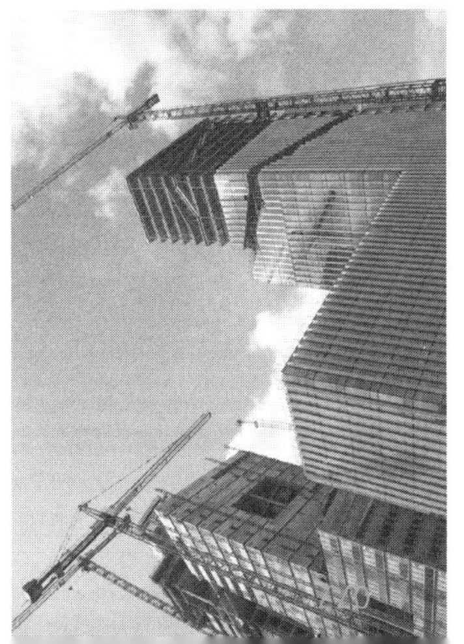

Barbara Visser

1

Hiding behind the Laptop

Despite its master plan, which suggests a pleasant coherence in the public space, the scale and the fragmentation of the Zuidas elicits agoraphobia.

Its name is actually Zuidas, without the 'the', but that is literally dumb. In five years, when we're used to it, no one will hear that it's missing an article. But it will have to be said without it for quite a long time first.

Don't panic. Take a deep breath. Concentrate on one element that mirrors the whole. There are mirrors aplenty. Surely fractal theory should be applicable here somewhere?

If you have to focus on one thing, why not ING House, the office building meant to be futuristic and saddled with numerous pejorative nicknames, yet considered fan-tas-tic by everybody?

The edifice has its own website, on which one can take a virtual tour. The descriptions of the building's architecture, furnishings and panoramic views evoke the atmosphere of the hypermodern office building Monsieur Hulot visits in the film *Playtime*,[1] leaving him completely bewildered. He repeatedly comes in con-

Barbara Visser

flict with the latest technological gadgets that pop up unexpectedly all over the building. Modernity presses in upon him to such an extent that he has great difficulty figuring out how to respond. Like the building, he begins to behave more and more strangely.

The other visitors in the film, on the contrary, seem to take on their role as extras effortlessly, allowing the star quality of the building to shine through.

030

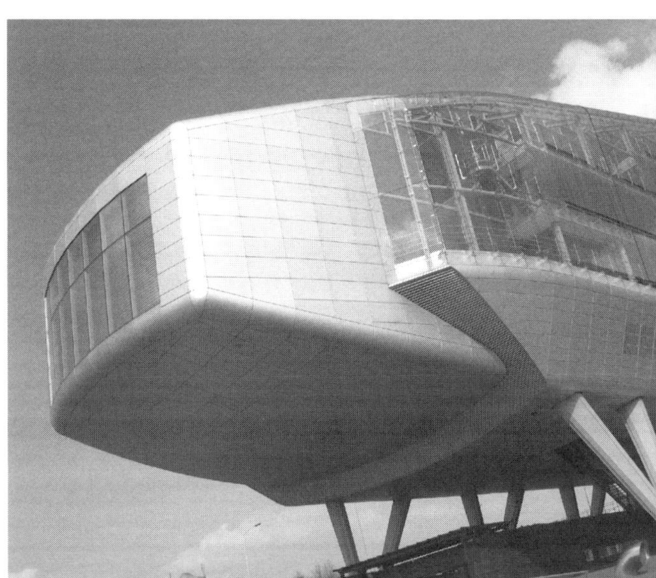

The website of ING House notes:

The Boardroom features a floor partly made of glass, which merges with a curved, angled glass wall. Wide slats serve as sunscreens. From here one looks out toward the west over the Nieuwe Meer and one has a view of a large section of the ring motorway. Schiphol Airport lies in the distance. The size of the conference table is adjustable.

ING House clearly differs from the office building in Tati's film in one respect: whereas Tati reduced the plant kingdom to one chrysanthemum on a lady's hat, in the ING spaceship plants are the X Factor. They symbolize quality, sustainability and growth, and will silence any criticism:

In the north loggia, a jungle atmosphere predominates. The garden links the east and west sections of this level. The inner gardens are considered the visual highlights of the building.
From this level, one has a view of the large outer patio, which begins on the 8th floor, in which eight Scots pines grow among royal ferns and heath berries.
Events such as retirement parties and anniversary receptions are held in the palm greenhouse, among the eight tall Livingstone palms planted in moveable pots. Their special design allows these to serve as tables as well. Not your run-of-the-mill reception room.

Barbara Visser

In reality, the building has been placed on a Teletubbie hill.

But the employees love working there, as evidenced by the quotes from the members of staff, from the highest to the lowest level, who were interviewed. Happy workers – it's finally been achieved. A member of the board of directors notes on the website:

There is so much more quality here than in the old building. I find it a fantastic work environment – really optimal, with an exceptional amount of room for interaction.
I use the glass staircases that link the 8th, 9th and 10th floors a lot – not just because of the short lines of communication, but to get some extra exercise as well.

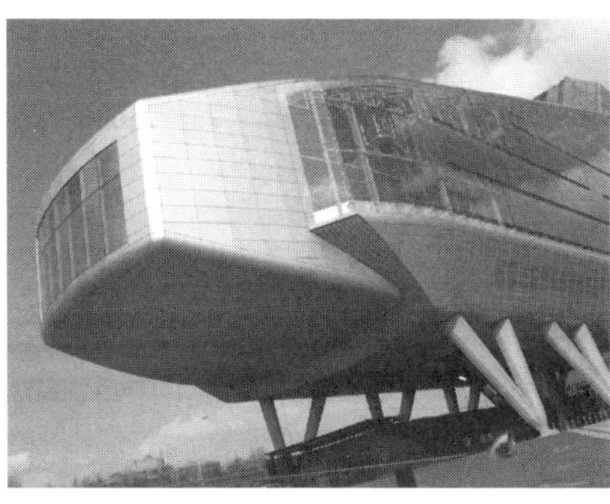

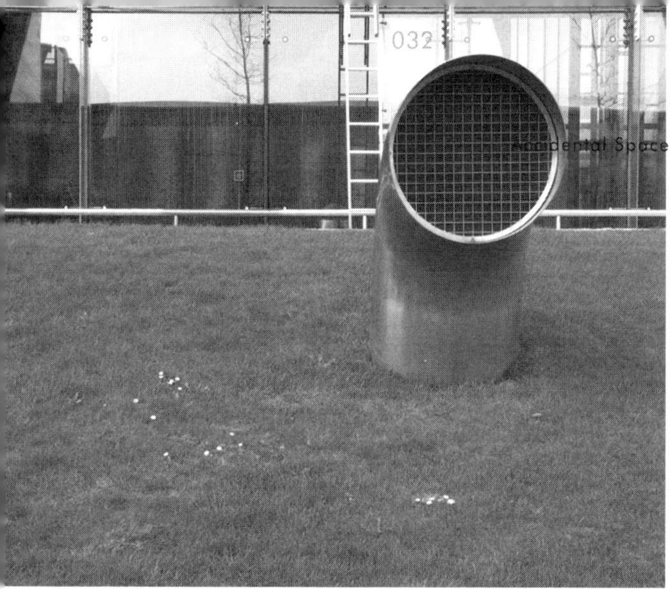

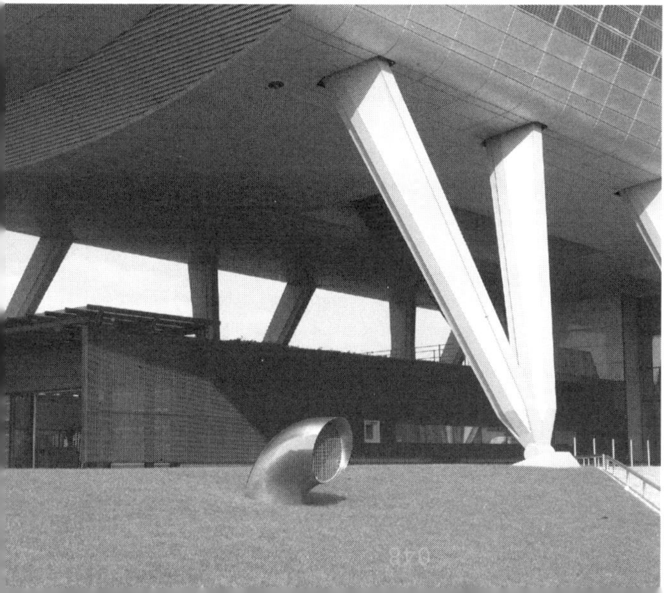

032

Accidental Space

Barbara Visser

2
Getting Out There

It is the 23rd of March and that's what the world outside looks like, too. I can't come up with any more good reasons to avoid the Zuidas. At the WTC-plein you're greeted by a forest of prescriptive and proscriptive signs. I'll quote one off the top of my head:

Those who do not leave their bikes in the permanently overcrowded bike rack will not be immediately shot, but the bikes go straight to the pound in Halfweg. NB: locks are not compensated for.

People in suits eat their ciabatta mozzarella sandwiches in the glaring sun, sitting on the broad rim of a plant container in which frail new saplings have been planted. Their name tags are wider than their trunks.

A photo shoot is going on in the gleaming sandwich shop on the ground floor. A girl holding an unused reflector screen is flirting with an older member of the crew. The screen twists and turns with her out of embarrassment. Here too, filming is waiting with glamour. The scene in question is about a guy in a sand-coloured suit eating a mozzarella sandwich. You can tell he's in the film from his suit: real people virtually never wear sand-coloured suits.

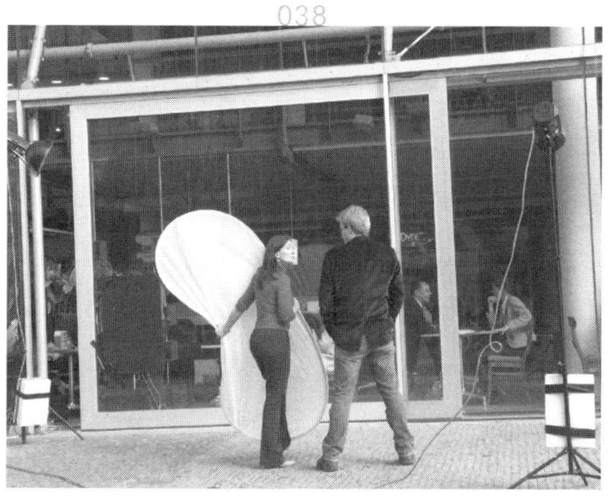

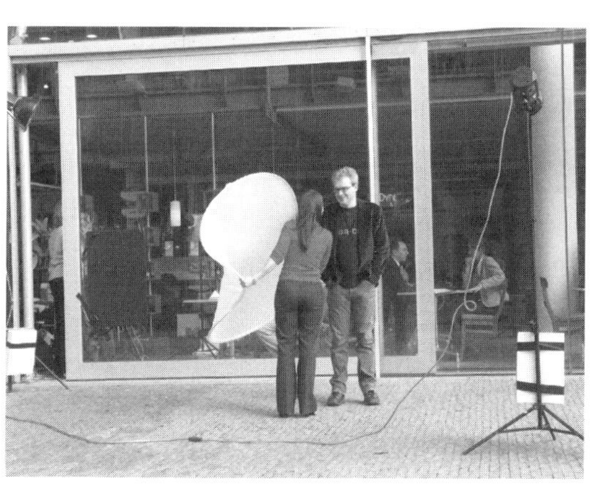

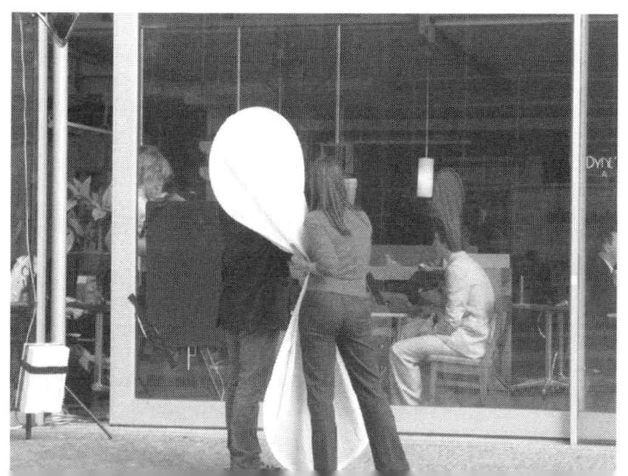

Barbara Visser

2.1
The Project Bureau

The project bureau stands out from the rest of the WTC design by its fragments of text on glass doors. Inside, three wall-sized images of the area are hung. On the left, a floor-to-ceiling aerial photograph, next to it an illustrated map, and on the wall to its right a schematic projection of Zuidas.

The human interfaces exchange lunch ideas over the office partition. On a pillar in the room are hung transparent holders containing glossy A4 brochures of the projects at the Zuidas: Gershwin, Vivaldi, Mahler. In the brochure, a just-completed building is still a utopian airbrush projection. It features a gleaming façade in which the cracks of terror are part of the design. Post-retro-modern seems the most applicable label. The brochure boasts about the fact that the building was erected in a little over a month using a sliding-form construction. This is achieved by pouring concrete 24 hours a day, from the bottom of the foundation to the current height of 95 metres: 3.166667 metres per day. It doesn't seem like much, but it is.

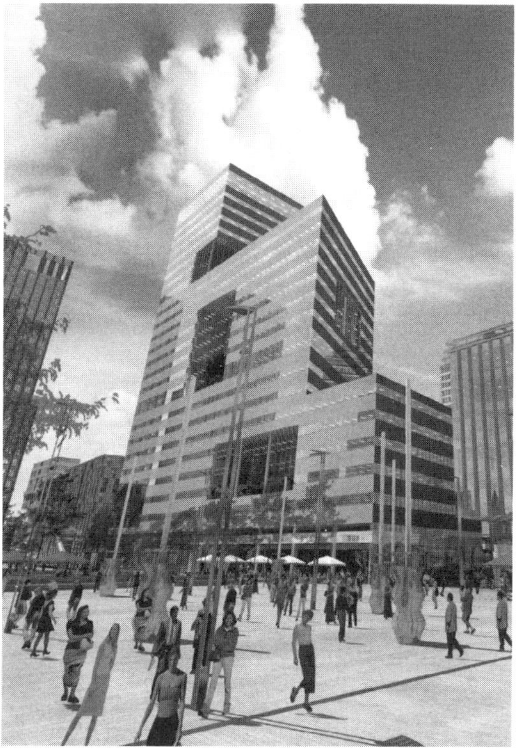

Hiding behind the Laptop

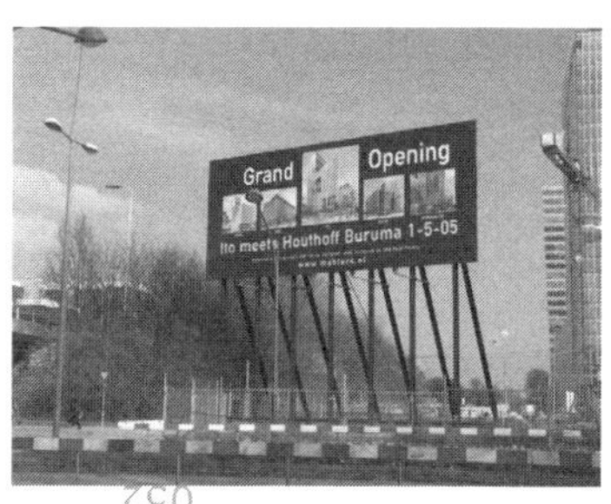

Barbara Visser

A large maquette takes up half of the floor space in the room. A change in scale is always welcome, especially if it makes you grow.

From this perspective, thinking about the rise of a future city centre (but not calling it that) is comfortable. The artist can only look sceptically on the haphazard way progress is being shaped here, but cynicism is not constructive in the light of progress.

Properly considered, the only function of an artificial structure is that it provides a framework for the element of chance. And the artist is there to intercept it. Without the use of staged chance – also known as added value – there remains an autistic 1:1 maquette in which only the wads of chewing gum on the street still represent chance. The artist races around the Zuidas, armed with a butterfly net, in search of possibilities.

Can we already say 'races around Zuidas', or do we still need the 'the'?

Let's take a quick photo in the foyer of the WTC. No security guards in sight – until you take a photo, of course. They suddenly appear out of nowhere, from every direction. Quick, put on the mask of the innocent tourist and, as a white woman, you're immediately cleared of suspicion.

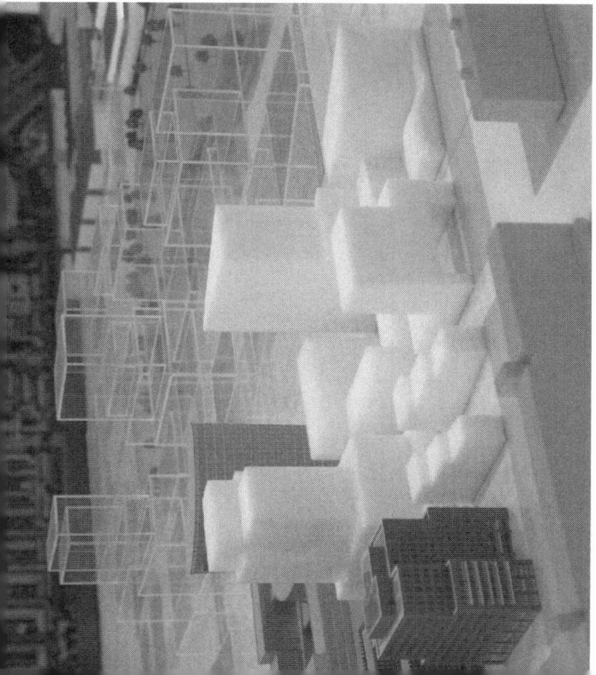

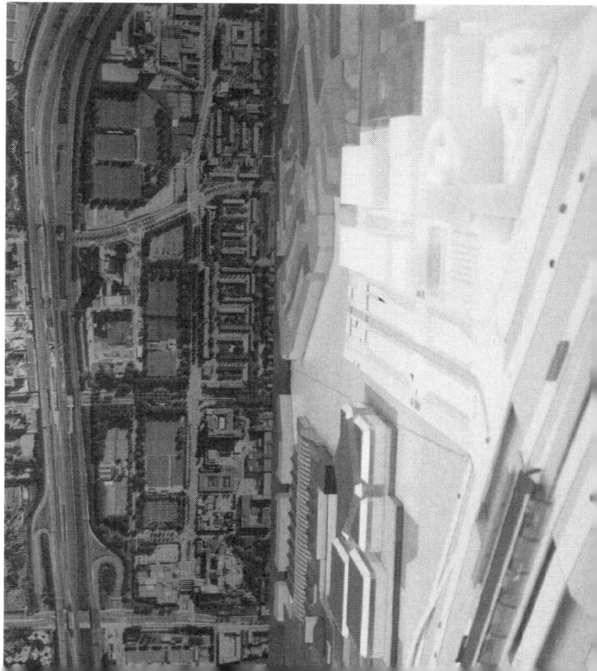

Barbara Visser

2.2
Wandering

What strikes you as you cycle across Zuidas is the ear-splitting noise. It's terrible. Unbearable. The construction, the motorway, the trains, the planes, the wind. Very few things can survive here. The word pandemonium spontaneously comes to mind, something it never does. The fact that the word was first used in John Milton's *Paradise Lost* doesn't help matters very much.

The optimist and the project developer think (other than about money, money and more money) that the building noises will eventually subside. And then? Then you'll hear Vivaldi, or Mahler's Fourth – 'Mahler-4', in Zuidas parlance.

Man may have perfected his habitat since the Stone Age, but according to science, he still operates, psychologically, at a rudimentary level.

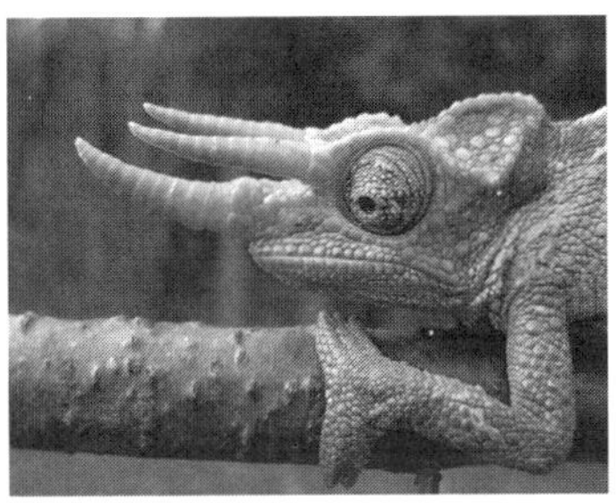

Imagine a pair of Jacksonii chameleons – an animal that looks like a prehistoric caricature of itself – placed in a scale-model version of a modern interior, instead of the usual simulation of mossy rocks. Their happiness and sadness are constantly recorded by a camera (where have we seen that before?). The apartment is decorated with the best scale-model Vitra furniture, an indoor fountain sculpture, and of course elements are applied in abstract form.

The graceful and taut movements of this animal fit in perfectly with the sleek design of the apartment, but the lifestyle of the chameleon, unchanged since primordial times, will eventually take a devastating toll on the environment: droppings, flies and half-eaten cockroaches will increasingly dominate the decor.
Could evolution be accelerated by placing these primeval creatures in a modernized environment? Would they acquire a different view of the world? Would they behave differently, develop a taste?
The most conspicuous features of the Jacsonii are three large horns on the snout. These horns are totally out of proportion with the rest of the body. These caricaturesque features make the animal seem highly unnatural. It looks like a rather unsuccessful Disney character, conceived by a cartoonist as a joke on a Friday afternoon.

Barbara Visser

The huge maquette of Zuidas could be an alternative biotope for our Jacksonii. The film that would be shot of this would be highly reminiscent of woodenly animated fantasy monster films like the 1933 version of *King Kong*, films that owe a great deal of their effect to the endearing nature of their technical limitations.

Back on the bike. I pass a white line drawing on the road. Not lines and arrows, but the outline of a human body, in the shape of a person leaping. The return of the human scale to Zuidas, albeit in a temporary form. An unlucky chance.

1. *Playtime*, 70mm feature film by Jacques Tati, 1967.

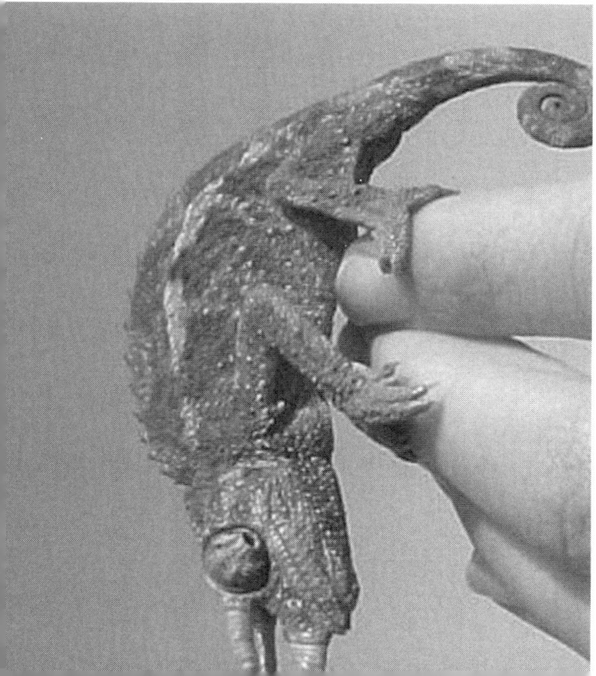

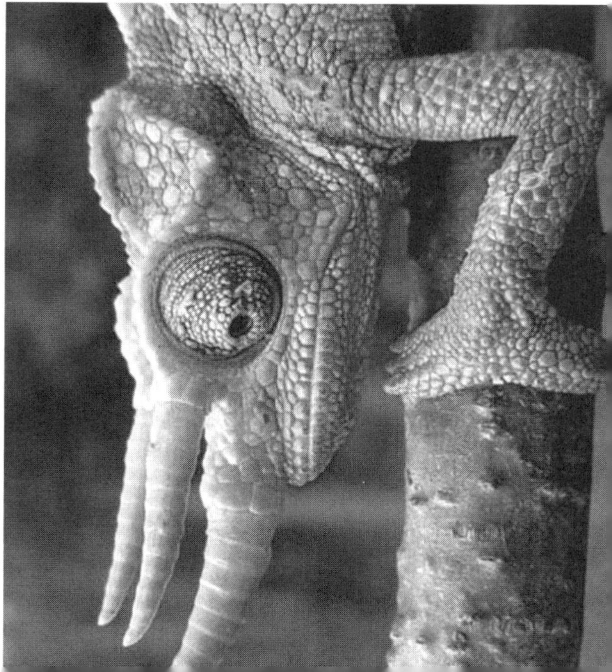

Barbara Visser

3
Zuidas ABC

(loosely based on Gustave Flaubert's *Diction-naire des idées reçues*)

A

Accessibility – These days, a quality in and of itself. Physically or virtually, you are nowhere without it.

Ambition – Comes with the start of every-thing. What comes with it, the story doesn't tell.

Art – Has it tough all over.

B

Banks of the IJ – The intellectual little brother of Zuidas.

Beethoven – Important composer. Plagued by deafness.

C

Charity – Still exists, apparently. See Sports Clubs.

Composer – Other than the word itself, has nothing to do with music composers.

Concept Vision – An idea with ambition, the content of which will be announced soon.

D

Desire Image – Something should be left to be desired.

Development – You can push the cart, or you can pull it.

Dock Model – When accessibility and aesthetics do not go together.

E

Energy – You can save this.

Environment – Doesn't mean setting here either.

F

Facilities – Everything has been thought of, especially what is being thought about now.

Function Mix – All parties benefit from this.

G

Gershwin – Important composer. The inspiration for grand building projects.

H

High Buildings – Great winds fall upon them. See Wind Nuisance.

Housing – Function intended to counter the spectre from the US.

I

Infrastructure – Always open to improvement.

ING House – What people used to think the future looked like. Popular building, in spite of its generally accepted ugliness.

K

Kiss & Ride – The limit of accessibility.

M

Mahler – Important composer. Putting a number after the name makes it a building designation.

Master Plan – Big idea, usually from one man. See Pi de Bruijn.

Museum Parcel – Plot of land that no bank wants.

N

Noord-Zuid Line – Line that also runs from South to North.

P

Peace and Quiet – What everyone is after.

Pedestrians – Mostly get underfoot. Make the decor in the brochures look good.

Pi de Bruijn – See Master Plan

Play – Something with marbles.

Principles – Ambition and Strategy translated into an A4.

Public Space – Not for bicycles outside the racks provided.

Q

Quarantine – Is usually the word for the Q.

R

Recreation – Important, apparently, but no one can explain why.

S

Spatial Planning – Term that takes away the fear of the new.

Sports Clubs – Charity. Are tolerated. See Function Mix.

Strategy – Contemporary method of predicting the future. Is necessary to success. See Ambition.

Sustainability – Word you use when you've had enough of the criticism that you only care about money.

T

Top Location – Does have something to do with height.

Traffic and Transport – See Accessibility. See Dock Model. See Environment. See

Infrastructure. See Kiss & Ride. See Noord-Zuid Line. See Public Space. See Spatial Planning.

Trial Zone – Plot of land where blunders can still be corrected.

V

Vivaldi – Important composer. Cannot be devalued.

Vision – Word that always does well in presentations.

W

Water – Man is 64 percent water.

Wind Nuisance – There are no problems, only challenges.

WTC – Used to stand in a wasteland. The building that started it all. See Ambition.

X

X Factor – Used to be called having *it*.

Y

Young Professionals – The more professional they are, the faster they age.

Z

Zuidas – Try to use it without the 'the' in front.

Hiding behind the Laptop

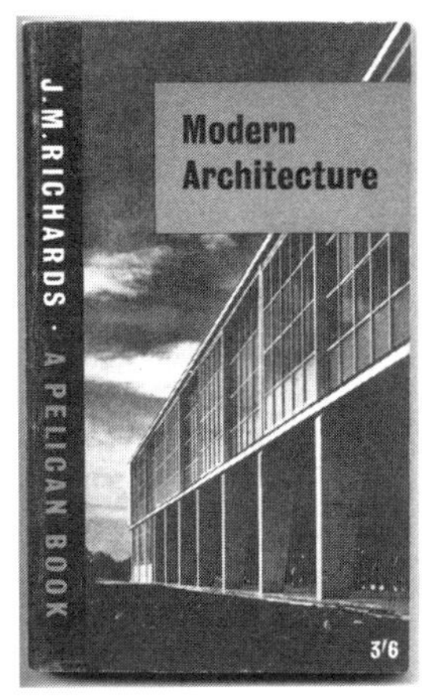

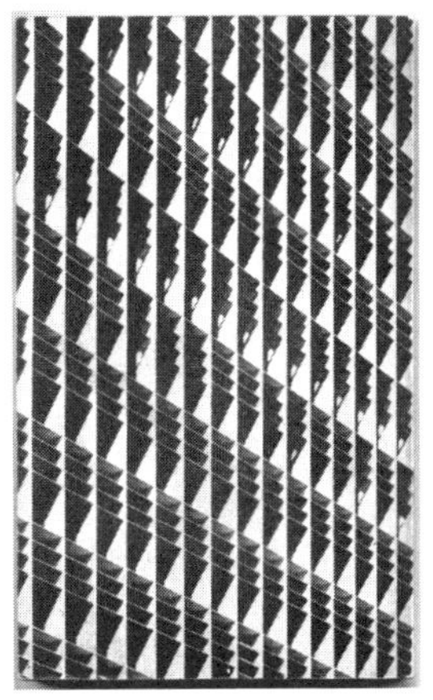

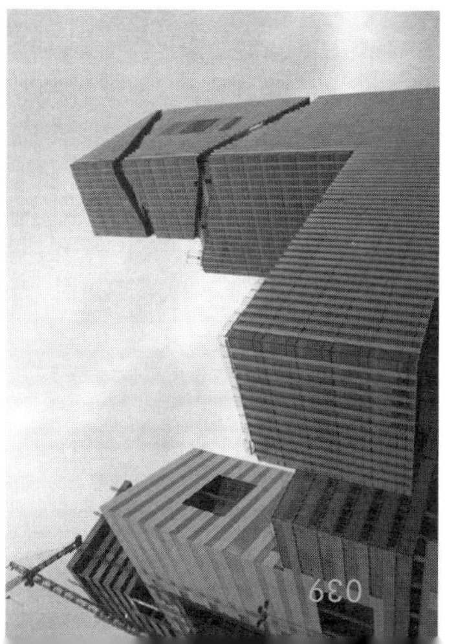

Joost Zonneveld

What Kind of City Centre Will the Zuidas Become?

The skyline on the south side of Amsterdam is slowly changing. Although it will be years before the Zuidas is 'finished', the new high-rises provide a glimpse of what is to be a new city centre for Amsterdam in 20 years' time.

At closer range, it is apparent that the Zuidas is still an incoherent whole. The WTC and the main offices of ABN-Amro and ING are juxtaposed with out-of-date stations, a university sports centre and vacant lots. In fact the Zuidas is merely at the beginning of an evolution whose goal is to redirect car and train traffic underground and to link Amsterdam-Zuid and Buitenveldert (the area next to Amsterdam-Zuid) through a new urban area dominated by high-rises. A new centre featuring one million square metres of office space, an equal amount of housing space and an additional 500,000 square metres for facilities are to be created on the Zuidas. Both Schiphol Airport and Amsterdam's historic city centre are a stone's throw away. Ultimately, the sports centre will disappear, there will be a major station for high-speed trains, regular trains and the metro, and there won't be any vacant lots on this high-priced land.

Joost Zonneveld

One only need utter the word 'Zuidas' and one hears about the enormous potential of the area – as a business centre, as an opportunity to lure highly desirable knowledge workers to the city and as a new centre for Amsterdam and the Randstad urban conglomeration. The mega-project will give Amsterdam a contemporary face and make it economically viable for the coming century. It even seems the economy of the Netherlands depends to a high degree on the development of the Zuidas. Residents of Amsterdam will benefit as well, through increased employment opportunities.

The question remains, however, whether the various ambitions of the government and market players can be reconciled in a balanced way. And whether a business centre can be effectively combined with the function of an urban centre. For whereas a top-flight business centre is mainly a visiting card for businesses, an urban centre has a function for all sections of a city's population. The presence of divergent functions such as housing, culture, business and sports does not necessarily mean that the Zuidas will actually evolve into an area embraced by the residents of Amsterdam as a city centre. Although the Zuidas is still mostly seen as an office location, more is needed than simply a mix of housing, culture and commerce.

Hustle and Bustle as a Selling Point

The Zuidas is supposed to grow into the new centre of Amsterdam, but the city authorities have not always shown much enthusiasm for the idea. In fact, Amsterdam was initially against the development of the Zuidas. The city was far more interested in the south bank of the IJ as a new location for office buildings. After all, as port activity declined, this area had to be given a new function. Moreover, the city feared for the competitive position of the inner city, because a location outside the old city centre might well carry negative economic consequences. However, market players involved in the development of the south bank of the IJ pulled out, and from the early nineteen-nineties, more and more businesses moved to the Zuidas, making the development of the area inevitable. Major banks set up their headquarters there, and the city ultimately decided to go along with the development. According to former alderman and current commissioner of the Zuidas Enterprise, Duco Stadig, 'the government capitulated to the market'. The Zuidas was to be the new top location, but in a way that would deliver added value for the city. Along with offices, the area would have to include housing and facilities.

The market forced the development of the Zuidas. Although the term did not yet exist in the early nineteen-nineties, it is an example of

Joost Zonneveld

what is now called 'development planology'. This is the new magic word when it comes to urban development, for the market and the government need each other to bring urban design projects to fruition. Thinking is based more on market demand, for the market, after all, knows what investors and consumers need. It is part and parcel of a society in which the demands of consumers are carrying increasing weight and the government is retrenching in all sorts of areas. Development planology is a method of development in which more of the emphasis is placed on implementation. In the past, many urban-design projects never got off the ground because the government made plans and then left implementation up to market players. Because this did not always come to pass, there is now an effort to take advantage of spatial and economic opportunities as they present themselves. The process no longer relies so much on a clear-cut plan as on visions, in order to be able to respond to changing factors. The aim is that urban-design projects be completed more quickly and that the spatial quality be increased. In the Netherlands, this way of working is a break with tradition, for Dutch spatial planning was long the exclusive purview of the state.

The involvement of private investors is necessary to finance a project like the Zuidas; the government cannot do it alone. As a result, the influence of market players on the development of urban-design projects like the Zuidas is significant. Sixty percent of the shares in the enterprise that is investing in installing the infrastructure underground are in the hands of private parties. The investors have already stipulated that their risk be fixed to a maximum figure. If financial setbacks exceed 350 million Euro, the loss is to be absorbed by the government. Recently, for fear of negative publicity, three banks have also offered to tie their profits to a maximum figure. Although this is a reasonable gesture, it is clear that the market has a major influence on the frameworks within the project.

Although it has been the wish of the Amsterdam city authorities, especially, that the Zuidas be more than simply a location for office buildings, it is inevitable that the representative quality of the area as a top location for business predominates. Precisely because the Zuidas is presented as an international top location, with the attendant real estate and rental prices, business interests have primacy. The urban environment that develops on the Zuidas, therefore, will be one dominated by these business interests. The proximity of a fancy restaurant and theatre make it attractive for businesses to take clients there. This makes the desired urban character a selling point for businesses on the Zuidas, and its urban functions will be dominated by economic interests.

Joost Zonneveld

What consequences this emphasis on representative quality can have is demonstrated by the irritation expressed by various businesses about the many bicycles randomly parked near the WTC. The typical Amsterdam bike spoiled the desired image; the bikes were said to make the Zuidas 'look messy'.

Function Mix on the Zuidas

Various reasons play a role in the ambition to turn the area into more than just a location for offices and to integrate it spatially into the city. At the moment, the area itself forms a physical barrier. The dike upon which the A10 motorway and the railroad tracks run draws a sharp line between Amsterdam-Zuid and Buitenveldert. Redirecting this – and future – infrastructure underground offers an opportunity to create a linked urban area (the dock variant). In addition, many more housing units and offices can be built. It is not yet entirely certain that the dock variant will be implemented. If it is not, the Zuidas can still develop into a top-flight office location. But if the dock does go ahead, it will mean a green light for the development of the desired urban centre. This will have to feature high quality and high density, taking Amsterdam's inner city as a reference. Spatially, separate sections of the city will be linked together. Whereas many other centres are becoming increasingly monofunctional by concentrating on one specific function, the aim on the Zuidas is to create a mix. This means, therefore, not a dull office park deserted after business hours, not a dormitory town containing only housing and not a centre devoted solely to entertainment, for instance. The added value of the area lies in the very combination of its functions. Moreover, it offers a chance to attract people from the surrounding region to the area with cultural facilities.

A mix in the area is important even based on purely economic interests. For if all that gets developed is an office park, the area becomes vulnerable to negative developments in the market. Linking offices to knowledge institutions such as universities and cultural facilities allows functions to complement one another, and there is a greater likelihood that the area will remain attractive as a location for the long term. Since the objective, moreover, is a top-flight urban area and an international environment, highly educated knowledge workers — the crucial target audience — from the Netherlands and abroad will be able not only to work on the Zuidas, but live there and spending their leisure time there as well. With the presence of restaurants, a musical theatre, museums, sports venues, parks and shops, they have at their disposal a complete package that suits their lifestyle. While there will also be facilities for day-to-day needs, the emphasis will be on an exclusive, high-quality assortment. You will not find cheap consumption stores on the Zuidas.

Targeting knowledge workers also means that a substantial portion of the housing stock is being developed in the top segment of the housing market. As Amsterdam is keen to have more such dwellings within city limits, this represents an opportunity to make up its shortfall. In addition to apartments, multi-story townhouses, penthouses and lofts, work-at-home dwellings, studios and publicly subsidized housing are being built.

In regard to the publicly subsidized housing, incidentally, the city has dropped its requirement of 30 percent publicly subsidized housing for the dock, bringing the percentage for the entire area down to just above 20 percent. Should costs rise, the publicly subsidized housing will be the first to see cutbacks. The Zuidas is primarily intended as an attractive area for international businesses and their employees. Amsterdam wants to establish a more prominent profile as a business, residential and cultural city. The Zuidas holds particular potential, as an icon in this domain, to counter the existing image of a city of drugs and backpackers.

Zuidas as a City Centre

Combining divergent functions plays an important role in the design of the new centre. Amsterdam's inner city is being used as a model. A similar mix of housing, employment and facilities, with a comparable density, is being sought, in order to create a bustling area. It is too easy to think, however, that an attractive centre emerges as long as functions are mixed and spatial densities are copied. Based on the plans, the potential for socio-cultural mix is particularly limited. The assortment of shops, the cafés, dwellings and offices will be aimed at residents and visitors with above-average incomes, turning the Zuidas into a centre for a specific group of Amsterdam residents. The park and the AFC football pitches may well attract a broader audience, but given the facilities on offer, it is difficult to imagine the average footballer sitting on the terrace in front of the WTC on a Sunday afternoon. Many different sorts of people will also use the area as a transit point, but that is of little predictive value as to the connection that people have to an area.

A city centre has a broader significance. One can only speak of such a centre once a section of the city appeals to people from the whole region, and people from different sections of the population live, work and spend their leisure time in that area. To put it concisely,

059

Joost Zonneveld

in the way the Zuidas is being promoted, the diversity of functions is highlighted, but not the diversity of people. The minimum quota of publicly subsidized housing, for instance, is primarily a political necessity, but it will have no impact on the elitist character of internationally oriented knowledge workers and financial institutions.

Of course living in Amsterdam's inner city is not within everyone's reach either, but the percentage of publicly subsidized housing is significant, there is a mix of high and low culture and various kinds of economic activity emerge that make the inner city a centre for all of Amsterdam's residents. Offering more groups room to live on the Zuidas and creating a more diverse assortment of facilities can bring about a more solid connection with the rest of the city. Whereas planners are currently banking on an 'exclusive and high-quality' assortment, an effort should be made to find a broader basis to realize a function like a city centre. Combinations such as an exclusive bookshop alongside a second-hand bookseller and a Moroccan bakery near an expensive sandwich shop increases diversity and lowers the threshold for a broader audience that has something to choose from and something to discover. In this way, the Zuidas can appeal to and serve different groups and in the process better connect to the rest of Amsterdam. If this does not happen, the Zuidas will eventually be spatially imbedded in the city, but it will form a socio-cultural island within it.

Forced Urbanness

Jan Winsemius, urban-design consultant, observes quite rightly that existing city centres like that of Amsterdam were never 'conceived' and certainly not with the question of 'how to bring urbanness into the area'. In today's urban development, this question does consistently come to the forefront, and attempts are made to add diversity in functions, so that the emergence of a multi-faceted and attractive urban environment flourishes as quickly as possible. By locating hospitality venues in the lower levels of buildings, by making intensive use of the space and by involving cultural institutions in the area, an urban climate is 'established' and an attempt is made to meet the needs of its residents and users. It is clear that the saleability of the Zuidas plays a major role. There is significant interest in creating a bustling city centre as quickly as possible. The consumer wants to live and work, immediately, in the attractive environment promoted in the brochures. Moreover, the Zuidas must meet the demands of representative quality, and money has to be made from the development of the area.

Joost Zonneveld

The result will be a forced urbanness, something that looks like the city centres we are familiar with, but that threatens to become a surrogate because of the significant economic interests involved. Not a centre that forms the nucleus of a great diversity of activities and people, but a cosmetic entity at the service of economic interests.

A desire to be a spotless billboard for the Netherlands and Amsterdam is strong. Because of the prestige associated with the Zuidas and the representative quality that the businesses located there want to exude with their office buildings, there will be no calls for more diversity any time soon. For the moment, visions for the future of the Zuidas still involve a new urban society of highly educated knowledge workers with a strongly international orientation, whereby the old Amsterdam, with its working-class neighbourhoods, immigrants and food-distribution banks, is completely taken out of the picture. The mix of functions may be borrowed from the old city, but preferably not its diversity of people. In so doing, the Zuidas, no matter how internationally oriented, will always lose out to the appeal of the familiar historic inner city.

Source
J. Winsemius, 'Economische maakbaarheid van stedelijkheid', in: *Leve(n) de stad* (The Hague: VROM, 2001).

064

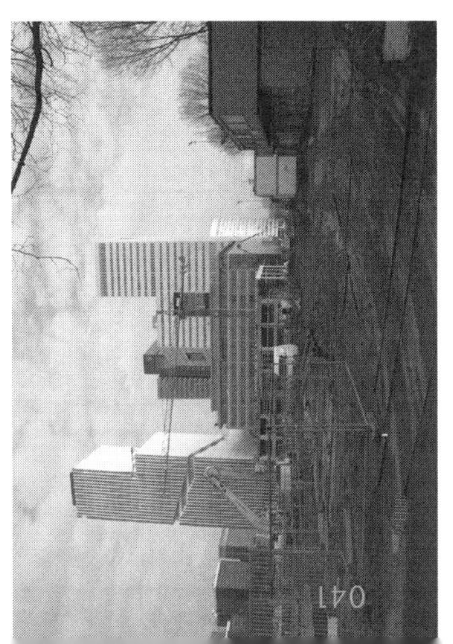

Stan Majoor

A Cultural Approach to City Building
Lessons from Forum Barcelona

Amsterdam-Zuidas is still struggling to give a cultural turn to a predominantly business-oriented urban development. The Forum project in Barcelona is an example of a completely different approach. Here the organization of an internationally-oriented cultural mega-event in the spring and summer of 2004 was one of the initial central pillars of a massive urban development scheme. The results were ambivalent however. On the one hand the cultural event helped to speed up the realization of different essential infrastructure projects for the area and added to the momentum for the transformation of a much wider part of Barcelona. It also created a lot of attention and visitors and resulted in additional regional, national and European subsidies for the transformation of the area. However, at the same time the physical result in the form of a large experimentally designed area is still difficult to appreciate three years after the event, while the cultural approach was criticized as being too politicized and eventually unable to create real and meaningful connections with wider groups in society. For the Zuidas, still aiming to

Stan Majoor

define the role of culture in its transformation, it is interesting to briefly review the story of Forum due to the central and integrative role this aspect had right from the outset. However it is not a straightforward 'best practice' and it teaches us in particular that if these large-scale transformations become socially disconnected, they will fail in the long term.

Barcelona is the city with probably one of Europe's most studied, discussed and praised strategies of urban interventions in the previous three decades.[1] Its strategies of urban transformation have certainly been interpreted as good practice by many visiting foreign politicians. The city's recent urban transformation took place in a very dynamic political, economic and social era after Spain's transition towards democracy at the end of the nineteen-seventies. Culture played an essential role in Barcelona's urban transformation in different ways. In the famous revitalization plans for the older, densely built neighbourhoods special attention was given to the creation of public spaces, the addition of places for local cultural institutions and the restoration of buildings with an important cultural function like indoor markets.[2] The Catalan identity was long suppressed during the Franco years and it could blossom again in these spaces, where old festivities were reintroduced. An extensive scheme of public arts was part of every neighbourhood transformation. At the same time a lot of emphasis was put on the restoration of buildings by some of Barcelona's most famous representatives of Catalan Art Nouveau–Jugendstil movement (*Modernisme Català*): Gaudí, Puig i Cadafalch and Domènech i Montaner. Additionally, some important new museums were realized to further promote the cultural dimension of Barcelona's transformation, both for the residents and for the outside visitor. During this phase of transformation social groups were extremely active and successful in advocating the preferences of the public and influencing the plans.[3] But the city witnessed an even more fundamental change due to the building programme for the 1992 Olympic Games. The games were not only used to create some world-class sporting facilities in the city. Their strategic goal was much more important. They created the momentum for political and financial investments from higher levels of government to much better use one of Barcelona's still secret assets: the Mediterranean coastline. Till then it had been hidden behind a barrier of infrastructure and mainly used for harbour and other industrial uses.[4] However, in less than a decade harbour activities were moved, most infrastructure was buried and water quality was improved. New beaches, public spaces, housing areas, marinas and complete enter-

Stan Majoor

tainment and shopping districts were realized. Barcelona and its steadily growing influx of tourists hungrily conquered the coastline as the new fashionable spot to be: a beach culture was born.

After the Olympics there was some time to reflect. Although the social, economic and physical changes had been large, Barcelona's transformation was certainly not 'finished'. However, it seemed necessary to redefine the goals and strategies of the city's development in a changing era in which competition between cities became a prominent issue. Barcelona city council responded with a whole series of strategic projects. The goal was to improve Barcelona's position in the advanced service economy, which was identified as a structural weakness of the city's economy.[5] It was in this context that the Forum project was initiated, as an attempt to repeat the Olympic success.[6]

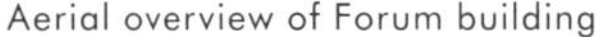

Aerial overview of Forum building

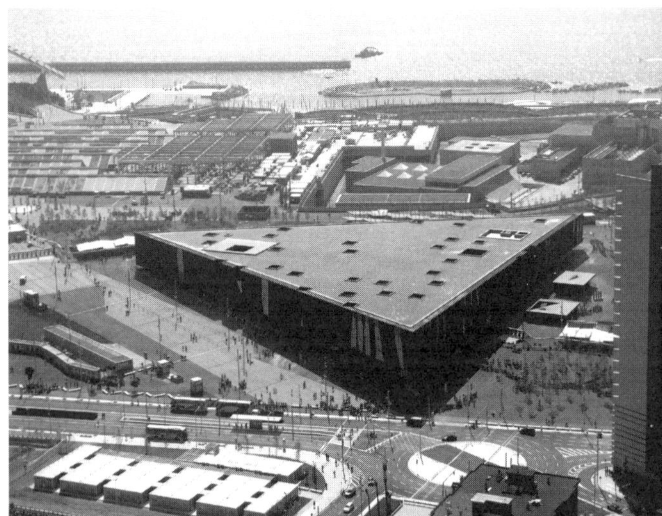

1.
The Three Goals of the Forum Project

The Forum transformation would be connected to a large public event in the spring and summer of 2004 which would mark the celebration of the 75th anniversary of the Universal Expo of 1929. This reference was more than symbolic. Just as the 1929 Expo gave Barcelona new public buildings and spaces around the Plaça d'Espanya and the slopes of the Montjuïc, the 2004 event was expected to function as a catalyst for the urban development of the city in a new timeframe.[7] The Forum site was planned in a dilapidated industrial area in the eastern section of the city, from where it was expected to eventually reinforce a much larger ensemble of projects. The location for this new prestigious project was extremely challenging: the site was occupied by a huge coal power plant, an incinerator and an exceptionally smelly wastewater treatment plant. To the east the area was bordered by the heavily polluted river Besòs, while on the north it adjoined two of the most disadvantaged neighbourhoods in Spain – La Mina and La Catalana. When analyzing Forum it is therefore important to make a distinction between the three sets of goals of the Forum project. It was (1) a physical regeneration project, (2) an (inter)national and local cultural event and (3) a project of major environmental investments.[8]

Stan Majoor

Forum as a Physical Regeneration Project

The long term strategic goal of the project was to urbanize an industrial area that was seriously blighted yet occupied a strategic coastal location. Forum was expected to become an area for visitors and tourists, with large public spaces, a marina and a bathing area. It would also contribute to the socio-economic regeneration of this part of the city with some key buildings, most importantly a new technological university campus and a huge convention centre with adjacent hotels. It was expected that the massive investment in public space and infrastructure would help alleviate the problems of surrounding disadvantaged neighbourhoods by improving their accessibility and the general image of the area. The adjacent Diagonal Mar area was being developed at the same time as a new mixed use residential and shopping area (see table 1). Together, these two projects were a small though strategic part of a revitalization and urbanization scheme for a much wider ring of projects on the eastern side of Barcelona. The most important was the 22@ project, aiming to redevelop the old industrial area of Poblenou into a vibrant mixed district with clean industries and an emphasis on the knowledge-based economy.[9]

Table 1:

Programme of urban investments in Forum and Diagonal Mar between 2001 and 2008, in square metres

Area	Area (ha.)	Housing	Hotels	Offices	Other commercial activities	Total programme
Forum	222	82,000	86,000	109,645[iii]	35,994	313,639
Diagonal Mar	23,5	169,978	58,000	57,000	87,000	371,978
Total	245,5	251,978[i]	144,000[ii]	166,645	122,994	685,617

i In the neighbouring poor housing areas of La Mina and La Catalana another 2,477 housing units will be built as part of the revitalization plans for these areas.

ii In Forum and Diagonal Mar 2315 hotel beds will be realized, mostly in the higher segments. Just outside the project area, along the coast, another 641 hotel beds have already been realized in recent years Ajuntament de Barcelona, *La reforma urbanística del Besòs* (Barcelona: Ajuntament de Barcelona, 2006), p. 109.

iii A large part of the offices in the Forum area are buildings for the university campus

Source: M. Tersol, 'La transformación del litoral de Barcelona en el área Fórum', in: *Ingeniería y Territorio*, vol. 67, 2004, pp. 54-63.

Stan Majoor

Forum as a Cultural Event

The Universal Forum of Cultures, to be organized in the area in the spring and summer of 2004, was expected to underline the city's international leadership in culture and to mobilize awareness and enthusiasm for the urban transformation. However, it also had a clear economic rationale. The prestigious cultural event had to result in political priority and money from other levels of government to finance the costly public investments that were expected to be beneficial to Barcelona's long-term economic growth.

Forum as a Project of Major Environmental Investments

The three installations in the area were crucial to the city. All three used outdated technologies and created a lot of air and water pollution. The open sewage treatment plant caused terrible odours in the area most of the time. Since it was extremely costly to move these installations to other parts of the city, it had been decided in an early stage to keep them in place, modernize them and integrate them in the urbanization strategy for the area. By making this operation an integral aspect of the Forum project, the city council hoped to secure additional outside funding for these operations – which had to be finished before

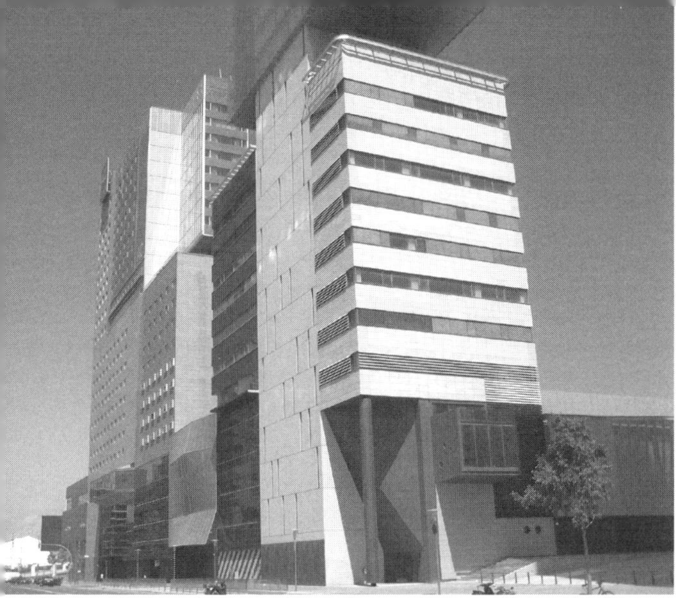

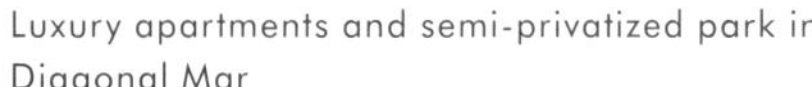

New offices and hotels at the fringe of the Forum area

Luxury apartments and semi-privatized park in
Diagonal Mar

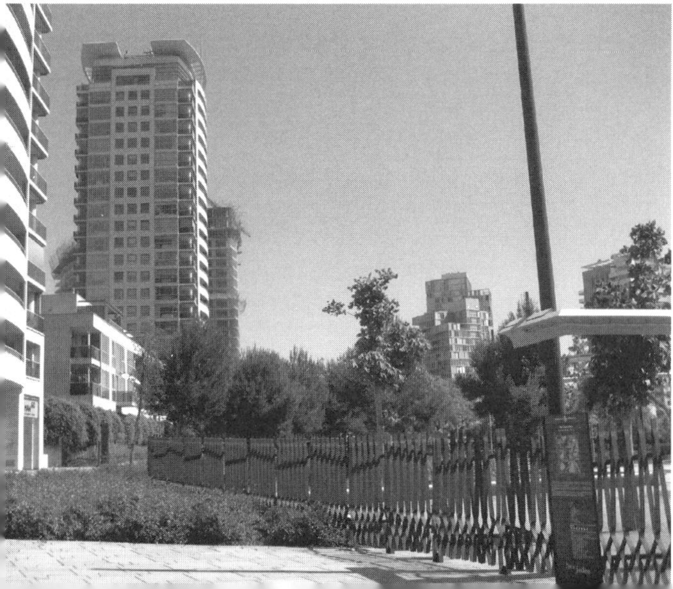

the Forum cultural event – and to give the whole transformation an ecological label.

The three different goals of the project were also reflected in the way the project was organized. One organization was responsible for the urban transformation and the environmental aspects, the *Consorci del Besòs*, while a different organization, the Forum Consortium, was initiated to organize the cultural event.

2.
Universal Forum of Cultures

Due to the specificity of the cultural dimension in Forum we dig a little bit deeper into this aspect now. It was eventually decided that the three main themes of the Universal Forum of Culture would be (1) sustainable development, (2) conditions for peace, and (3) dialogue of cultures. The Forum Consortium was governed by the three most important public financers of the Forum transformation, the Barcelona city council ruled by the *Partit dels Socialistes de Catalunya*, the regional government of Catalonia with the conservative *Convergència i Unió* in the majority and central government controlled by the right wing *Partido Popular*. These three were supported by UNESCO, the United Nations Educational Scientific and Cultural Organization. The event had a total budget of 318 million euros.

A Cultural Approach to City Building

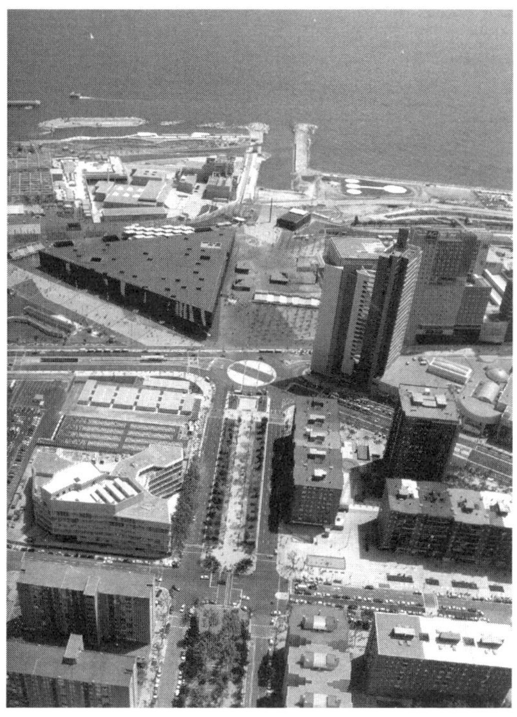

Forum as Barcelona's newest waterfront project

Stan Majoor

The event was scheduled for a period of almost five months in the spring and summer of 2004, but its preparation phase in the years before the Forum was almost as important. It was expected by the initiators that Forum could work as an 'Olympic Games for culture' and that instrumental connections could be realized with social and civic groups.[10] This is an interesting thought, because most comparative research on large-scale development projects shows that the connection of these initiatives with citizens' and cultural groups is a weakness.[11] In the case of Forum many cultural and neighbourhood groups were invited to participate in the preparation of the event. The plan was to generate an open dialogue on its main themes rather than pushing forward with the realization of spectacular shows and festivals. However, the objective to create a successful connection to different parts of the population and to realize a form of civic pride failed almost completely at the end. The reasons seem to be in a combination of specific circumstances related to this particular event and a wider unease about the way large-scale development projects are conceived, planned and executed in many cities.

If we start with the Universal Forum of Cultures it is clear that in the initial phase there was just too much uncertainty about the direction of the event. As something that had never

A Cultural Approach to City Building

been organized before, many were unsure what its meaning was. Although this could be a perfect start for a more organic approach to the organization, in the case of Forum it resulted mainly in inertia. The themes of diversity, peace and sustainability were very broad, lacking content and a clear purpose, leading many people to believe that the whole event was just a 'trick' by the relatively poor Barcelona city council to get higher government funding for the urban transformation, rather than a serious attempt to involve people or create a fundamental debate or event about its themes.[12]

However, during the build up to the invasion of Iraq in the spring of 2003, the lethargy of the broader public concerning Forum quickly disappeared, though certainly not in the way the initiators hoped. The credibility of the event was at stake when the invasion was supported by the ruling Partido Popular. Although one of themes of Forum was 'conditions for peace', the result was that the Forum Consortium could not speak against this invasion due to the political character of its governing board, which included Partido Popular politicians. This resulted in much anger since most Barcelonese supported the social democrats who objected to the invasion. The polemic debates that followed negatively influenced the preparatory stages of the event: 'how can you organize an

Stan Majoor

event about peace when your country is in a war?' angry protesters asked.[13] One of the results was that Barcelona's influential federation of neighbourhood organizations, the *Federació d'Associacions de Veïns i Veïnes de Barcelona* (FAVB), which had been the first to appreciate the project, eventually decided to become a strong opponent and set up the *Assemblea de Resistències al Forum 2004*. The reasons for rejecting Forum were not only related to the war issue but also included the expected property speculation caused by the project in neighbouring poor housing areas and the strong business sponsorship of the event by companies that did not comply with the values of the Forum in their daily practices.[14]

So while the urban transformation was moving ahead full swing to create the site for the 2004 event, the preparatory stage of the event resulted in the opposite of the expected enthusiasm and support. The organizing Forum Consortium had to move forward however, and finally a cultural event was organized with much more emphasis on large exhibitions and shows, and hardly any on participatory events and critical debates. The convention centre was used for two large exhibitions: 'Cities, Corners' (on urban development), and 'Voices' (on the value of the diversity of languages in the world). Two other big exhibitions were 'The warriors of Xi'an' (Chinese funerary art) and 'Inhabiting the world' (about sustainable development). The Forum building hosted a large exposition about the urban development of Barcelona – a typical example of the way the city is very strong in building its own legacy. This building was also used for the Forum dialogues in which prominent politicians and intellectuals expressed their views on the Forum's themes. A part of the Esplanade, the largest open space in the area, was used for a market where different international organizations were present (although many cancelled their participation). Two amphitheatres were regularly used for outdoor shows. Around the harbour – which was used for different spectacles as well – was a concentration of restaurants. Tickets for the event were 23 euros a day. In total the event was visited by around three million people, 7.5% of them from abroad. Critics argued that Barcelona's Forum eventually only presented a popular commodification of culture, with no lasting intellectual or cultural value.[15] However, the concept of a 'Universal Forum of Cultures' continues in the fall of 2007 in Monterrey, Mexico, with a similar event of congresses, shows and exhibitions.[16]

Stan Majoor

3. Decontextualizing the Critical Reactions

The critical reactions to the Universal Forum of Cultures were not only related to its preparatory processes and the final event itself, and certainly not limited to its alleged cultural dimension. They were much wider and have to be understood as an expression of a critical discourse on the development of cities and the particular role of large-scale development projects in this process.[17] Although Barcelona has created a favourable image of itself and in many respects has been very successful in its social, economic and physical transformation, there is also a growing critical opposition to its development. The drift towards business-friendly planning and large public private partnerships that are responsible for large 'flagship' developments in the city, without much citizen influence, has been especially criticized.[18] In Barcelona, as in other places, there seems to be a growing contrast between the glamorous development of these kinds of places and the persistent and rising inequalities between groups of people, the increased difficulty of finding affordable housing for large groups in the city, and problems with immigration.

Forum gives a warning about the results of very closed introvert policy circles in which plans are conceived and developed. The public consortium that had to realize most of the Forum before the 2004 event had to move extremely quickly. Its closed style of governance was enhanced by the lack of existing users and inhabitants in the area and a planning culture in which architects have a very powerful position.[19] In this context the Forum event area became a playground for experimental architecture, both in public spaces and in buildings. The Esplanade, advertised as the second biggest square in the world, is the physical backbone of the area. Two landmark buildings were realized in Forum. The 120,000 m² Convention Centre by Barcelona architect

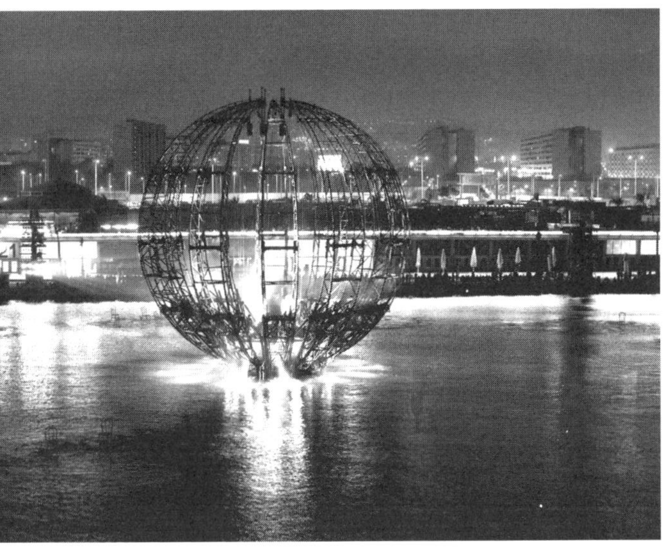

2004 Universal Forum of Cultures event

Stan Majoor

Josep Mateo and the 70,000 m² Forum building by Jacques Herzog and Pierre de Meuron from Switzerland. The triangular shaped Forum building is especially eye-catching. It seems to float, giving it a rather untouchable mystic feel. The large convention centre is completely internally organized as well. Next to the Forum event area, Diagonal Mar was developed quickly around the turn of the century. In this case the city council was so happy that a private party was finally investing in this dilapidated part of the city that it gave them almost absolute freedom regarding the programme and design of the site. Diagonal Mar is being developed with high-rise luxury condominiums in a semi-public park, a large shopping mall, some office buildings and several hotels. Although it is a commercial success, it is generally disliked by Barcelonese due to its 'American style' physical appearance that forms the antithesis of the compact Mediterranean city.

Both projects can be interpreted as examples of situations were one actor was capable of intervening very independently, without facing public or civic scrutiny. The results are spaces that are difficult to read and comprehend. Some critics see its virtue as '. . . departure from the careful "good taste" that has often limited the aesthetic ambition of Barcelona design, and an opening towards rougher, freer, more lucid and expressive forms that

A Cultural Approach to City Building

organize and focus the urban territory'.[20] However, three years after the Forum event has finished, the reality is that the area is only used once in a while for large concerts. Outside these moments it has a really deserted feel. The marina in the meantime has been privatized and fenced off while the landmark Forum building has hardly been used. The lack of urban functions in the area and the poor design result in a dominant feel of emptiness and an enduring post-event depression. Although Barcelona was successful in realizing the physical aspects of the project – the environmental benefits are especially impressive – it is safe to conclude that it has failed to create a publicly appreciated and used urban area till now. The Forum cultural event was instrumental in aligning the investment priorities of three levels of government and triggering some private investment as well, but it hardly added value for the transformation and even created a lot of negative publicity that remains associated with the development. Before, during and after the event the cultural value was extremely limited.

The results are forcing Barcelona to rethink its strategies for urban development and the role of culture in it in particular. The city still has many cultural trump cards in its hand. However, it seems to have difficulty in adapting to a situation where general consensus on the

Stan Majoor

direction of the city's urban development is fading away. It is interesting to explore what role culture can play in this context and to explore a new consensus on the direction and programme of urban transformations in its future development.

4. Lessons for the Zuidas?

What can the Zuidas, currently exploring its cultural dimensions, learn from Barcelona?[21]

Barcelona taught us that using culture as a pillar for a large-scale transformation can certainly be very beneficial to achieving higher level political priority, short-term (inter)national exposure and, although this largely failed, a potential discourse that gives meaning to the development. The Zuidas would love to borrow these three aspects, since these are weaknesses the project has been struggling with for the last decade.[22] However, it is very questionable whether Barcelona's cultural approach is the one to follow for the Zuidas. What Barcelona did was try to copy the Olympic Games event formula with culture as a substitute for sports. It was therefore not culture that was the central strategy; it was the mass 'happening' that would draw people to the new area to be entertained. Although the initial intentions were different, culture was finally reduced to a form of content, a catchy theme of this event, commodified in popular shows and mass exhibitions. In our opinion there are three lessons.

A Cultural Approach to City Building

The first is related to the event-based strategy, set aside if the theme is culture, sports or something else. Although such a strategy can surely reinforce the focus on the urban transformation and can also be instrumental from a political or economic perspective, the post-event gap is always waiting. In Forum there are now extremely large public areas in desperate search of a use. This is something the Zuidas should definitely not want. If it should want large public events, it should

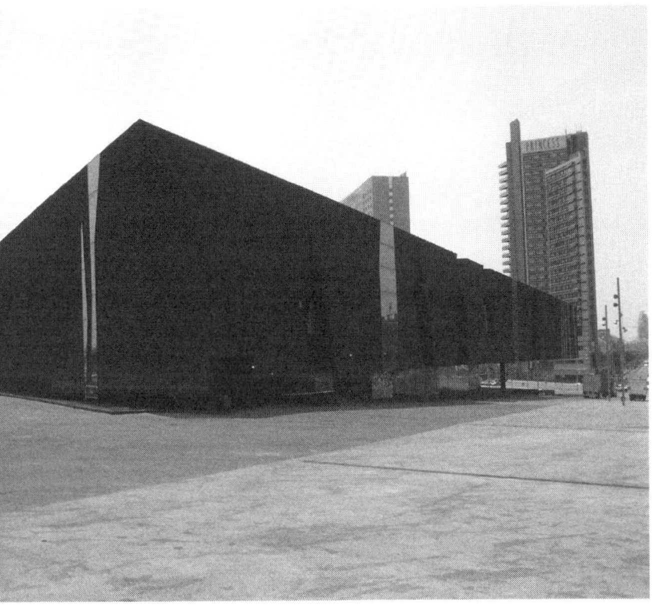

The Forum building by Herzog and De Meuron

Stan Majoor

always think about carefully embedding these kinds of initiatives in the current or future urban fabric, or give them a more enduring nature.

The second lesson from Barcelona is that a specific focus on culture as a major pillar of development can also get very tricky. An essential part of culture is the inherent struggle about interpretations, styles and good taste. Forum teaches us that when culture links up with heated political themes, it can get easily out of control and result in the whole development project having negative connotations for the public.

Thirdly, the cultural approach in Barcelona was eventually almost completely disconnected from the urban transformation. Seen purely from a cultural perspective this is not a problem. However, it strongly diminishes the capacity of culture in any form to add value to the transformation. The Universal Forum of Cultures was a generic cultural event which could have been held anywhere. It was only successful in supporting the physical makeover of the area in a political and economic sense and did not add any cultural value to it.

In the Zuidas it is therefore important to be restrictive with both the 'large event' and 'generic cultural approach' strategy of Barcelona. Obviously, due to its location and appearance, the Zuidas can be the ideal place to exhibit modern art and more experimental

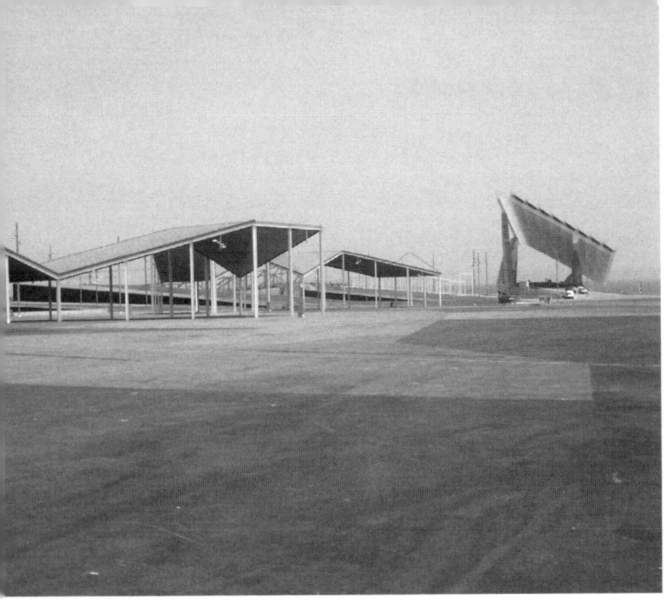

The Forum building by Herzog and De Meuron

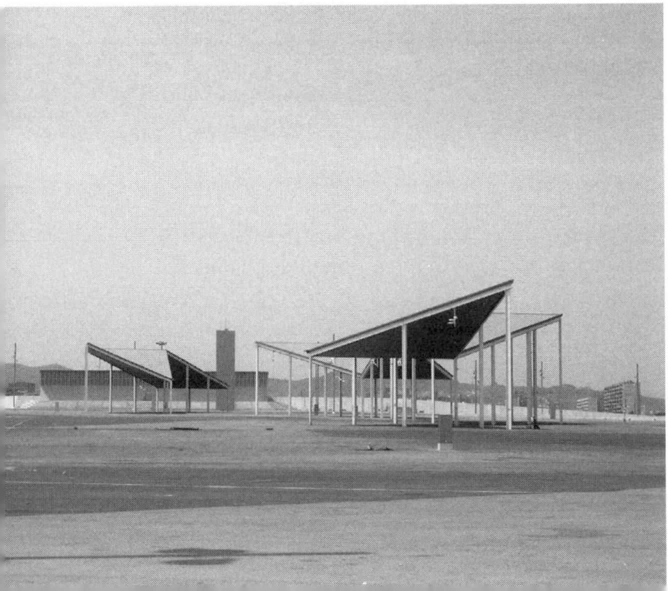

Stan Majoor

forms of art. However, if the aim is to connect culture to the development of the area, it seems relevant to complement this with an approach to give the whole urban transformation of the area a more cultural dimension. This can be done by letting the cultural programme revolve more strongly around themes like 'construction/change', 'modern architecture', 'flows of money, goods, people and ideas' or 'green buildings'. These are themes that are related to the current or emerging culture of the Zuidas as a distinctive place in Amsterdam. This gives a basis to link them to (the interests of) its current and future inhabitants and users. Although it is outside the scope of this article to develop this line of reasoning into a full cultural agenda for the Zuidas, it is our conviction that, with these kinds of themes, culture has a much better chance to become a characteristic yet more natural aspect of the transformation. It can be potentially much better aligned with the peculiarities of this space in transition than when much more general cultural themes such as 'diversity' or 'peace' are addressed. This can also help to deal with a more fundamental problem that we pointed out in the previous section: the latest generation of large-scale urban development projects like the Zuidas is initiated to serve very abstract strategic goals. Enhancing the 'competitive position' of a city is the most essential example.

The problem is that these goals — relevant as they might be — are quite far removed from the direct short-term needs of most citizens. Adopting an approach like the one we suggest can contribute to a more piecemeal, organic and essentially more human style of development when these global strategic goals are enlightened and enriched with a more cultural interpretation of physical and social change. It is in this respect that Barcelona has failed this time to set international standards. Maybe the Zuidas can pick up the gauntlet?

Notes
1. Tim Marshall (ed.), *Transforming Barcelona* (London and New York: Routledge, 2004).
2. Joan Busquets, *Barcelona: the Urban Evolution of a Compact City* (Rovereto: Nicolodi editore, 2005).
3. Nico Calavita and Amador Ferrer, 'Behind Barcelona's Success Story: Citizen Movements and Planners' Power', in: Marshall (ed.), op. cit., pp. 47-64 (see note 1).
4. Han Meyer, *City and Port: Transformations of Port Cities London, Barcelona, New York, Rotterdam* (Utrecht: International Books, 1999).
5. Marisol García and Miria Claver, 'Barcelona: Governing Coalitions, Visitors, and the Changing City Center', in: Lily M. Hoffman, Susan S. Fainstein and Dennis R. Judd (eds.), *Cities and Visitors: Regulating People, Markets and City Space* (Malden/MA: Blackwell, 2003).
6. J.L. Luzón and J. Vila, 'Universal Forum of Cultures 2004, a Cultural Event as Catalyst of a Major Urban

Stan Majoor

Regeneration', in: Willem Salet and Enrico Gualini (eds.),
*Framing Strategic Urban Projects. Learning from Current
Experiences in European City Regions* (London: Routledge,
2007).
7. Josep Acebilllo, 'Una nueva geografía urbana. Las
cinco ideas programáticas del proyecto del Fórum', in:
Architectura Viva, vol. 94-95, 2004, pp. 44-53.
8. Stan Majoor, 'Transformerend Barcelona', in:
Stedebouw & Ruimtelijke Ordening, vol. 87, no. 1, 2006,
pp. 55-59.
9. Cordula Gdaniec, 'Cultural Industries, Information
Technology and the Regeneration of Post-industrial Urban
Landscapes. Poblenou in Barcelona – a Virtual City?', in:
GeoJournal, vol. 4, No. 50, 2000, pp. 379-387.
10. Beatriz García, 'Urban Regeneration, Arts Program-
ming and Major Events: Glasgow 1990, Sydney 2000 and
Barcelona 2004', in: *International Journal of Cultural
Policy*, vol. 10, no. 1, 2004, pp. 103-118.
11. Frank Moulaert, Arantxa Rodríguez and Erik
Swyngedouw (eds.), *The Globalized City: Economic
Restructuring and Social Polarization in European Cities*
(Oxford: Oxford University Press, Oxford, 2003);. Salet
and Gualini (eds.), op. cit. (see note 6).
12. Salvador Clarós, 'L'objectiu real del Forum', in: *La
Veu del Carrer*, vol. 84, 2004, pp. 16-17.
13. E. Fernandez and M. Andreu, 'Preguntes i crítiques al
Forum', in: *La Veu del Carrer*, vol. 84, 2004, p. 4.
14. Luzón and Vila, op. cit. (see note 6).
15. Fernandez and Andreu, op. cit. (see note 13).
16. See www.monterreyforum2007.org
17. Stan Majoor, 'Paradox van grote projecten', in:
Rooilijn, vol. 38, no. 2, 2005, pp. 57-63.
18. Mari Balibrea, 'Urbanism, Culture and the Post-
industrial city: Challenging the "Barcelona Model",' in:

A Cultural Approach to City Building

Marshall (ed.), op. cit., pp. 205-224 (see note 1).
19. Ibidem.
20. D. Cohn, 'Magma diagonal, la collision geológica de la ciudad con el mar', in: *Architectura Viva*, vol. 94-95, 2004, pp. 40-43.
21. Interestingly enough, Amsterdam was once interested in hosting one of the future Forum events, expected to be held once every three years now, and ordered a consultancy firm to investigate the possibilities.
22. Willem Salet and Stan Majoor, 'Reshaping Urbanity in the Amsterdam Region', in: Salet and Majoor (eds.), *Amsterdam Zuidas. European Space* (Rotterdam: 010 Publishers, 2005), pp. 19-40.

Many thanks go to Dr Francesc Carbonell and to Marc Pradel. The fieldwork for this study was financially supported by the City of Amsterdam, the Van Eesteren, Fluck & van Lohuizen Foundation, the Province of North Holland and by an EU Cost Action A 26 Short Term Scientific Mission Grant.

The research on Barcelona was conducted as part of a PhD thesis on new urbanity in three large-scale development projects: Zuidas in Amsterdam, Ørestad in Copenhagen and Forum in Barcelona. This study will be published at the beginning of 2008.

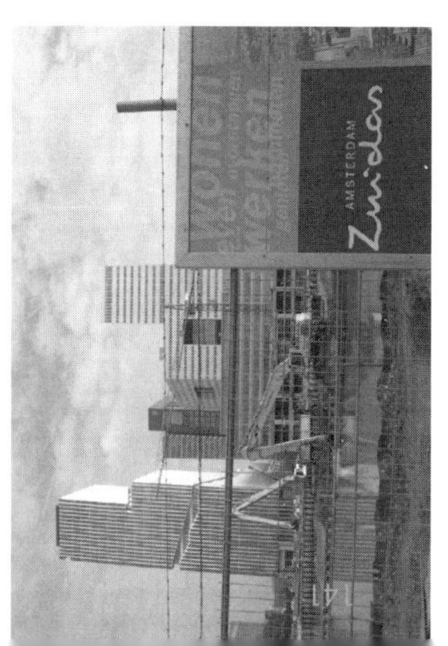

wonen
werken
AMSTERDAM
Zuidas

Roemer van Toorn

Looking through the Space
The Politics of Appearance

There are philosophers and critics who make extremely negative pronouncements about our image culture. Images are deceiving. They can be interpreted in multiple ways and therefore are not capable of telling the truth. Therefore we would do better, according to Paul Virilio, to concentrate on the word.[1] According to Guy Debord, our culture of spectacle even ensures that the spectator becomes passive in the extreme: an optimal consumer.[2] In short, despite the enormous influence, the pleasure and the significance we derive from our image culture, many theorists prefer to renounce the image instead of taking its complex nature seriously. Rather than putting out yet more critical analyses on the negative aspects of spectacle or develop yet more strategies that destabilize our image culture by taking refuge in the sensual, for instance, Paul Toornend and Jelle Post of Untitled_Space and I – at the invitation of Jeroen Boomgaard and Henk de Vroom of the Research Group Art and Public Space – looked into what realities might be revealed when you look through the space. This premise was not so much predicated on a position of 'if you can't beat 'em, join 'em' as on the conviction that spectacle, and with it

Roemer van Toorn

the image, can also generate other kinds of experiences. Or to put it another way, the essentially pornographic dimension of the visual,[3] the mindless appeal of the image, which seduces us into staring at the world as if it were a nude body, can also be used to see things differently. We do not want to disqualify the virtual reality that has become so important, we want to embrace it – because its ambivalent ambiguity, its appeal, and yes, even its false and dirty beauty can take the audience on a journey along alternative paths.

The consequences of such a perspective are nothing to sneeze at. The designed object, in this case, can no longer be seen as a self-asserting, autonomous and formal structure, separate from a specific time and place. It is not about the object but about the connections that the object makes with a given everyday context and about its relationship with the spectator. The moment you look through the space, the object can no longer appear autonomously through the many reflections operating in the confines of the Untitled_Space. Thinking in ready-made dialectic oppositions, representation versus tactility, technique versus content, and for instance good versus evil, can be discarded, as well as design methods that declare the outcome of a specific process sacred according to a tried method of expertise. Nothing is certain, and that's the whole point. What considerations, attitudes toward the profession, possibilities and limits can our virtual intervention at the Zuidas lead to – those are the questions I want to address in the following text.

Beyond Autonomous Reflection

Today, all sorts of doom scenarios fill us with fear.[4] Instead of resisting this – and appealing to our social history of democratic experiments – many, through lack of vision, fall back into forms of fundamentalism. There are architecture critics[5] who forget that championing a better living environment is more than making propaganda for ecological materials or user participation.[6] Now that consumerism is robbing the world of its sensual depth, philosophers, artists, critics and architects are resorting to the experience of real life. They no longer base themselves on critical considerations but merely on what they feel. To them it's more about what's in your bones than what's in your head. And this while technical science is only interested in the measuring and weighing of an object. In short, it comes down to a fundamentalist division between what things are as measurable facts and how we experience them from a subjective perspective. And this while aesthetics, as the science of concrete living, in fact links the rational with everyday experience, in our view. This is also the reason Bruno Latour prefers to

Roemer van Toorn

speak of 'matter-of-concerns' instead of 'matter-of-facts'.[7] You could say that a good work of art, like a good building, should be based on a sensual logic. It is reason, as it were, brought home, a reason linked to experience. In other words, projects are not about imagination or utopias, but about actual possibilities for living and models for action that are developed in negotiation with the complexity of our reality.

In Untitled_Space's first experiment,[8] a virtual space, that is to say an abstract, empty space – built out of glass walls and standards of mostly reflective material, à la Mies van der Rohe's Barcelona Pavilion – is constructed on a computer and then placed in a landscape setting. In the book *Untitled_Space* we see photographs of how this digital house absorbs and mirrors a Holland landscape. These are digital abstractions that look just like our analogue world, but that under the influence of the laws of light and the subjective recordings of a photographed reality, invite the viewer to look through the space.

How can we best interpret this sensual logic when we deliberately go beyond the autonomous view of the architectural form? And when an investment is made, in fact, in how external references, such as those of social reality, can bring the building to life and make it accessible to the user? What the Untitled_Space experiment seems to emphasize is that architecture, as a cultural object, has a subjective presence, within a preconceived sustainability such as the one we find in the tectonics of the building. According to architecture critic Michael Hays, Mies van der Rohe's Barcelona Pavilion can in fact only be understood – like the Untitled_Space – as a simultaneity of self-aware form and existing in the world.[9] Van der Rohe, says Hays, created an internal order open to the possibilities and uncertainty of life in the metropolis, to the unexpected and the inexplicable. The pavilion comes to life through the many reflections in its glass walls. It is the reflections that give the pavilion its critical quality. The image of reality is distorted: the virtual and real worlds are difficult to distinguish from each other; they show how chaotic modern life is. It is this reflective effect, according to Hays, and according to Manfredo Tafuri as well, that creates a silent theatre of the world, even as the pavilion maintains its critical distance from the world.

Reflections of reality in a building may be a source of confusion, but it remains to be seen whether they can be considered critical. Robin Evans rightly points out that Mies is mainly interested in reflecting his own construction, more than the surroundings in which it is located.[10] Rather than looking through things with a directed gaze, Mies creates coherence in his pavilion. According to Evans – and in this I agree with

Paul Toornend
and Jelle Post
UNTITLED_SPACE_14/01,
Zuidas, Amsterdam (NL),
May 2007

Paul Toornend
and Jelle Post
UNTITLED_SPACE_14/02,
Zuidas, Amsterdam (NL),
May 2007

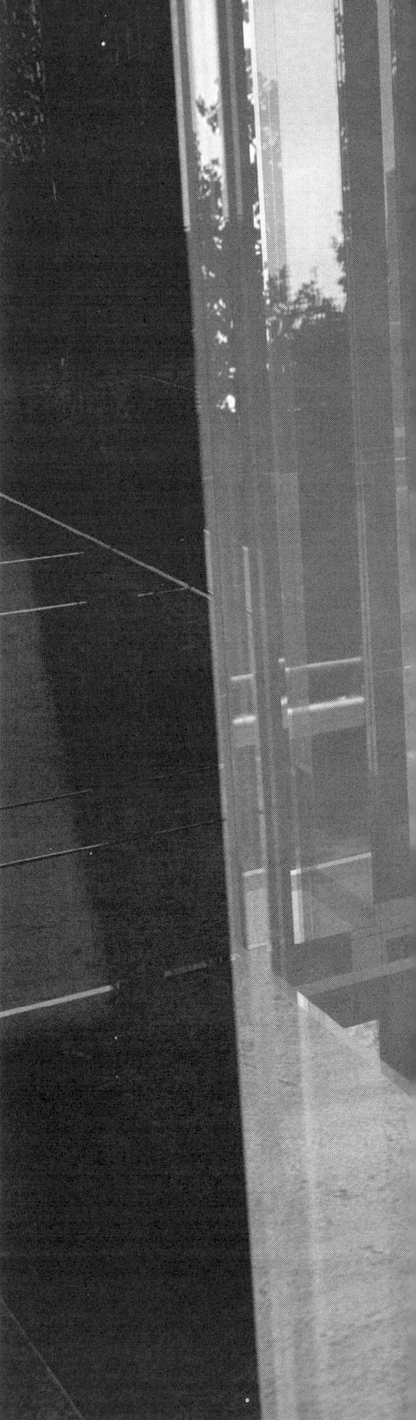

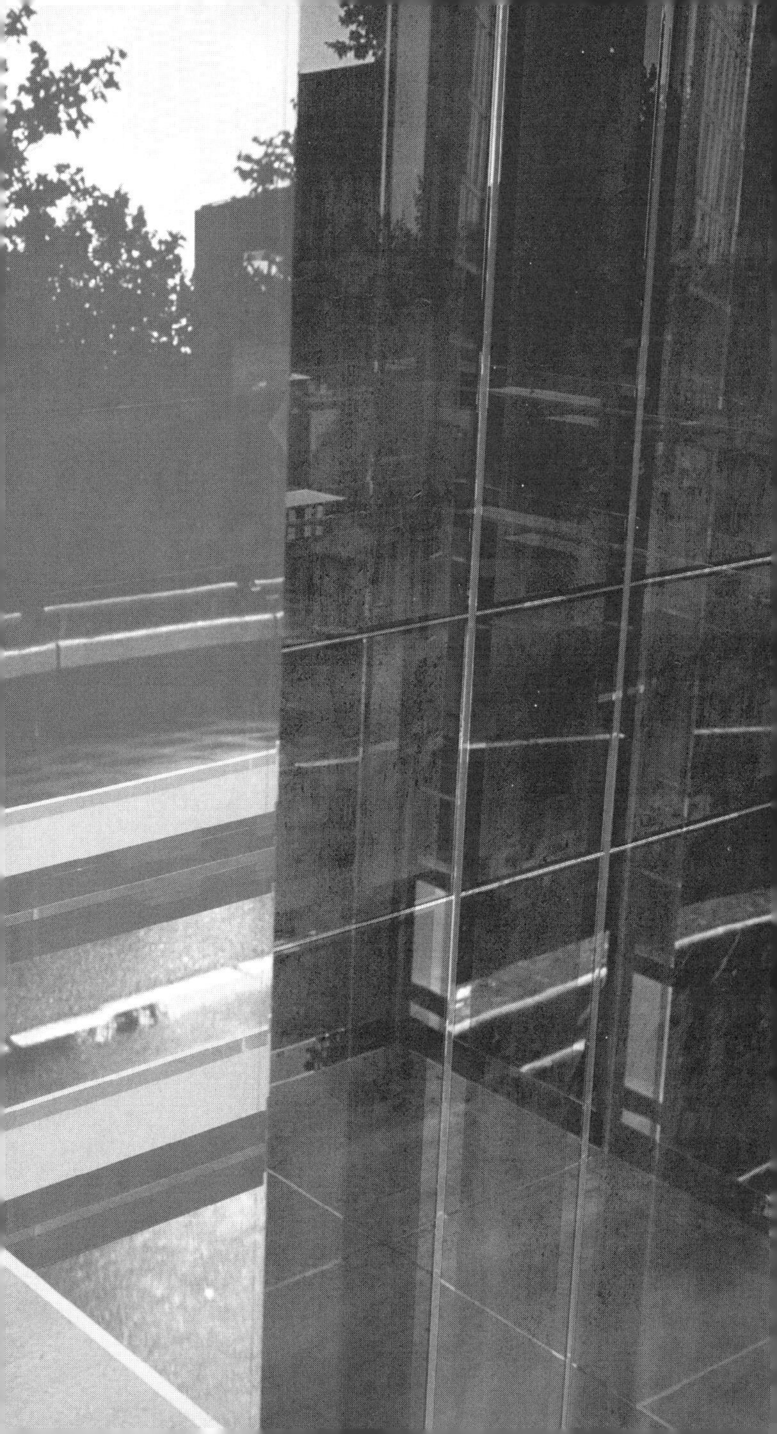

Paul Toornend
and Jelle Post
UNTITLED_SPACE_14/03,
Zuidas, Amsterdam (NL),
May 2007

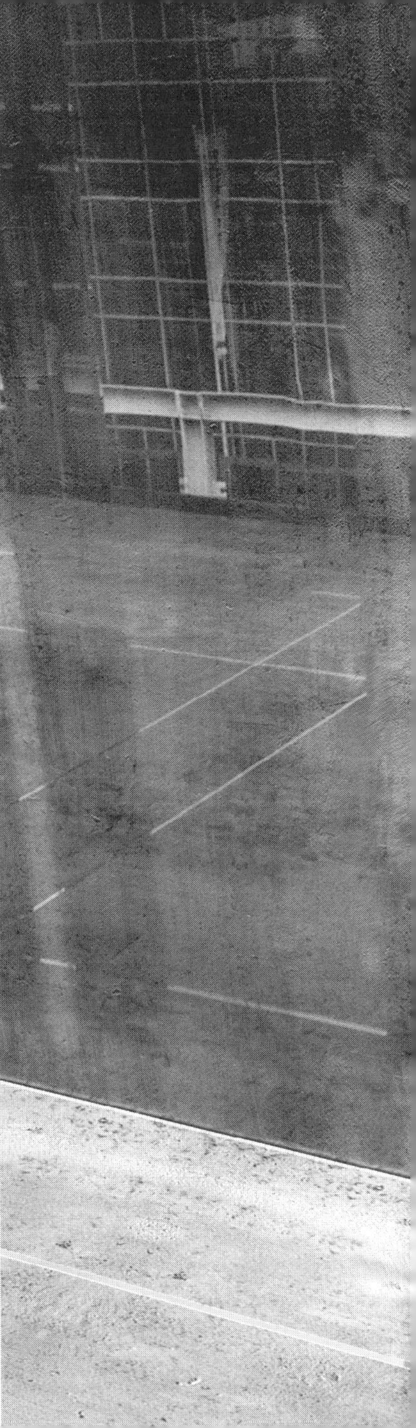

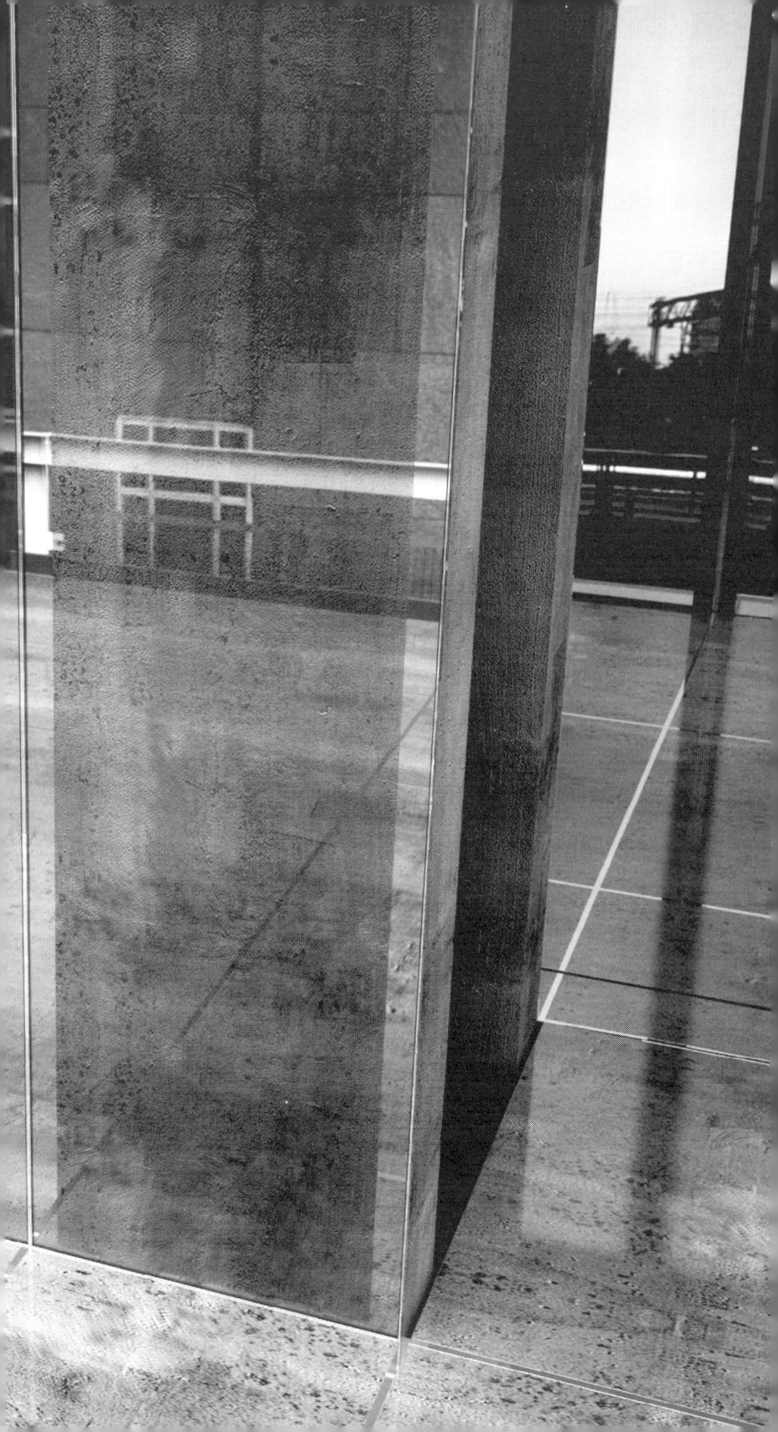

Roemer van Toorn

him – Tafuri and Hays confuse the idea of aesthetic distance with that of critical distance. Mies keeps the world at arm's length. He makes everything so beautifully abstract, imbues it with so much beauty, everything is so perfected, that the everyday – that of use – has no chance of taking possession of it by discovering or recognizing something in it. It is the reflection of amnesia – what Evans calls the beauty of the forgotten – that Mies van der Rohe propagates in the Barcelona Pavilion. Rather than the pavilion turning the spectator into an active investigator, the spectator is forced to identify with the pavilion by means of the many reflections he or she sees. In so doing Mies objectifies his reality, and the spectator can only identify with the beauty of the pavilion itself. It is a way of looking that, despite the dynamic interaction of reflections, operates in a dominant fashion, instead of mediating between inside and outside. Alternative levels of interpretation are excluded. Finding out just what is fixed must be open to interpretation, in order to bring the many contradictions that abound in reality into focus, might well be highly relevant to break through the impasse of the autonomous reflection in Mies's work.

Amateurism

Initially – when I first saw the publication *Untitled_Space* – I thought I detected the same obsession as Mies's propagated beauty. On closer examination, however, I saw that the abstract building that Paul Toornend and Jelle Post had designed on the computer hardly matters as an autonomous object. It is nothing else than a three dimensional camera that absorbs light in search of what specific reflections a space creates when reality enters it. The point is not the beauty of the object – as evidenced by the everyday objects, like a ball, a meadow, a bush or other kinds of reflections that enter the Untitled_Space. Instead of architecture framing life – making beautiful paintings of life in an architectural *Mies-en-scène* – everyday reality enters in heaps and unframed. In contrast to Mies van der Rohe, the Untitled_Space is not about the architecture itself; what is at stake is not the autonomous object but what it can set into motion at a specific spot in space. How architecture is continually able to change the perception of reality – in an unexpected and startling way. Mies van der Rohe's architecture clings to what is certain, while uncertain life is separate from it. He makes a roof so that life can have free range on it. Dealing with doubt, let alone with complex contradictions that might provide direction to a space, is not Van der Rohe's strong point. Untitled_Space, on the

Paul Toornend
and Jelle Post
UNTITLED_SPACE_14/04,
Zuidas, Amsterdam (NL),
May 2007

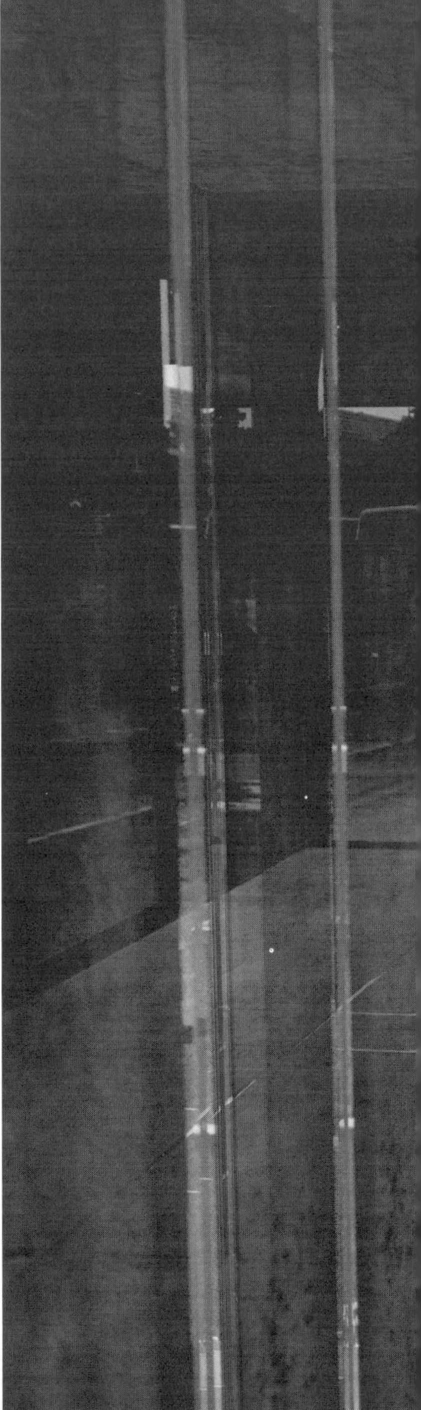

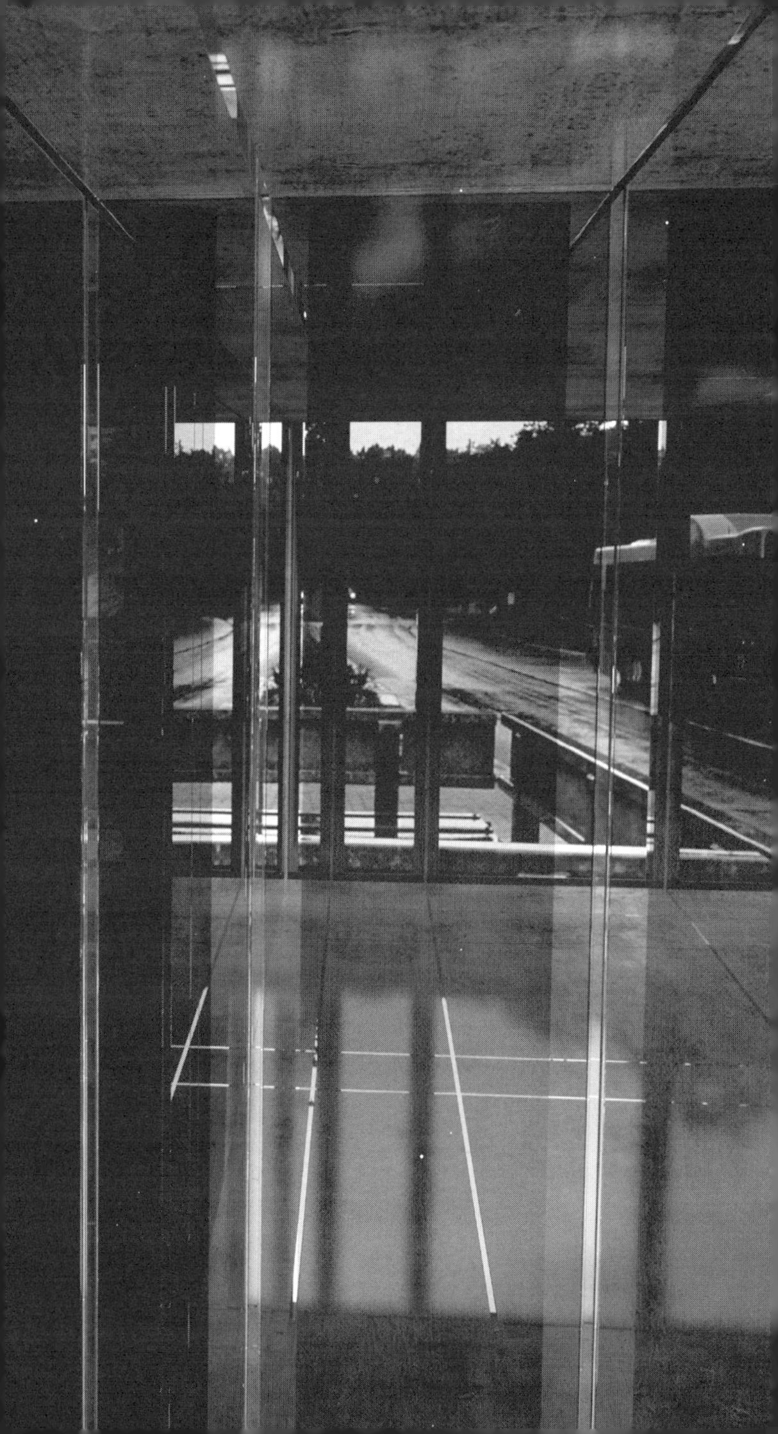

Paul Toornend
and Jelle Post
UNTITLED_SPACE_14/05,
Zuidas, Amsterdam (NL),
May 2007

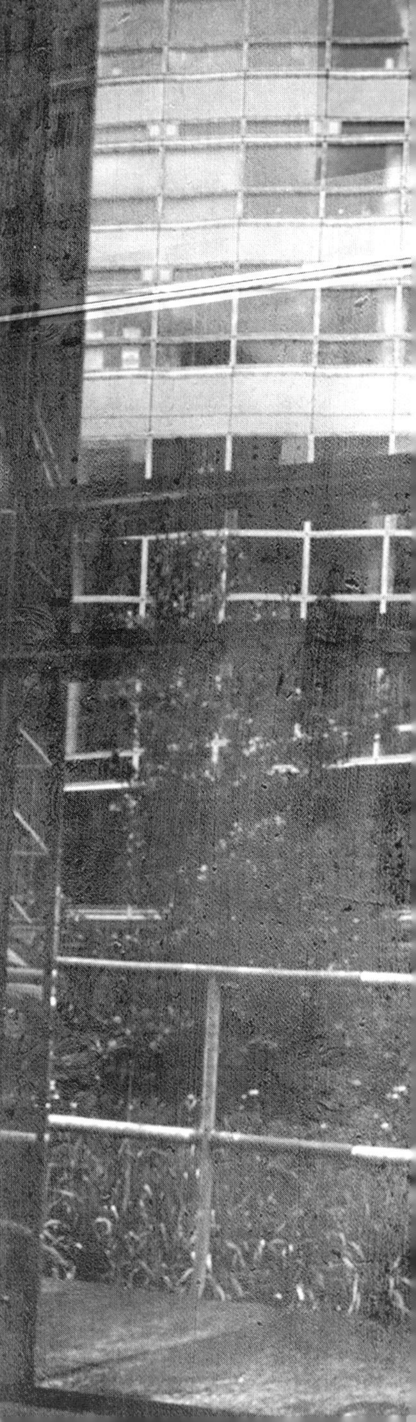

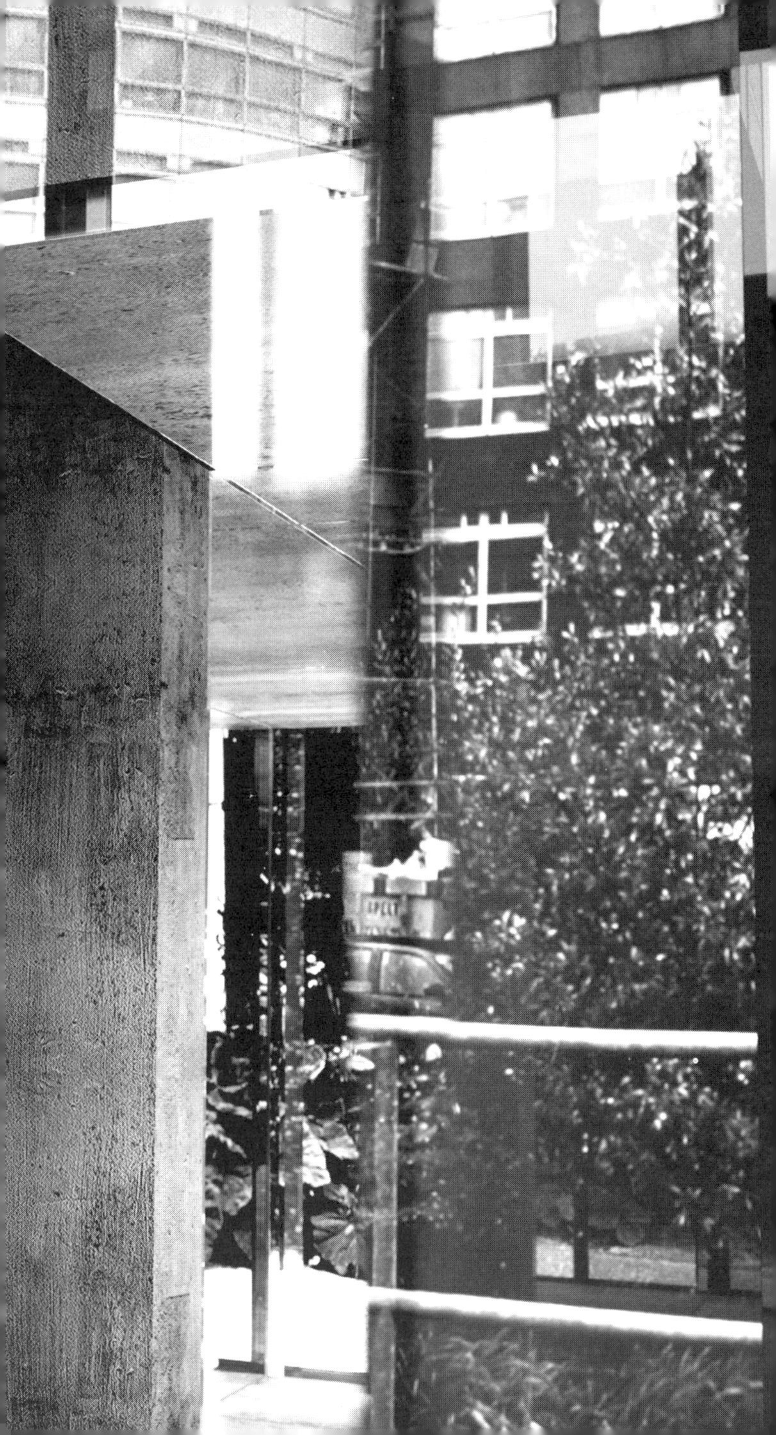

Paul Toornend
and Jelle Post
UNTITLED_SPACE_14/06,
Zuidas, Amsterdam (NL),
May 2007

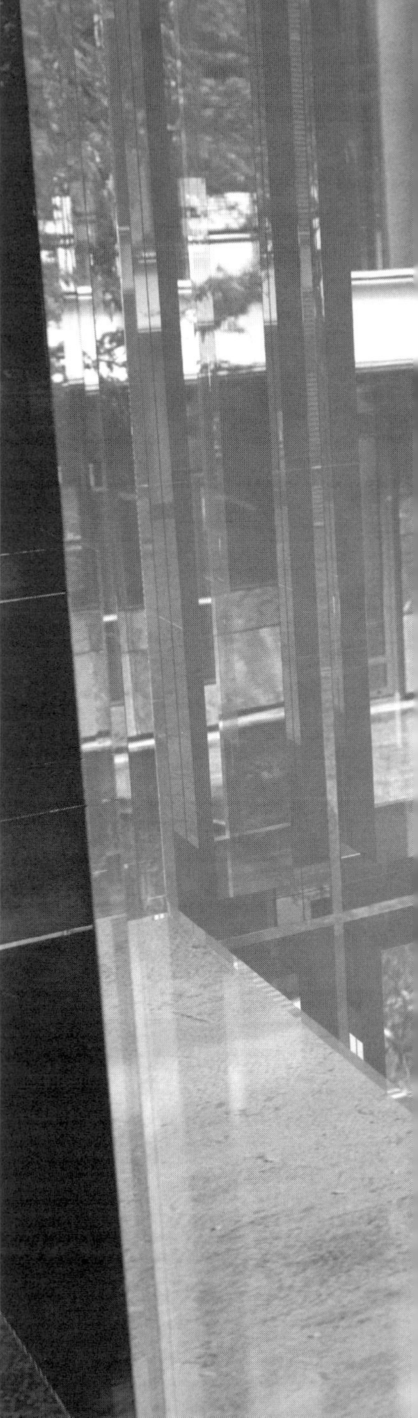

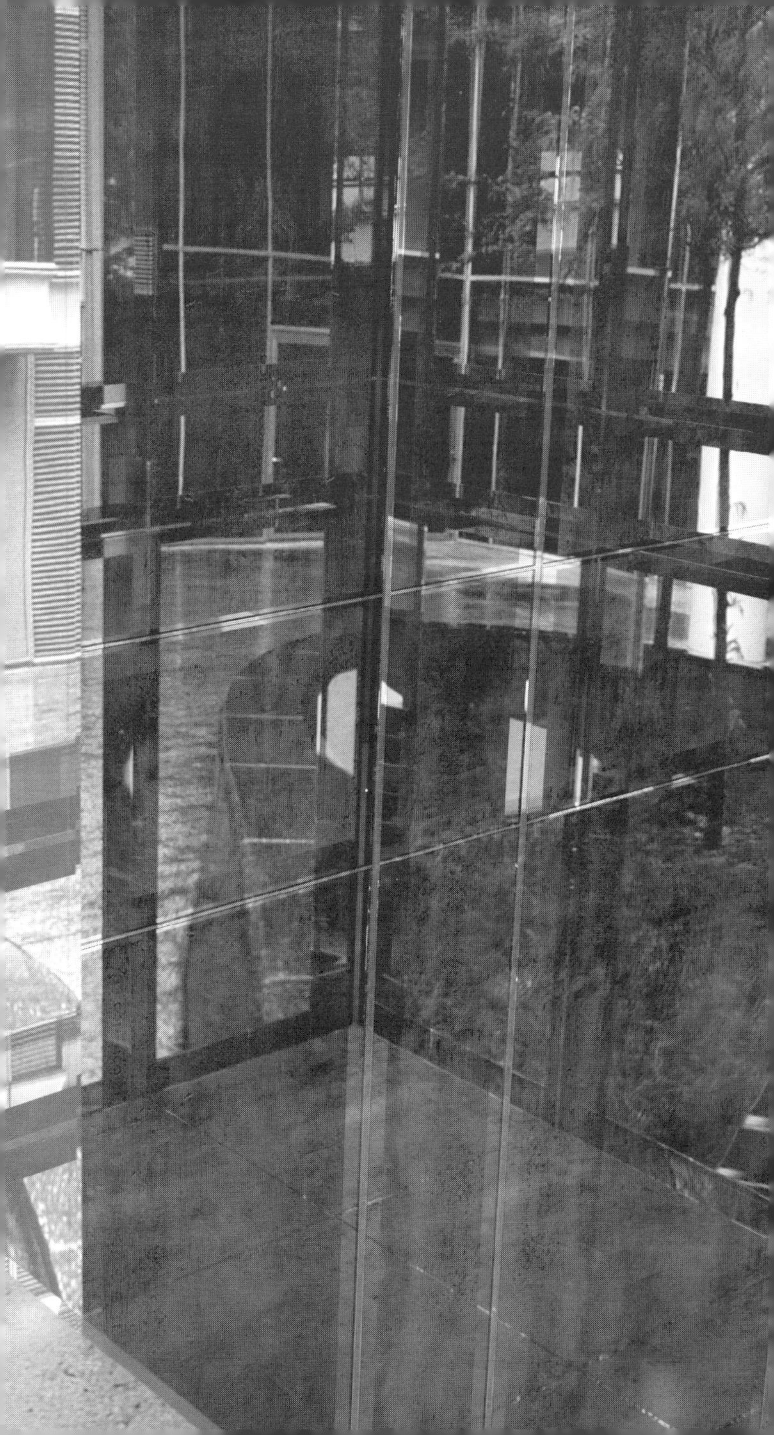

contrary, is not about the permanence of the architecture, but looks into what it sets into motion. In the Untitled_Space tectonics, collage and photography meet in a surprising way. Toornend and Post are looking for what the moving eye sees beyond Mies van der Rohe's framed gaze. What draws their attention is not what is static, but what changes under the influence of the permanent in the architecture. In so doing they are entering unknown territory and deviating from institutional paths. And they open the door to a necessary amateurism. Experts are certified professionals who, by collaborating with the right authorities, realize institutionally correct and in particular profitable projects according to the norm. The amateur, on the contrary, is nourished by care, affection instead of profit, self-interest and limited specialization. The amateur resists the blindness of the expert; he does not merely follow the procedural route dictated by technical competence, but instead is prepared to take risks precisely because he wants to relate to the public sphere. In essence the amateur is asking, how does one speak the truth, and what truth? For whom, and why?

On to the Zuidas

In terms of outlook and method I can follow Toornend and Post. But how were we to confront the new work and residential city of Zuidas with the concept of Untitled_Space? When we went to look at the Zuidas we were struck by how shabbily and unimaginatively neoliberalism manifests itself in the Netherlands. The mediocre architecture we were presented with, based on an urban-design plan stripped to the bone, is fairly hopeless. We saw a public space that is nothing more than a cheap display for Amsterdam's corporate business, with neutralized art as decorative kitsch, a public space lacking any form of urban conflict befitting a real city. We felt something had to be done. We saw lifts whiz by like Untitled_Spaces, into which different realities can be projected, like those encountered at La Défense. We thought buildings on a 50-cm plinth, with a light ticker with stocks and news information, like those we know from the CNN news scroll, would be a good idea. That way, at least, it would be clear what these urban centres are based upon: the permanence of virtual economic speculation. Or should we do something with the ideology of the lobby on the Zuidas?

We weren't satisfied with these proposals. We ran into a problem: our critical commentary

Paul Toornend
and Jelle Post
UNTITLED_SPACE_14/07,
Zuidas, Amsterdam (NL),
May 2007

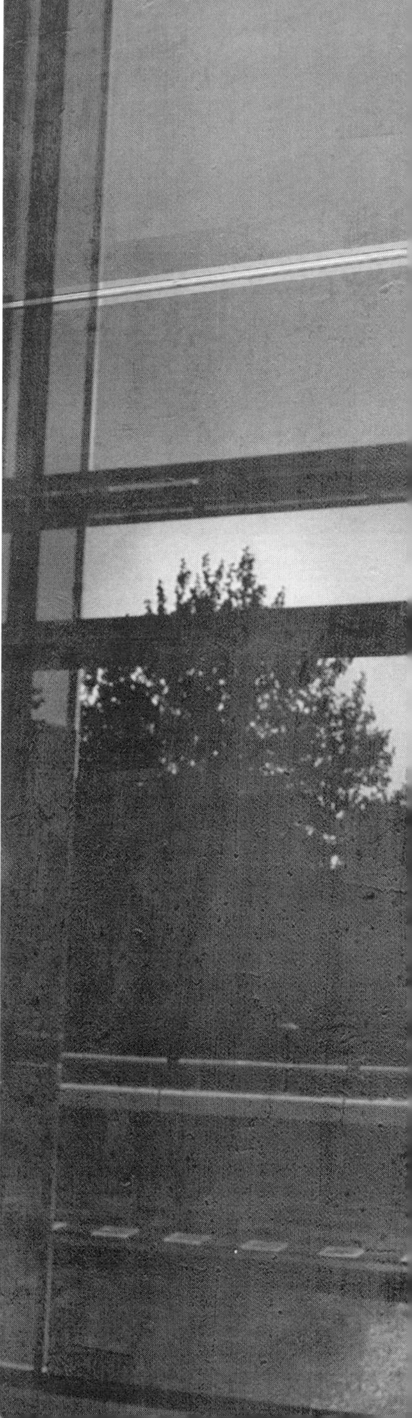

Paul Toornend
and Jelle Post
UNTITLED_SPACE_14/08,
Zuidas, Amsterdam (NL),
May 2007

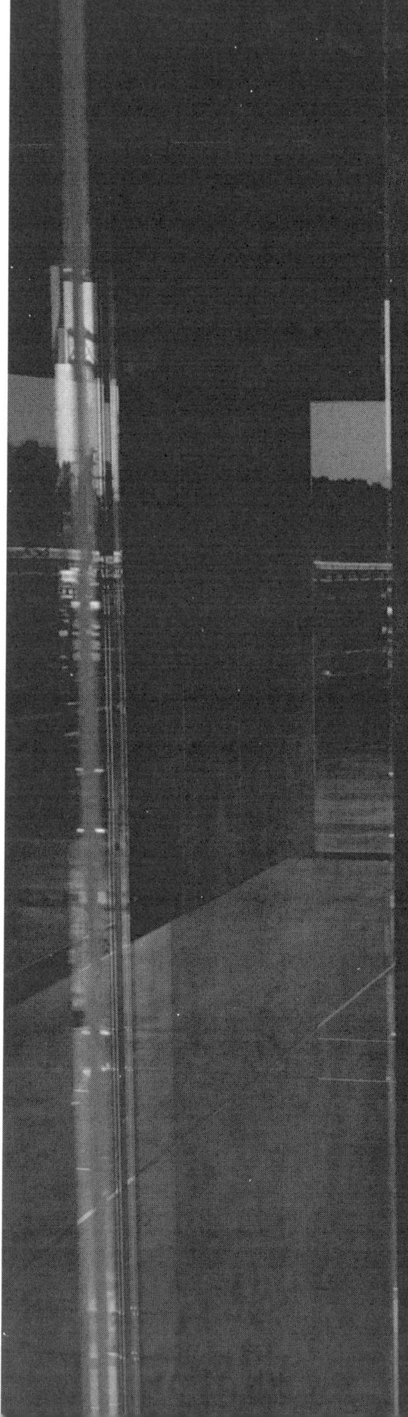

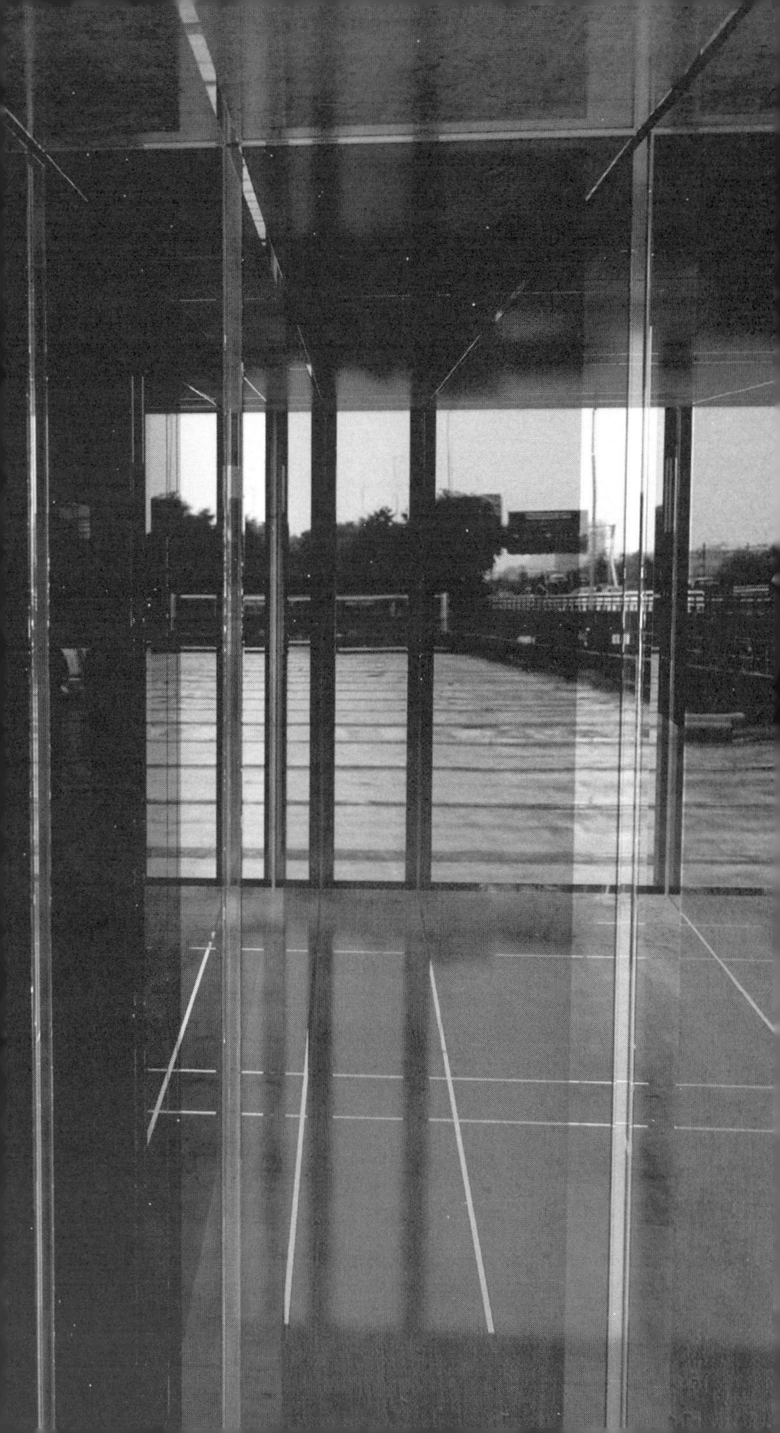

Paul Toornend
and Jelle Post
UNTITLED_SPACE_14/09,
Zuidas, Amsterdam (NL),
May 2007

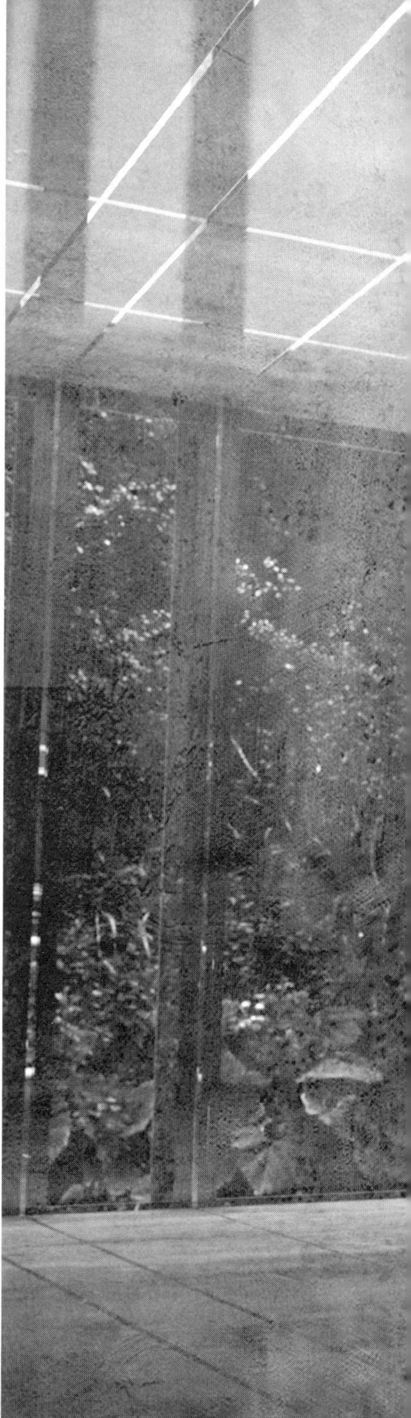

seemed too literal. The spectator no longer needs to experience, discover or interpret anything personally. When you set theories or opinions loose on a project, the risk arises that the project will become an illustration of an idea or a critique, whereas the project itself should be able to stimulate through the experience of looking. Toornend and Post went back to their tried method of the Untitled_Space. They took photographs of the Zuidas and set them loose on their space without features, constructed on the computer. After many hours of computing time, unexpected images appeared. Yet how exactly were we supposed to interpret this mountain of subjective images of the Zuidas? How were we supposed to decide which spaces of the Zuidas were interesting and which were not, which were a secret and which were not, which would elicit commentary and which would not? Here the tried method of the Untitled_ Space failed us. The amateur gaze had to be precisely directed, that is to say we had to rely on our viewpoints to make a definitive selection. A selection that addresses the multiple cultural meanings of the Zuidas, beyond the subjective gaze that the method of the Untitled_Space generated on the computer. This method entailed Toornend and Post looking, by means of the computer, from various camera angles through the Untitled_Space at locations on the Zuidas: through a door, through a room, you see a hangar-like space, or the Zuidas is reflected by a wall. Operating procedurally, all the angles are neatly aligned, but what perceptions and emotional effects the combinations of images can stimulate in the viewer through colour, subject, sensation, visual rhyme, contradiction, emptiness and imagination – as a theatre of the city – that is what Toornend, Post and I care about. However elaborate and clever a method might be, a trick does not make art. By means of our professional amateurism, we found out, together, by choosing ever-changing combinations of angles and locations, that a series of four triptychs with varying angles best captures the actual character of the Zuidas. The combination creates multiple connections among the images. In other words, a certain mediation takes place between the different contents contained within the image and activated by the act of looking.

Not Seeing, but Looking

The promise of the Untitled_Space experiment lies in the opportunity to look at reality with different eyes. This is not about seeing the facts – the stereotypical image of the Zuidas advertising likes to propagate – but about an act of looking that shows the familiar and the apparently trivial in a different way. Experiencing and evaluating – judging through looking – generated more rewarding reactions than

Paul Toornend
and Jelle Post
UNTITLED_SPACE_14/10,
Zuidas, Amsterdam (NL),
May 2007

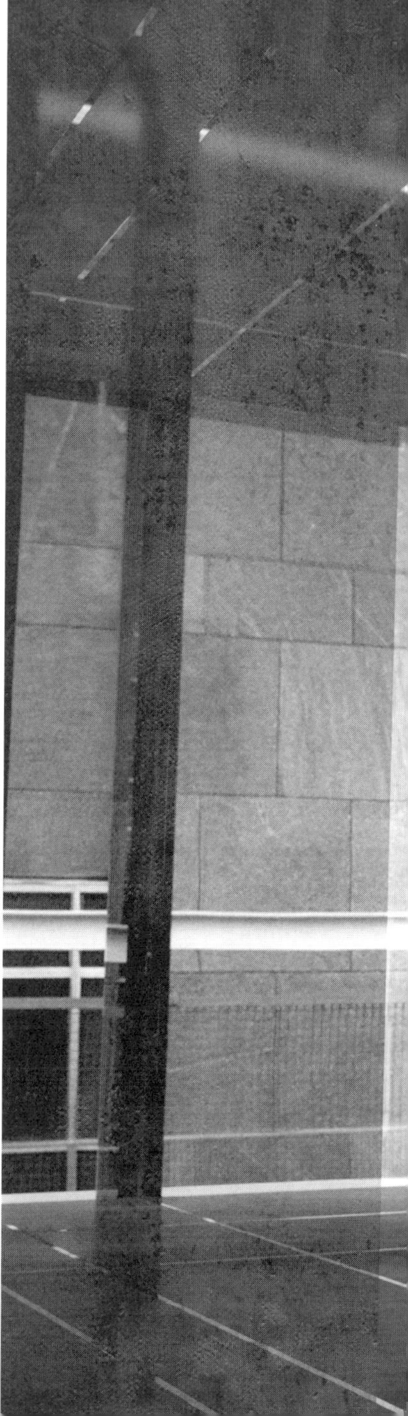

Paul Toornend
and Jelle Post
UNTITLED_SPACE_14/11,
Zuidas, Amsterdam (NL),
May 2007

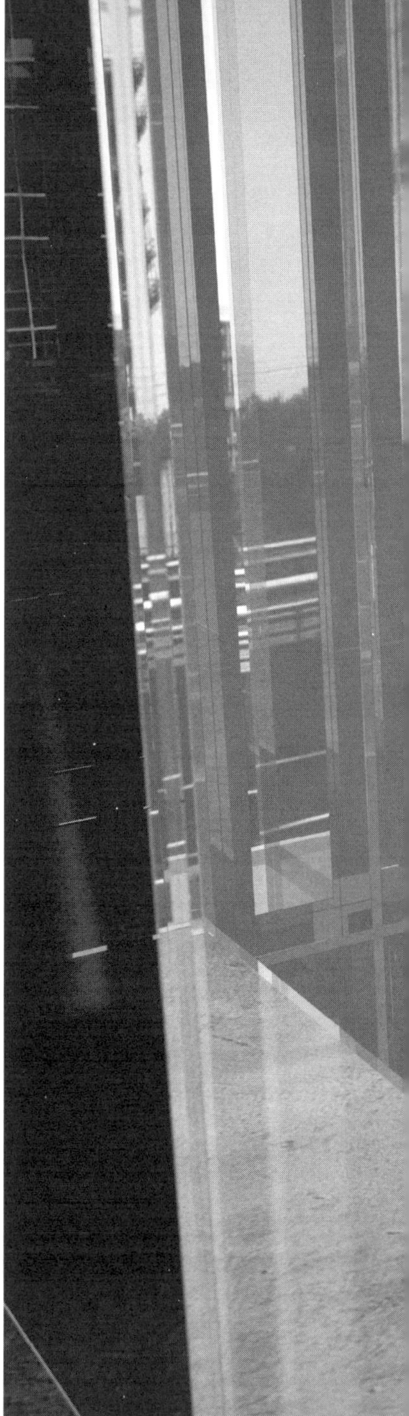

Paul Toornend
and Jelle Post
UNTITLED_SPACE_14/12,
Zuidas, Amsterdam (NL),
May 2007

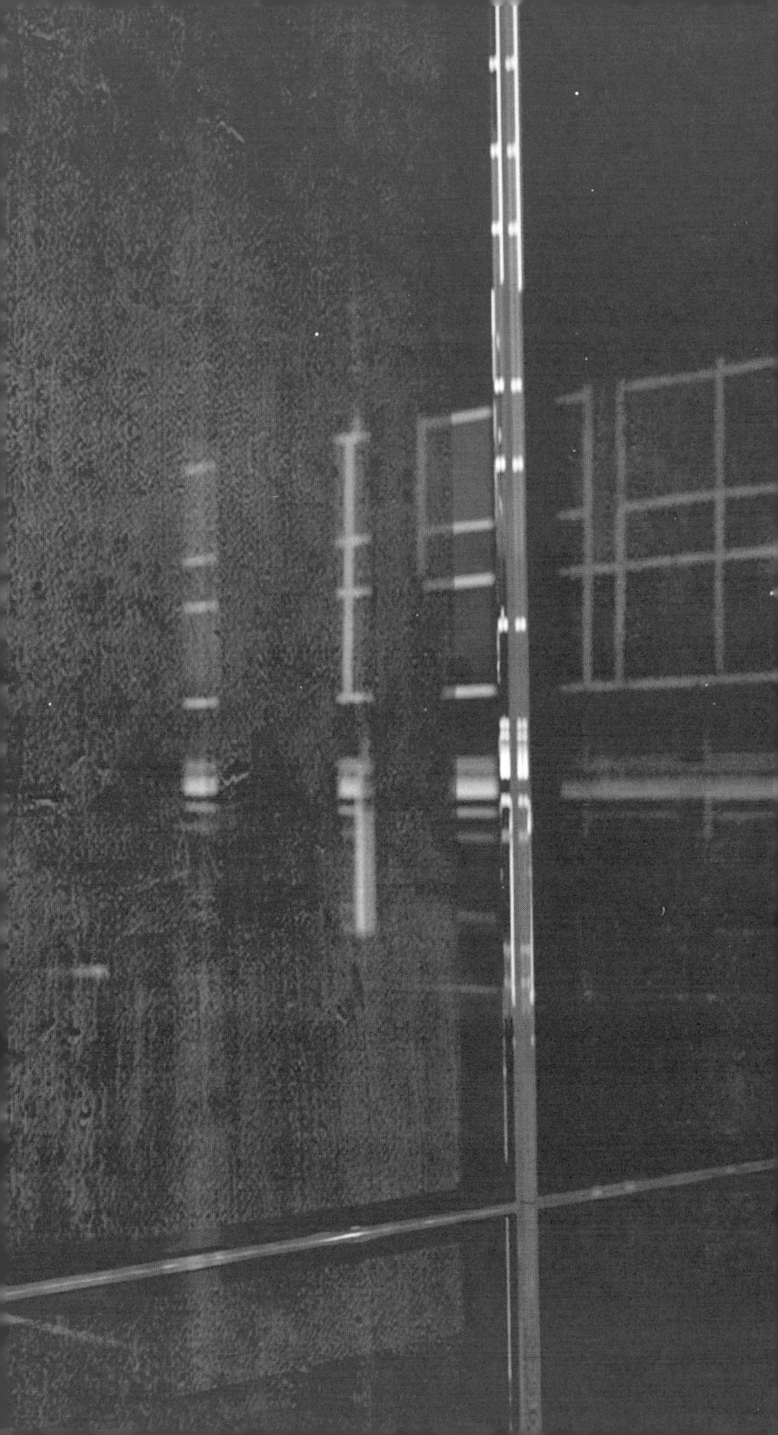

Roemer van Toorn

reading and understanding a method or the theoretical exposition of a work. By experiencing the images and not understanding them – if everything goes right – a moment in time filled with ambiguity opens up. If you could see that the Untitled_Space images were in fact computer montages, our plan would fail. It is not the computer, but the amateurish method that should control the process: open up the gaze onto reality. Each image in the series should evoke a tension between subjective construction and documentary recording, so that the audience begins to investigate. Like the spectacle, these four triptychs command all attention (certainly when they are exhibited, the smoothness of the surface, the use of colour, the sterility and reflection of the Untitled_Space will strike the viewer), but it is no authoritarian spectacle, no spectacle that merely seduces, but rather a spectacle that poses questions. It is like an inward-facing Mesdag panorama.[11] Instead of looking at a panorama from a single elevated point, from a distance, the various panoramas of the Zuidas are unlocked within the three-dimensional interior of the Untitled Space. The gaze does not stretch to the horizon, but light reflections of what is taking place outside are interconnected by the rough framing of the space – by doors, windows, walls, floors, ceilings and materials – awaiting the reflections of the spectator. In the four triptychs, various main themes of the Zuidas are highlighted. There is a kind of narcissist, almost autistic beauty through which the architecture is annexing the surroundings and turning them into a religion of pure abstraction associated with a sublime form of luxury. In a surprising way – with surreal and sometimes even Baroque aspects – the wild and the designed greenery of the Zuidas invades the abstract order at certain moments. At other moments we seem to find ourselves in Jean-Luc Godard's sinister 1965 science-fiction film, *Alphaville*. And this while in another triptych the world of the infrastructure is strung together in fragments or the emptiness in all its indeterminacy begs to be put to use.

In an earlier experiment, the space without features (Untitled_Space)[12] changed into a luxury villa with transparent storeys and reflections of everyday use in the Holland landscape. Here the Untitled_Space could still be read as an actual villa, built and inhabited. With the experiment on the Zuidas, it has long ceased to be about floor plans, elevations, façades or entrances – it doesn't matter whether you find yourself in a villa, a high-rise or a lobby. The point is how an abstract modern order – a space without features such as that encountered on the Zuidas – with its endless corporate interior – generates a series of multiple reflections through which it says a great deal about its use and the city. As far as I'm concerned the point is not the beauty

Roemer van Toorn

of the Untitled_Space on the Zuidas, but how the method of the Untitled_Space reveals the actual character of the Zuidas through its spatial reflections of its immediate surroundings. By looking through the Untitled_Space we see that architecture is too important to be left to the architectural object itself. Architecture is always more than that which the autonomous object places in the foreground: architecture is a relational aesthetics. A politics of appearance in space. A viewing machine that directs the gaze. Not from a single point but with a simultaneous gaze. One that produces, as well, instead of simply representing. What we need is a re-appreciation of looking, image and spectacle, of how we can use the act of looking by the active spectator to better understand the architecture we produce and use.

Looking through the Space

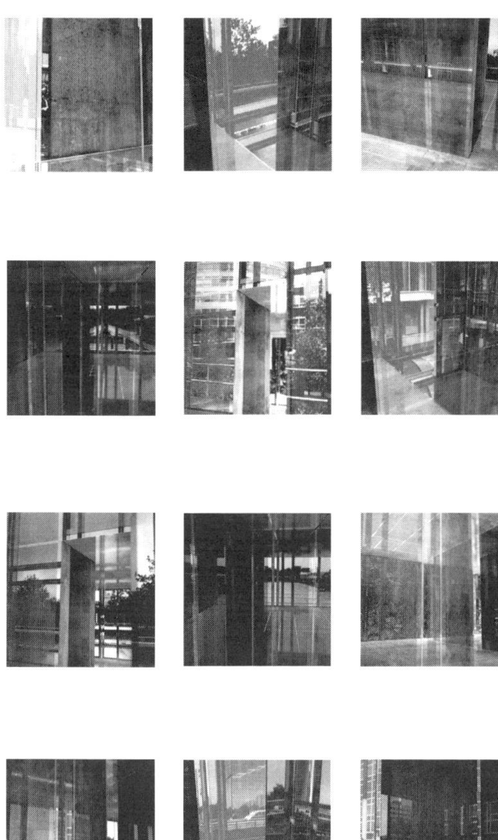

Roemer van Toorn

Notes
1. 'Der Paparazzo, das sind wir', interview with Paul Virilio in: *Der Spiegel* (37, 1997), 08.09.1997.
2. Guy Debord, *Comments on the Society of the Spectacle* (London/New York: Verso, 1998).
3. Fredric Jameson, *Signatures of the Visible* (New York: Routledge, 1992).
4. The world is headed for a global environmental catastrophe, Islam will engulf our Christian culture, the devaluation of our society through the free market and super-individualism is destroying the public sphere, and so on and so forth.
5. See for example Harm Tilman, 'Architecten moeten pleitbezorgers worden voor een betere leefomgeving', interview with Anthony Vidler in: *de Architect*, January 2007; Kenneth Frampton, 'Architecture in the Age of Consumption', in: Power: *Producing the Contemporary City*, catalogue of the International Architecture Biennale Rotterdam (Rotterdam: NAi Publishers 2007).
6. Such as in the work of Jeanne van Heeswijk and many other artists who take pity on everyday reality and set to work outside the walls of the museum. The alibi for their art lies in a passion for reality.
7. Bruno Latour and Peter Weibel (eds.), *Making Things Public: Atmospheres of Democracy* (Cambridge/MA: MIT Press, 2005).
8. Paul Toornend and Jelle Post, *Untitled_Space* (Amsterdam: Architectura+Natura, 2005).
9. Michael Hays, 'Critical Architecture: Between Culture and Form', in: *Perspecta 21*, 1984.
10. Robin Evans, 'Mies van der Rohe's Paradoxical Symmetries', in: Ibidem, *Translations from Drawing to Building and Other Essays* (Cambridge/MA: The MIT Press, 1997).
11. In The Hague, the Netherlands, www.panorama-mesdag.nl
12. Toornend and Post, op.cit. (see note 8).

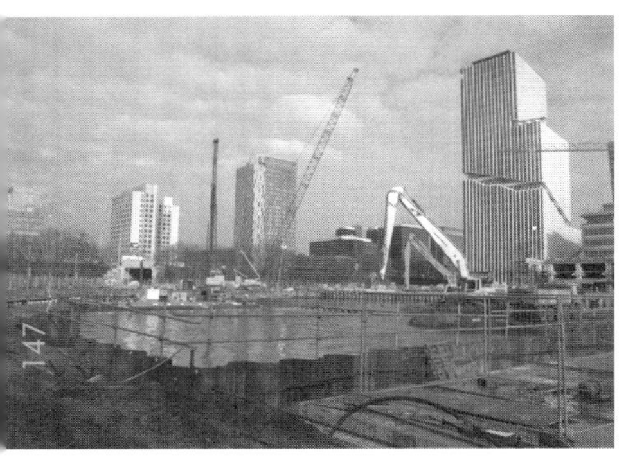

147

Chantal Mouffe

Public Spaces and Democratic Politics

What interests me in different uses of 'public' is a reference to democratic politics in the sense of the common, publicity or openness and it is the aspect that I want to emphasize in the reflections that I will develop, focusing on the idea of the 'public space'. As far as I am concerned, what is at stake in this debate is the kind of public space that those who want to foster the radical democratic project should try to establish, a space of deliberation and consensus or a space of agonistic confrontation.

To begin, I need to delineate the theoretical framework which will inform my approach. Its main tenets have been developed in several of my previous publications[1] and here I will limit myself to the aspects that are relevant to my argument about 'the public'. Let's start with the distinction I have proposed making between 'politics' and 'the political'. In ordinary language it is not very common to speak of 'the political' but I think that such a distinction opens important alleys for reflection and a variety of political theorists are making it. The difficulty, though, is that no agreement

Chantal Mouffe

exists among them concerning the meaning attributed to these different terms and that may cause some confusion. Commonalities exist, however, and they can provide some points of orientation. For instance, to make this distinction suggests a difference between two types of approach – political science, which deals with the empirical field of 'politics', and political theory, which is the domain of philosophers who enquire not about the facts of 'politics' but about the essence of 'the political'. If we wanted to express such a distinction in a philosophical way, we could, borrowing the vocabulary of Heidegger, say that politics refers to the 'ontic' level while 'the political' has to do with the 'ontological' one. This means that the ontic has to do with the manifold practices of conventional politics, while the ontological concerns the very way in which society is symbolically instituted.

But this still leaves the possibility of a lot of disagreement about what constitutes 'the political' and that has important consequences for the way 'the public' is envisaged. Some theorists like Hannah Arendt envisage the political as a space of freedom and public deliberation, while others see it as a space of power, conflict and antagonism. My understanding of 'the political' clearly belongs to the second perspective. More precisely this is how I distinguish between 'the political' and 'politics'. By 'the political' I refer to the dimension of antag-

Public Spaces and Democratic Politics

onism which I take to be constitutive of human societies, while by 'politics' I refer to the set of practices and institutions through which an order is created, organizing human coexistence in the context of conflictuality provided by the political.

The Political as Antagonism

I want to take as the point of departure of my reflection about the public space our current incapacity to envisage the problems facing our societies in a *political* way. Political questions are not mere technical issues to be solved by experts. Properly political questions always involve decisions which require making a choice between conflicting alternatives. This incapacity to think politically is to a great extent due to the uncontested hegemony of liberalism. 'Liberalism', in the way I use the term in the present context, refers to a philosophical discourse with many variants, united not by a common essence but by a multiplicity of what Wittgenstein calls 'family resemblances'. There are to be sure many liberalisms, some more progressive than others but except for a few exceptions (Isaiah Berlin, Joseph Raz, John Gray and Michael Walzer among others) the dominant tendency in liberal thought is characterized by a rationalist and individualist approach which is unable to adequately grasp the pluralistic nature of the social world, with the conflicts that pluralism entails; conflicts for which no rational solution could ever exist, hence the dimension of antagonism that characterizes human societies. The typical liberal understanding of pluralism is that we live in a world in which there are indeed many perspectives and values and that, due to empirical limitations, we will never be able to adopt them all, but that, when put together, they constitute a harmonious and non-conflictual ensemble. This is why this type of liberalism must negate the political in its antagonistic dimension. Indeed, one of the main tenets of this liberalism is the rationalist belief in the availability of a universal consensus based on reason. No wonder that the political constitutes its blind spot. Liberalism has to negate antagonism since, by bringing to the fore the inescapable moment of decision – in the strong sense of having to decide in an undecidable terrain – what antagonism reveals is the very limit of any rational consensus.

When we examine the different perspectives existing within contemporary liberal thought, we can single out two main paradigms. The first one, sometimes called 'aggregative', envisages politics as the establishment of a compromise between competing forces in society. Individuals are portrayed as rational beings, driven by the maximization of their

Public Spaces and Democratic Politics

own interests and as acting in the political world in a basically instrumental way. It is the idea of the market applied to the domain of politics which is apprehended with concepts borrowed from economics. The other paradigm, the 'deliberative' one, developed in reaction against this instrumentalist model, aims at creating a link between morality and politics. Its advocates want to replace instrumental rationality by communicative rationality. They present political debate as a specific field of application of morality and believe that it is possible to create in the realm of politics a rational moral consensus by means of free discussion. In this case politics is not apprehended through economics but through ethics or morality. In both cases what is left aside by this rationalist approach, be it on the mode of instrumental rationality or communicative rationality, is the crucial role played in the field of politics by what I call 'passions', the affective dimension which is central to the constitution of collective forms of identification, identifications without which it is impossible to grasp the construction of political identities. Political identities are always collective identities and this is another reason why liberalism with its methodological individualism is unable to grasp the specificity of the political. In politics we are always dealing with a 'we' opposed to a 'them' and, as I will show in a moment, this is why antagonism cannot be eliminated.

I contend that it is only when we acknowledge 'the political' in its antagonistic dimension that can we pose the central question for democratic politics. This question, pace liberal theorists, is not how to negotiate a compromise among competing interests, nor is it how to reach a 'rational', i.e. fully inclusive consensus, a consensus without any exclusion. Despite what many liberals want us to believe, the specificity of democratic politics is not the overcoming of the we/them opposition, but the different way in which it is established. What democracy requires is drawing the we/them discrimination in a way compatible with the recognition of the pluralism which is constitutive of modern democracy.

In developing this point I have found the notion of the 'constitutive outside' particularly useful because it unveils what is at stake in the constitution of identity. This term has been proposed by Henry Staten[2] to refer to a number of themes developed by Jacques Derrida around notions like 'supplement', 'trace' and 'difference'. The aim is to highlight the fact that the creation of an identity always implies the establishment of a difference, which is often constructed on the basis of a hierarchy, for example between form and matter, black and white, man and women etc. Once we have understood that every identity is relational and that the affirmation of a difference is a precondition for the existence of any identity, i.e. the perception of something 'other' which constitutes its 'exterior', we can understand why politics is concerned with the constitution of a 'we' which can only exist by the demarcation of a 'them'. This does not mean of course that such a relation is necessarily one of friend/enemy, i.e. an antagonistic one. But we should realize that, in certain conditions, there is always the possibility that this we/them relation can *become* antagonistic. This happens when the 'them' is perceived as putting into question the identity of the 'we' and as threatening its existence. From that moment on, as the case of the disintegration of Yugoslavia testifies, any form of we/them relation, be it religious, ethnic, economic or other becomes the locus of an antagonism.

Let's draw a first theoretical conclusion from the previous reflections. What we can assert at this stage is that the we/them distinction, which is the condition of possibility of formation of political identities, can always become the locus of an antagonism. Since all forms of political identities entail a we/them distinction, this means that the possibility of emergence of antagonism can never be eliminated. It is therefore an illusion to believe in the advent of a society from which antagonism would have eradicated. Antagonism is an ever present

Chantal Mouffe

possibility, the political belongs to our onto-logical condition and when we envisage the public space this is something that needs to be taken into account.

Politics as Hegemony

Next to antagonism, the concept of hegemony is, in my approach, the other key notion for addressing the question of 'the political'. To acknowledge the dimension of 'the political' as the ever present possibility of antagonism requires coming to terms with the lack of a final ground and the undecidability which pervades every order. It requires in other words recognizing the hegemonic nature of every kind of social order and the fact that every society is the product of a series of prac-tices attempting to establish order in a context of contingency. As Ernesto Laclau indicates, 'the two central features of a hegemonic inter-vention are, in this sense, the "contingent" character of the hegemonic articulations and their "constitutive" character, in the sense that they institute social relations in a primary sense, not depending on any a priori social rationality.'[3] The political is linked to the acts of hegemonic institution. It is in this sense that one has to differentiate the social from the political. The social is the realm of sedimented practices, that is practices that conceal the originary acts of their contingent political institution and which are taken for granted, as if they were self-grounded. Sedimented social practices are a constitutive part of any possible society; not all social bonds are put into question at the same time. The social and the political have thus the status of what Heidegger called *existentials*, i.e. necessary dimensions of any societal life. If the political – understood in its hegemonic sense – involves the visibility of the acts of a social institution, it is impossible to determine a priori what is social and what is political independently of any contextual reference. Society is not to be seen as the unfolding of a logic exterior to itself, whatever the source of this logic could be: forces of production, development of the Spirit, laws of history, etc. Every order is the temporary and precarious articulation of contingent practices. The frontier between the social and the political is essentially unstable and requires constant displacements and renegotiations between social agents. Things could always be otherwise and therefore every order is predicated on the exclusion of other possibilities. It is in that sense that it can be called 'political' since it is the expression of a particular structure of power relations. Power is constitutive of the social because the social could not exist without the power relations through which it is given shape. What is at a given moment considered as the 'natural' order – jointly with

Chantal Mouffe

the 'common sense' which accompanies it – is the result of sedimented hegemonic practices. It is never the manifestation of a deeper objectivity exterior to the practices that bring it into being.

Summarizing this point, every order is political and based on some form of exclusion. There are always other possibilities that have been repressed and that can be reactivated. The articulatory practices through which a certain order is established and the meaning of social institutions is fixed are 'hegemonic practices'. Every hegemonic order is susceptible of being challenged by counter-hegemonic practices, i.e. practices which will attempt to disarticulate the existing order so as to install another form of hegemony.

As far as collective identities are concerned, we find ourselves in a similar situation. Identities are the result of processes of identifications and they can never be completely fixed. We are never confronted with 'we/them' oppositions expressing essentialist identities preexisting the process of identification. Moreover since, as I have stressed, the 'them' represents the condition of possibility of the 'we', its 'constitutive outside', this means that the constitution of a specific 'we' always depends of the type of 'them' from which it is differentiated. This is a crucial point because it allows us to envisage the possibility of different types of we/them relation according to the way the 'them' is constructed.

Which We/Them for Democratic Politics?

Once the ever present possibility of antagonism is acknowledged, one can understand why one of the main tasks for democratic politics consists of defusing the potential antagonism that exists in social relations. If we accept that this cannot be done by transcending the we/them relation, but only by constructing it in a different way, then the following question arises: what could constitute a 'tamed' relation of antagonism, what form of we/them would it imply? How could conflict be accepted as legitimate and take a form that does not destroy the political association? This requires some kind of common bond to exist between the parties in conflict, so that they will not treat their opponents as enemies to be eradicated, seeing their demands as illegitimate, which is precisely what happens with the antagonistic friend/enemy relation. However, the opponents cannot be seen simply as competitors whose interests can be dealt with through mere negotiation, or reconciled through deliberation, because in that case the antagonistic element would simply have been eliminated. If we want to acknowledge on the one hand the

145

permanence of the antagonistic dimension of the conflict, while on the other hand allowing for the possibility of its 'taming', we need to envisage a third type of relation. This is the type of relation which I have proposed calling 'agonism'.[4] While antagonism is a we/them relation in which the two sides are enemies who do not share any common ground, agonism is a we/them relation where the conflicting parties, although acknowledging that there is no rational solution to their conflict, nevertheless recognize the legitimacy of their opponents. They are 'adversaries' not enemies. This means that, while in conflict, they see themselves as belonging to the same political association, as sharing a common symbolic space within which the conflict takes place.

What is at stake in the agonistic struggle is the very configuration of power relations around which a given society is structured, it is a struggle between opposing hegemonic projects which can never be reconciled rationally. The antagonistic dimension is always present. It is a real confrontation but one which is played out under conditions regulated by a set of democratic procedures accepted by the adversaries. An agonistic conception of democracy acknowledges the contingent character of the hegemonic politico-economic articulations which determine the specific configuration of a society at a given moment. They are precarious and pragmatic constructions which can be disarticulated and transformed as a result of the agonistic struggle among the adversaries. Contrary to the various liberal models, the agonistic approach that I am advocating recognizes that society is always politically instituted and never forgets that the terrain in which hegemonic interventions take place is always the outcome of previous hegemonic practices and that it is never a neutral one. This is why it denies the possibility of a non-adversarial democratic politics and criticizes those who, by ignoring the dimension of 'the political', reduce politics to a set of supposedly technical moves and neutral procedures.

The Public Space

It is time now to examine the consequences of the agonistic model of democratic politics that I have just delineated for envisaging the public space. The most important consequence is that it challenges the widespread conception that, albeit in different ways, informs most visions of the public space conceived as the terrain where consensus can emerge. For the agonistic model, on the contrary, the public space is the battleground where different hegemonic projects are confronted without any possibility of final reconciliation. I have spoken so far of the public space, but I need to specify straight away that we are not dealing here with one single space. According to the agonistic approach, public spaces are always plural and the agonistic confrontation takes place on a multiplicity of discursive surfaces. I also want to insist on a second important point. While there is no underlying principle of unity, no predetermined centre to this diversity of spaces, diverse forms of articulation always exist among them and we are not faced with the kind of dispersion envisaged by some postmodernist thinkers. Nor are we dealing with the kind of 'smooth' space found in Deleuze and his followers. Public spaces are always striated and hegemonically structured. A given hegemony results from a specific articulation of a diversity of spaces and this means that the hegemonic struggle also consists of the attempt to create a different form of articulation among public spaces.

My approach is therefore clearly very different from the one defended by Jürgen Habermas, who when he envisages the political public space, which he calls the 'public sphere', presents it as the place where deliberation aiming at a rational consensus takes place. To be sure Habermas now accepts that it is improbable, given the limitations of social life, that such a consensus could effectively be reached and he sees his ideal situation of communication as a 'regulative idea'. However, according to the perspective that I am advocating, the impediments to the Habermasian ideal speech situation are not empirical but ontological and the rational consensus that he presents as a regulative idea is in fact a conceptual impossibility. Indeed it would require the availability of a consensus without exclusion, of a we without a them, which is precisely what I have shown is impossible.

To support my argument about the impossibility of such a rational consensus I have referred to Derrida and the constitutive outside, but I could also have reached the same conclusion with the help of different thinkers. We can for instance also use Wittgenstein's insights to undermine Habermas's conception of procedures and the very idea of a neutral or rational dialogue. In order to have agreements about opinions, there must first be agreement on the language used, and this, as Wittgenstein points out, implies agreement about forms of life. According to him procedures only exist as a complex ensemble of practices. Those practices constitute specific forms of individuality and identity that make possible the allegiance to the procedures. It is because they are inscribed in shared forms of life and agreements on judgments that procedures can be accepted and followed. They cannot be seen as rules, created on the basis of principles, and then applied to specific cases. Rules for Wittgenstein are always abridgments of practices. They are inseparable from specific forms of life. Therefore distinctions between 'procedural' and 'substantial' or between 'moral' and 'ethical', which are central to the Habermasian approach cannot be maintained.

Still another way to problematize the very possibility of the notion of the 'ideal speech situation' conceived as the asymptotic ideal of intersubjective communication, free of constraints and where the participants arrive at consensus by means of rational argumentation, is to follow the lead of Slavoj Žižek, through Lacan. Indeed a Lacanian approach reveals how discourse itself, in its fundamental structure, is authoritarian since, out of the free-floating dispersion of signifiers, it is only through the intervention of a master signifier that a consistent field of meaning can emerge. For Lacan the status of the master signifier, the signifier of symbolic authority, founded only on itself, is strictly transcendental: the gesture that 'distorts' a symbolic field, that 'curves' its space by introducing a non-founded violence is in the stricter sense correlative to its very establishment. This means that, if we were to substract from a discursive field its distortion, the field would disintegrate, it would 'de-quilt' to speak in Lacanese. This clearly undermines the very basis of the Habermasian view, according to which the inherent pragmatic presuppositions of discourse are non-authoritarian since they imply the idea of a communication free of constraints where only rational argumentation counts.

I also want indicate that, despite the similar terminology, my conception of the agonistic public space also differs from the one of Hannah Arendt which has become so popular recently. In my view the main problem with the Arendtian understanding of 'agonism' is that, to put it in a nutshell, it is an 'agonism without antagonism'. What I mean is that while Arendt puts great emphasis on human plurality and insists that politics deals with the community and reciprocity of human beings who are different, she never acknowledges that this plurality is at the origin of antagonistic conflicts. According to her, to think politically is to develop the ability to see things from a multiplicity of perspectives. As her reference to Kant and his idea of 'enlarged thought' testifies, her pluralism is not fundamentally different from the liberal one because it is inscribed in the horizon of an intersubjective agreement. Indeed what she looks for in Kant's doctrine of the aesthetic judgment is a procedure for ascertaining intersubjective agreement in the public space. Despite significant differences between their respective approaches, Arendt ends up like Habermas envisaging the public

Chantal Mouffe

space in a consensual way. To be sure, as Linda Zerilli has pointed out, in her case the consensus results from the exchange of voices and opinions (in the Greek sense of doxa) not from a rational 'Diskurs' like in Habermas. While for Habermas consensus emerges through what Kant calls 'disputieren', an exchange of arguments constrained by logical rules, for Arendt it is a question of 'streiten', where agreement is produced through persuasion, not irrefutable proofs. However neither of them is able to acknowledge the hegemonic nature of every form of consensus and the ineradicability of antagonism, the moment of 'Wiederstreit', what Lyotard refers to as 'the differend'. It is symptomatic that, despite finding their inspiration in different aspects of Kant's philosophy, both Arendt and Habermas have in common that in Kant's aesthetic they privilege the aspect of the beautiful and ignore his reflection on the sublime. This is no doubt related to their avoidance of 'the differend'.

The Public as Publikum

To end I would like to share with you some thoughts concerning the relation between the Public as 'Öffentlichkeit' and the Public as 'Publikum'. It is clear that we are not dealing with two preconstituted entities facing each other but that there exists a relation of mutual implication. The very identity of a given public space is a function of its public and recipro-cally the identity of the public is at stake in the way the public space is constructed. Since I am focusing here on the political aspect of this relation, the question I would like to address concerns the implications of this discursive construction for the political role that progres-sive critical arts practices could play.

I want to stress at the outset that when I think about the relation between art and poli-tics, I do not see it in terms of two separately constituted fields, art on one side and politics on the other, between which a relation would need to be established. There is an aesthetic dimension in the political and there is a polit-ical dimension in art. This is why I never speak of political art because I consider that one cannot make a distinction between political and non-political art. From the point of view of the theory of hegemony, artistic practices play a role in the constitution and maintenance of a given symbolic order or to its challenging and this is why they necessarily have a political dimension. The political, for its part, concerns the symbolic ordering of social relations, what Claude Lefort calls 'the mise en scène', 'the mise en forme' of human coexistence and this is where its aesthetic dimension lies.

The real issue concerns the possible forms of *critical* art, the different ways in which artistic practices can contribute to the questioning of the dominant hegemony. Once we accept that identities are never pre-given but that they are always the result of processes of identification, that they are discursively constructed, the question that arises is the type of identity that critical artistic practices should aim at fostering. Clearly those who advocate the creation of agonistic public spaces, where the objective is to unveil all that is repressed by the dominant consensus, are going to envisage the relation between artistic practices and their public in a very different way from those whose objective is the creation of consensus, even if this consensus is seen as a critical one. I am for this reason very suspicious of the current tendency to promote 'commemorative' art because, even when the intention is a critical one, it tends to impose one accepted way of seeing things instead of opening up the debate and facilitating an agonistic confrontation. According to the agonistic approach, critical art is art that foments dissensus, that makes visible what the dominant consensus tends to obscure and obliterate. I do not think, however, that critical art only consists of manifestations of refusal, that it should be the expression of an absolute negation, a testimony of the 'intractable' and 'unrepresentable'. We witness today a certain infatuation with the 'sublime' which leads to dismissing the importance of proposing new modes of coexistence, of contributing to the construction of new forms of collective identities. There is too much emphasis on 'dis-identification' at the expense of 're-identification'. This perspective, while claiming to be very radical, remains trapped within a very deterministic framework according to which the negative gesture is in itself enough to bring about the emergence of a new form of subjectivity. As if this subjectivity was already latent, ready to emerge as soon as the weight of the dominant ideology would have been lifted. Such a conception is in my view completely anti-political. It fails to come to terms with the nature of the hegemonic struggle and the manifold of practices, discourses and language games through which identities are constituted. I am convinced that it is only by recognizing the need for a plurality of forms of interventions, taking place in a variety of public spaces, that critical artistic practices can contribute to the constitution of a variety of agonistic spaces where a radical and plural conception of democracy could be fostered.

Chantal Mouffe

Notes
1. Ernesto Laclau and Chantal Mouffe, *Hegemony and Socialist Strategy. Towards a Radical Democratic Politics* (London: Verso, 1985); Chantal Mouffe, *The Return of the Political* (London: Verso, 1993); Chantal Mouffe, *The Democratic Paradox* (London: Verso, 2000).
2. Henry Staten, *Wittgenstein and Derrida* (Oxford: Basil Blackwell, 1985).
3. Ernesto Laclau, *Emancipation(s)* (London: Verso, 1996), p. 90.
4. This idea of 'agonism' is developed in my book *The Democratic Paradox*, op. cit., chapter 4 (see note 1). To be sure, I am not the only one to use that term and there are currently a variety of 'agonistic' theorists. However, they generally envisage the political as a space of freedom and deliberation, while for me it is a space of conflict and antagonism. This is what differentiates my agonistic perspective from the one defended by William Connolly, Bonnig Honig or James Tully.

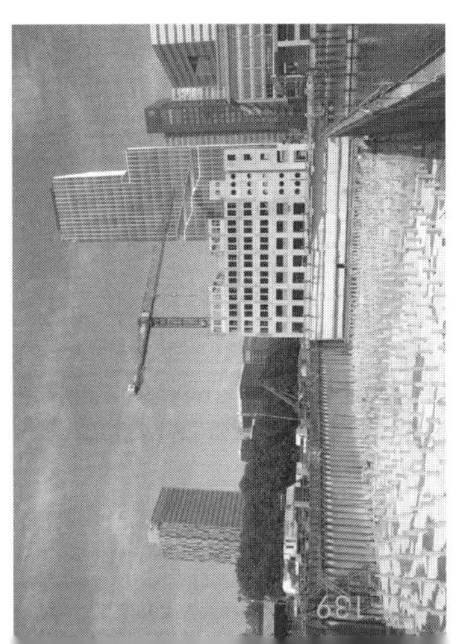

Gerard Drosterij

Art and Public Space
The Question of Artistic Publicness

This article deals with the ambivalent relationship between art and public space. On the one hand art is seen as a human expression which awards public spaces with precious insights. On the other hand it is said that art – especially public art – is more and more encapsulated by the hegemony of big institutional players. The question arises how art can stay relatively independent while remaining publicly influential. In other words, how to define art's position in public space?

Some say that a solution to the above dilemma is to challenge powerful social hierarchies. Because artists are worried that art is getting trapped between commercialism and state patronage, an agonistic approach to art in public space is seen as the only way out. Unravelling the structure of knotted power might turn art into a new counter culture; and in a time of raging global capitalism, many would welcome this.

I have reservations about the agonist conception of public space, however, and will propose an alternative conception. In my opinion the power of art in public space lies in its capacity to create a sense of publicness: to suggest, through its very particularity, a connection between the addressee's aesthetic impressions and his or her ideas of the world at large. If an art work succeeds in evoking a sense of publicness, it might create a public space among a greater audience. In any case, art has no obligation to entertain a political commitment, that is, to understand itself to be socially interdependent and embedded in power relations, which consequently needs to be communicated to its audience.

I will explain this thesis by comparing different conceptions of public space, but will concentrate on the agonist conception since it has become rather influential in current discourses about art and public space – not least concerning the debate about art and the Amsterdam-Zuidas.

Documenta 12: Aesthetic Challenge or Perverse Conservatism?

If something was absent in documenta 12, it was rhetorical and visual bombast. Some even complained about the lack of thematic and literary direction whilst visiting the exhibition. Documenta 12 caused confusion and a loss of direction. The Aue-Pavillion – a huge glass house construction with metallic curtains and brown floors – was an especially unwelcome place, it was said, a place where orientation was annoyingly difficult.[1] Although I had the same experience, initially, I started to appreciate the inside absence in the Aue-Pavillion of preordained destinations and museological contextualizations. It took some effort to accept the crisscross positioning of the art objects, but ultimately it was challenging to be thrown back on just observing, thinking, memorizing and associating. The horizontal architecture of the pavilion forced the visitor to concentrate on the works of art themselves, and to make the connections himself. The visual result was a wandering attendance that was magically blended with the works of art.

I guess that a visit to documenta 12 gave way to the sensation that director Roger M. Buergel and curator Ruth Noack had in mind by creating its 'inherent formlessness':[2] to invite visitors to choose their own path. In Buergel's portrayal: 'They tend to feel the challenge deeply and they counter this challenge by seeking for identity. But how does one keep the balance between identification and fixation? Art can teach us that discipline ... This is aesthetic experience in its true sense: the exhibition becomes a medium in its own right and can thus hope to involve its audience in its compositional moves.'[3] Not the form of the exhibition itself but the form of its art was to the concern of Buergel and Noack. After a barrage of political engagement during the former documenta, they choose to let art speak for itself. A rather daring gesture; to reposition art in the centre of attention and see how it speaks of the world.

Documenta 11 was different. Its message outweighed the medium. Not art itself but the socio-political context in which art operated stood at the forefront – in the words of director Okwui Enwezor 'yet another turbulent time of unceasing cultural, social, and political frictions, transitions, transformations, fissures, and global institutional consolidations.'[4] How art was supposed to deal with this constellation was documenta 11's question. It was, Enwezor wrote, the 'challenge of making meaningful articulation of the possibilities of contemporary art in such a climate, as well as the disciplinary, spatial, temporal, and historical pressures to which it has been subjected, represent the diagnostic, deliberative process out of which the full measure of documenta 11 has been engaged.'[5] Documenta 11 burdened art with politics. Art had to render account of its message. 'In the democratic system', Enwezor stated, 'the demands of citizenship place strong ethical constraints on the artist, based on his or her commitment to all "forms of life." The practice of art presents the artist with the task of making such commitment.'[6] Enwezor only saw two courses for art to steer: clear of or towards politics. Yet, in effect the former option is out of this world, it is 'not only perversely conservative but, more importantly, misunderstands the nature of the critical energy that drives the conditions of artistic production ... '[7]

Buergel and Noacks's intention has been somewhat more laid-back than Enwezor's almost aggressive stand.[8] Instead of focusing on today's world wide web of complexities – art's inescapable theater – they have taken a big step back by posing the classic art question of the 'internal dynamic destinies of form'.[9] Thinking of documenta 12, Buergel said he wanted to be 'idiotic': acknowledging his ignorance, and moving away from the burden of current public conventions.[10] 'Wir vertrauen der Kunst'[11] is a remark that stands in sharp contrast to Enwezor's political perception of artistic commitment.

Modernity and Three Conceptions of Public Space

The idea that art needs to challenge the socio-political status quo is quite a popular thought today; but in my opinion in need of some serious assessment. Why should artists have to think of their art as stemming from a political disposition? And why does art have to be activist and critical in order to be called truly public? Below I will compare several conceptions of public space and thereby hope to illustrate that these assumptions are not satisfactory. Art can do perfectly well in public space without a political mission statement.

We could say that ever since Beethoven – while having a walk with Goethe – decided not to bow to the approaching Archduke Rudolph,[12] the discourse about the arts changed into the question about art's meaning for free citizens. Or as Robert Hughes has put it: 'The idea of a cultural avant-garde was unimaginable before 1800. It was fostered by the rise of liberalism. Where the taste of religious or secular courts determined patronage, "subversive innovation" was not esteemed as a sign of artistic quality.'[13] Beethoven undoubtedly represented this subversive innovative spirit[14] as he was everything but obedient to political power. Beethoven was a democrat[15] and personified a new kind of freedom, namely to be free in one's artistic creations from political directives.

At the same time, modern artistic freedom raised the question about its public implications – what was it for? As the sovereign became the public, a wide discussion about art's quality was inevitable. A public sphere in the world of art emerged,[16] with the salon as its central place.[17] The discussion about the public meaning of art has never stopped, and especially today, during a time of great international turbulence, it is seen as more critical than ever to hold.

At present agonist theory is rather influential in explaining art's role in public space. An important defender of this theory is Chantal

Mouffe, whose writings (together with Ernesto Laclau) have unmistakably helped to prepare documenta 11's conceptual framework.[18] According to Mouffe the prime function of art in public space is to radicalize democratic society, to bring into the open its inherent power struggles. The idea that public art should challenge and agonize hegemonic interests stems from Mouffe's basic belief that '[a]ny social objectivity is constituted through acts of power. This means that any social objectivity is ultimately political and has to show the traces of the acts of exclusion that govern its constitution ... '[19] Hence, public space is the domain in which we need to transform antagonistic power relations into agonist relations: 'Antagonism is struggle between enemies, while agonism is struggle between adversaries.'[20]

The idea of agonism goes back to the late nineteen-fifties. It was the time of intense emancipatory impulses (e.g. existentialism, Beat Generation, feminism) and in art of the rise of the 'neo-avant-garde'.[21] The general worry of artists and intellectuals was the disappearance of public space, be it in relation to artistic innovation, democratic legitimacy, or public morals. The creation of a counter culture was needed, vital to shake off the tarnished legacy of Western bourgeois culture (capitalism, universalism, neo-colonialism etc.). The term 'agonist' stems from Hannah Arendt, who was deeply inspired by Greek publicness, which she characterized as 'a fiercely agonal spirit'.[22] Greek publicness was a manifestation of individuality and particularity, a result of the belief that 'man is capable of action [and] that the unexpected can be expected from him, that he is able to perform what is infinitively improbable.'[23] Arendt formulated her agonist conception of public space as an alternative to the dominant liberal conception of public space, characterized by a technocratic idea of politics on the one hand, and a materialistic understanding of interests and ideas that were exchanged in public on the other. The idea that a political elite, being democratically elected, could wisely aggregate the preferences of the people[24] was increasingly seen as a false neutralization of the political status quo. The public was made private as it were, being left out of political decisions that surely were of its concern. Democratic politics could not be limited to the occasional voting of political representatives. A strong democratization was called for which needed to take place through a political injection of public space.

Next to agonist theory, a second political alternative to the aggregative approach of public space was formulated during the early nineteen-sixties: deliberative theory, as represented by Jürgen Habermas.[25] Instead of Arendt's expressivist solution Habermas wanted to improve public space by rational deliberation. The opinion of the public needed to be taken seriously by setting up networks of communicating citizens. The object was to reach rational consensus about core values of democratic politics. So, while Arendt returned to the classical ideal of public excellence in order to reclaim public space, Habermas returned to the Enlightenment idea of public reason.

However, Mouffe stresses that her theory breaks with Arendt's. She criticizes Arendt for still being influenced too much by Western universalism and for maintaining a liberal idea of diversity and plurality.[26] Mouffe, in contrast, proceeds from the idea of 'the hegemonic nature of every form of consensus and the ineradicability of antagonism'.[27] Because antagonism is part and parcel of contemporary societies, consensus will always be artificial, identities fluid, and instability forever present. Public space activity is therefore centred on challenging political dominance. And, by making 'visible what the dominant consensus tends to obscure and obliterate', art can be of help with this assignment, she thinks.[28]

To be sure, both the deliberative and agonist conception of public space are political. Despite their different intellectual backgrounds they contemplate an approach to public space in which meaning needs to be publicly challenged. Words, acts and identities should be publicly discussed or agonized since they are effectively non-neutral; their meaning is expressed within a context of power and domination and needs to be subjected to publicity, accordingly. Hence, aesthetics becomes politics, or *Dasein* becomes *Design*, as Henk Oosterling has stylishly put it.

The difference between the deliberative and agonist conceptions, however, lies in their definition of the political *purpose* of public space. According to deliberative theory it should be focused on a rational discussion based on democratic values (e.g. sincerity, truthfulness, equality) with the aim of reaching social consensus and harmony. Since the nineteen-nineties the deliberative approach to public space has revived and led to a wide array of communicative and interactionist art. This art is lead by the 'ideal of social renewal by cultural challenge'[29] and is often process-based: it examines whether its activities empower a democratic culture, whether they promote understanding, toleration, interculturality etc. Jeroen Boomgaard has stressed the difference between the dominant agonist engagement of the nineteen-sixties and today's communicative (or deliberative) engagement: 'The basis for much committed action in public space is no longer the disruption of the system or the erosion of structure, but individual contact or interaction with a limited and clearly

Art and Public Spacee

circumscribed group. The emphasis is on participation in everyday life, not on action that unmasks everyday and exposes the hypocrisy of power.'[30]

Still, like the agonist conception of public space, deliberative engagement in public is seen as political. The ideal-typical understanding of public deliberation is democratic: identity and meaning are constituted in a process of communication and interactivity.[31] So, whether deliberative or agonistic, both models believe that theorizing public space is essentially political. They have left the classical liberal public/private approach that started in Beethoven's age, which made a principal difference between artistic publicness and political publicness – and which located real freedom in the former.

Introducing a Fourth Conception of Public Space

I have strong reservations about a political characterization of public space in general, and in relation to art in particular. The very value of an artistic public space lies in the freedom not to think about political decision-making. It is nonsensical to demand democratic responsibility of art, to expect that it should determine its position regarding political issues.

Gerard Drosterij

Public space activities in general should be concerned much less with questions about power modification, policy making or problem solving, but rather with contemplating, comparing and demonstrating. The sensation of publicness, and what a public space should safeguard, does not lie at the end of the epistemic spectrum – politics – but at its very beginning; namely, with the imagination of subjective experience.

I therefore suggest a different approach to public space. And if we put the three conceptions of public space that I have sketched below in a scheme, my preferred conception of public space will become automatically clear. A fourth conception of public space remains to be discussed.[32]

Intention \ Status	Non-political	Political
Rationalist	Aggregative	Deliberative
Ontological	Civil	Agonist

Four conceptions of public space

The aggregative model – whose influence today is still prevalent, of course – defines public space as an economical and technical way to optimally aggregate ideas and interests. The market is the prime mechanism to do this because it is seen as a rational and fair device. Furthermore, according to this model public space is not specifically political because people's interests are being defined and discussed in society itself. This makes the model unmistakably (neo)liberal. It stresses that, relatively independent from political decision making, a wide array of non-political ways of human interaction exists (art, trade, industry etc.). It is the task of political institutions to rationally aggregate all these different preferences.

Although the deliberative model also defines public space as a rational mechanism, it is seen as distinctively political. Merely aggregating ideas and interests will not lead to legitimate democratic decisions. Social theorist Jon Elster has written: 'The core of [deliberative] theory, then, is that rather than aggregating or filtering preferences, the political system should be set up with a view to changing them by public debate and confrontation.'[33] Reason should improve the democratic quality of society.

The agonist model shares with the deliberative model a political conception of public space; however, not with the intention to rationally discuss ideas and interests but to agonize them in order to lay bare their hidden power structure. This cannot be done rationalistically since to understand reality is, in Mouffe's words, not to bring mere arguments and justifications to the fore but to especially acknowledge that power constitutes social reality. This is an ontological position (a conception of human reality) and stands at the basis of a political definition of public space.

Now, in line with the aggregative conception of public space, I argue for a nonpolitical conception of public space. I believe that publicness is in no way automatically political. I consider the analytical difference between public space and politics as the essence of democracy since it provides citizens – and not least artists – with the freedom and opportunity to independently express their imagination, craft and intelligence. I call it therefore a civil conception of public space because public space activities evolve around the institutionalization of civil society.

Importantly, I share Mouffe's critique of a rationalist portrayal of public space and prefer an ontological understanding instead. Yet my idea of ontology is exactly the reverse of Mouffe's agonist publicness. An ontology is not a priori related to the intrinsic political constitution of social reality (embedded in power relations), as Mouffe would have it, but is related to man's particular reflection on aspects of human existence that cannot be put in a scientific language. As Otto Duintjer has written: 'Ontological statements do not refer to the reality in itself, but clarify our understanding of what we take as "existence" or "reality", given the context of a certain praxis, or broader, given a dominant world view within a certain time and culture.'[34] An ontology is constituted by the dialectic between our particular sensations and general impressions of the world. While the world is 'filled' with socially constructed artefacts, underneath these 'architectures' particular intuitions and experiences play a crucial role in understanding them. Civil publicness is centred on the reflection on this very dialectic, which is, as Habermas once wrote, 'a process of self-clarification of private people'[35] – of a people independent from political or social imperatives.

Artistic Publicness

A civil conception of public space is most sympathetic to thinking about art's position in society. The idea that publicness is an ontological sensation in a non-political environment goes well with the idea of artistic publicness. Works of art may invite the public to contemplate their particular aesthetic sensations in question, through which a different or deeper understanding of the world might be

Gerard Drosterij

achieved.[36] Buergel writes: 'Artists educate themselves by working through form and subject matter; audiences educate themselves by experiencing things aesthetically. How to mediate the particular content or shape of those things without sacrificing their particularity is one of the great challenges of an exhibition like the documenta.'[37] This requires an open mindset, and accepting '[t]he possibility of not understanding, of a total failure to relate . . . in order to enable other ways of understanding, other forms of relation'.[38]

In this respect a political conception of artistic publicness is deficient for it does not acknowledge the many other public expressions, actions and manifestations of art that are not focused on challenging dominant power relations. The virtue of publicness in general is not to agonize social reality per se, but to understand it, to theorize it, and even to classify it. The purpose is to develop different forms of organization in which the dialectic of publicness (in which private sensations are indispensable) can prosper.

Documentas 11 and 12 have demonstrated the difference between a political and non-political conception of artistic publicness. In the end, I think, art's potential to carry political statements only will increase if we discard any a priori political single-mindedness. As Boomgaard has put it: 'Art should be concerned about the world, but artists must continue to create their own platform and not allow themselves to become string puppets in the official commitment show.'[39]

Bringing back artistic publicness caused Buergel to tone down documenta's ambitions (or not, you could say), and to return to the 'simple' issue of the relation between the public, art and the world. Whether he has succeeded or not is less important than what he has tried to do, I think. In this respect it is telling how he writes about the first documenta (1955), which he compliments for being 'a form of organization.'[40] The exhibition raised the question of where art stands and where we stand, Buergel explains. And although he acknowledges documenta's very particular post-war context, he sees it as exemplary because it 'took place neither on the basis of the country's [West Germany, GD] new consti-tution, nor on the basis of religious or political beliefs ... Within the context of documenta, the public constituted itself on the groundless basis of aesthetic experience – the experience of objects whose identity cannot be identified. Here there was nothing to understand, in the true sense, no preconceptions, which is precisely why it was possible and essential to talk about everything, to communicate about everything. The exhibition was, in short, an act of civilization.'[41]

Public space is not inherently political. That has been the basic argument of this article. Likewise, public art in no way needs to be political. The expression and experience of publicness arises in all sorts of ways, relates to a collection of topics. It does not necessarily include a commentary on authority or domination. The essence of public space lies in the organization of publicness. It should provide for a spatial perpetuity, an enduring architecture, that is inviting to artistic publicness: the striking experience of the human condition through particular aesthetic expressions. An understanding of how such publicness can be evoked by art – unexpectedly, emotionally, dramatically, unanticipatedly[42] – shows precisely its distinctive (and tragic) beauty. A civil conception of public space stresses that the organization of artistic publicness is nonpolitical and ontological.

Art and Public Spacee

Notes
1. See e.g. Janneke Wesseling, 'Door een gat in de ruit',
in: *NRC Handelsblad*, Cultureel Supplement, 22 June
2007, p. 22 and Holland Cotter, 'Asking Serious
Questions in a Very Quiet Voice', in: *The New York Times*,
22 June 2007.
2. Roger M. Buergel and Ruth Noack, 'Preface', in:
Catalogue Documenta Kassel 16/06 – 23/09 2007
(Cologne: Taschen. 2007), p. 10.
3. Ibidem, pp. 11-12.
4. Okwui Enwezor, 'Preface', in: *Documenta11_Platform 5:
Exhibition, Short Guide* (Ostfeldern-Ruit: Hatje-Cantz.
2002), p. 6.
5. Ibidem.
6. Okwui Enwezor, 'The Black Box', in: *Documenta11_
Platform 5: Exhibition, Catalogue,* (Ostfeldern-Ruit: Hatje
Cantz, 2002), p. 54.
7. Ibidem, p. 53.
8. In his introduction to *Platform1_Documenta11:
Democracy Unrealized*, Enwezor does not mention art
once. Elsewhere he states: 'To understand what constitutes the avant-garde today, one must begin not in the
field of contemporary art but in the field of culture and
politics, as well as in the economic field governing all
relations that have come under the overwhelming
hegemony of capital.' Enwezor, 'The Black Box', op. cit.,
p. 45 (see note 6).
9. Buergel and Noack, 'Preface,' op. cit., p. 12
(see note 2).
10. Roger M. Buergel in: Hanno Rauterberg, 'Revolte in
Kassel', in: *Die Zeit*, 12 April 2007.
11. Ibidem.
12. As Ludwig van Beethoven explained in a letter to
Bettina Brentano in 1812. In: Romain Rolland, *Het leven
van Beethoven*, 1927 (Wereldbibliotheek, 1948) p. 36.

Gerard Drosterij

13. Robert Hughes, *The Shock of the New: Art and the Century of Change* (London: Thames and Hudson, 1980, 1993), p. 372.
14. 'Kings and Princes may install learned men and secret councils; and bestow them with titles and knighthoods; they cannot produce great men, giant minds that rise above the world's muck.' Beethoven in: Rolland, op. cit., p. 36 (see note 12), my translation.
15. Recall the 'Eroica tale': Beethoven originally dedicated his Third Symphony *Eroica* to Napoleon but later removed his name from the front page when Napoleon proclaimed himself emperor.
16. Magnificently set out by Habermas. See: Jürgen Habermas, *Structural Transformation of the Public Sphere: An Inquiry into a Category of Bourgeois Society*, translation: Thomas Burger (Cambridge: Polity Press, 1962, 1996), original title: *Strukturwandel der Öffentlichkeit: Untersuchungen zu einer Kategorie der bürgerlichen Gesellschaft.*
17. 'The bourgeois audience did not invent the salon but it did create the permissions within which the artistic variety that the salon, by 1820, had come to express could ferment an *avant-garde*.' Hughes, op. cit., p. 373 (see note 13).
18. Her article 'For an Agonistic Public Sphere' was published in: Okwui Enwezor (ed.), *Platform 1_Documenta11: Democracy Unrealized* (Ostfeldern-Ruit: Hatje-Cantz, 2002).
19. Chantal Mouffe, 'Democracy, Power, and the "Political"', in: Seyla Benhabib (ed.) *Democracy and Difference: Contesting the Boundaries of the Political* (Princeton: Princeton University Press, 1996), pp. 245-256. See also Chantal Mouffe, *The Democratic Paradox* (London/New York: Verso, 2000) p. 98.

20. '[An adversary is] somebody whose ideas we combat
but whose right to defend those ideas we do not put in
question.' Mouffe, *The Democratic Paradox*, ibidem,
p. 102. See also Mouffe's article elsewhere in this volume.
21. Hal Foster, *The Return of the Real: The Avant-Garde at
the End of the Century* (Cambridge/MA: MIT Press, 1996),
pp. 3 ff.
22. Hannah Arendt, *The Human Condition* (Chicago: The
University of Chicago Press, 1958, 1998), p. 41.
23. Ibidem, p. 178.
24. 'The democratic method is that institutional arrangement for arriving at political decisions which realizes the
common good by making the people itself decide issues
through the election of individuals who are to assemble in
order to carry out its will.' Joseph Schumpeter, *Capitalism,
Socialism and Democracy* (London: Unwin Paperbacks,
1943, 1987), p. 250.
25. 'Tendencies pointing to the collapse of the public
sphere are unmistakable, for while its scope is expanding
impressively, its function has become progressively
insignificant.' Habermas, op. cit., p. 4 (see note 16).
26. '[Arendt] never acknowledges that this plurality is at
the origin of antagonistic conflicts. According to Arendt,
to think politically is to develop the ability to see things
from a multiplicity of perspectives.... Despite significant
differences between their respective approaches, Arendt,
like Habermas, ends up envisaging the public space in a
consensual way.' See Chantal Mouffe, 'Artistic Activism
and Agonistic Spaces,' in: *Art & Research: A Journal of
Ideas, Contexts, and Methods*, 1/2, Summer 2007. See the
parallel from an art historic perspective when Enwezor
defends a third perspective of art, which he calls
postcoloniality, next to modernism and avant-garde: '[I]n
a sense, the avant-garde and formalist art [modernism,

GD] share a common assumption in the completeness of
their vision, which is to say: to secure the past and
maintain tradition, or to depart vigorously from the past
and renovate tradition.'
27. Mouffe, 'Artistic Activism and Agonistic Spaces',
ibidem. To be sure, I have strong doubts about Mouffe's
interpretation of Arendt, but lack of space forces me to let
this issue rest.
28. Ibidem.
29. Hughes, op. cit., p. 365 (see note 13).
30. Jeroen Boomgaard, 'The Platform of Commitment',
in: Jeroen Boomgaard et al., *One Year in the Wild*,
(Amsterdam: Gerrit Rietveld Academie/Universiteit van
Amsterdam, 2004), p. 46. Hal Foster's idea of the
'ethnographic turn': 'Only with the ethnographic turn in
contemporary art and theory... is the turn from medium-
specific elaborations [modernism] to debate-specific
projects so pronounced.' Foster, op. cit., p. xi
(see note 21).
31. For a Dutch example of a deliberative or communicative conception of public space, see René Boomkens,
*Een drempelwereld: moderne ervaring en stedelijke
openbaarheid* (Rotterdam: NAi Publishers, 1998), p. 53;
for a conception of public space that balances between
deliberative and agonistic, see Henk Oosterling,
'Grootstedelijke reflecties: De verbeelding van de
openbare ruimte', in: Henk Oosterling and Siebe Thissen
(eds.), *Grootstedelijke reflecties: Over kunst & openbare
ruimte*, InterAkta 5, 2002, p.11; Henk Oosterling,
'Bouwen voorbij gated communities en no go areas: of
hoe onherbergzaam zijn hedendaagse individuen?' in:
Dennis Kaspori and Henk Oosterling, *Bewoningsinterven-
ties: een prospectus voor alternatieve woningbouw*
(Rotterdam: The Maze Corporation, 2003), pp. 97-139;

Dennis Kaspori, 'Een communisme van ideeën: Naar een open source architectuurpraktijk', in: *Archis*, no. 3, 2003.
32. I have analyzed these models of public space in relation to political theory in depth elsewhere: Gerard Drosterij, 'Mind the Gap: Three Models of Democracy, One Missing; Two Political Paradigms, One Dwindling', in: *Contemporary Political Theory*, 6/1, 2007, pp. 45-66.
33. Jon Elster, 'The Market and the Forum: Three Varieties of Political Theory', in: James Bohman and William Rehg (eds.), *Deliberative Democracy: Essays on Reason and Politics* (Cambridge/MA: The MIT Press, 1986, 1997), p.11.
34. Otto Duintjer, *Rondom metafysica: over 'transcendentie' en de dubbelzinnigheid van de metafysica* (Meppel: Boom, 1988). pp. 7-8, my translation.
35. Habermas, op. cit., p. 29 (see note 16).
36. Cf. Richard Sennett, *The Fall of Public Man* (New York/London: W.W. Norton & Company, 1974, 1992),p. 4
37. www.documenta12.de/leitmotive.html?&L=1, last visit: 13 September 2007.
38. Roger M. Buergel, 'The Origins', in: *Modernity, Documenta 12 Magazine* (Köln: Taschen, 2007), pp. 25-39.
39. Boomgaard, 'Platform of Commitment', op. cit., p. 51 (see note 30).
40. Buergel, 'The Origins', op. cit., p. 32 (see note 38).
41. Ibidem, p. 31.
42. Cf. Jeroen Boomgaard, 'An Injection of Planlessness', in: Jeroen Boomgaard et al., *One Year in the Wild*, op. cit., pp. 9-18 (see note 30).

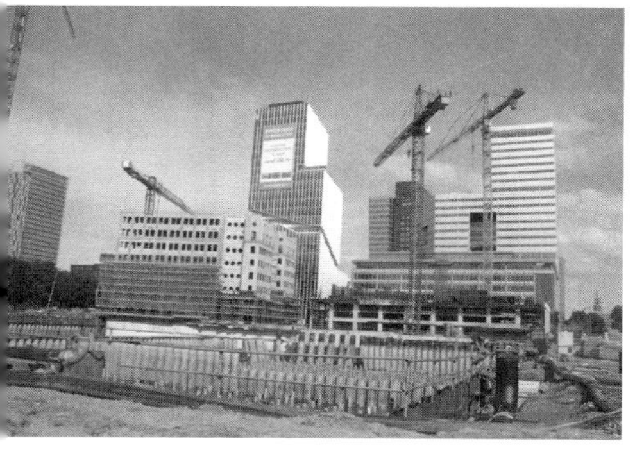

Orgacom
Zuidas in 2030

'30 years of mud.' That was the answer to the question Teike Asselbergs and Elias Tieleman of Orgacom – an artists' initiative that works on visualizing organization cultures by means of contemporary visual art – posed to students at the Vrije Universiteit (VU) in Amsterdam in 2000, about how they saw the future of the Zuidas, their campus and its environs. For the VU students, the focus lay not on the end result of a completed Zuidas, but on the mud along the way. The Research Group Art and Public Space inviting Orgacom to undertake an artistic investigation of the Zuidas in May 2003 provided an opportunity for the artists' initiative to delve deeper into the Zuidas. The premise of the Research Group's brief was a reflection on what is happening with the art projects in the Zuidas from the standpoint of the art. Orgacom subsequently wondered about the assumptions of the people involved in the development of the Zuidas and what consequences these assumptions have for the art and the artistic parties in this area.

In order to document this, Orgacom initiated a series of interviews, in which people who are influential in what the Zuidas will look like are asked to offer their vision of the processes concerning the Zuidas. The 'shapers' of the area were as open as the political situation allowed and were willing, in spite of their busy schedules, to speak to Orgacom. From the thirty people Orgacom interviewed during the investigation, five workshops, each involving a maximum of six people, were formed. The objective of these workshops is to get a clear picture of just where priorities lie within a number of oft-cited and therefore significant dilemmas. The themes of the workshops are:

Workshop 1: Do all parties share a desire to bring the Zuidas positive attention? What is the actual perception of end users?

Workshop 2: Does art contribute to an aestheticization of the area? Is there room for newcomers to 'occupy' space with meanings?

Workshop 3: Private domains are urbanizing and public spaces are privatizing. Is this visible in the security discourse and what is the place of art within this?

Workshop 4: What is the professional proposition of art? What should remain open within this, and what can be formalized?

Workshop 5: What is the best conceivable organization of artistic parties? And who gets to have a say about art in the Zuidas?

Workshop 6: Whom is the art actually for? Can the Zuidas be simultaneously exclusive and for everybody?

Orgacom uses the interviews and the workshops to get a feel for the way people who work in the area normally think. Orgacom does not want to adopt an outsider's position, but instead, by means of empathy, reflect on the processes that play a role in the creation of art in this area.

To return to the verdict of the VU students – '30 years of mud' – Orgacom wonders what potential 'mud' might have. Physically, mud is an amorphous substance, but it can simultaneously have numerous colours and aspects. In metaphorical language, mud is often used to describe unclear and/or emotionally charged situations: 'mud slinging' or 'getting your feet muddy'. Mud can flow in slides or take on solid forms.

In 2030 the Zuidas will be 'finished'. What will be the state of the mud when the mudslides are finally channelled? Who will be living in the Zuidas once the dust settles? What societal changes will have taken place there? What will be the role of art in this context? What aspects of the present vision of the Zuidas will have been achieved and which will have become obsolete? What kind of Zuidas will exist in 2030? What effects can the current situation have for the long term, and how aware of these are we in our day-to-day life? A resident of the Zuidas in 2030 probably has no idea of all the people and processes that brought his or her house into being. He or she lives there, happily or not, and experiences the area as a neighbourhood where you go grocery shopping, children go to school and where public transport is fully available.

Orgacom concludes the investigation by contributing a future vision of the Zuidas in the form of a series of fictional messages from 2030, such as a newspaper article, a blog text, minutes of an internet meeting, a legal document, an AT5 (local radio / television station) transcript, a change of address form, a postcard, the website of the borough council and the invitation to an art prize: a sample of the stream of information and personal messages we are barraged with on a daily basis. Orgacom's future vision is like a scoop out of a pile of post addressed to a Zuidas resident in 2030. It is neither a clear-cut utopia or dystopia, but a snapshot of the mudslides of the future.

Zuidas in 2030
Artists-Uni Gets a Veto

As every week, the members of the work group 'positive attention to the Zuidas' are meeting online. The Chinese Han Group, which has purchased half of the Zuidas, and the (Chinese or partly Chinese) developers associated with the group have just concluded their monthly progress meetings with all the Amsterdam parties.
Since the Chinese became majority shareholders in the Zuidas, financial problems have arisen, because construction is proceeding faster than anticipated and Dutch bureaucracy cannot keep up with the growth. Chairman Yen (cultural management at UvA) welcomes Kunay Raadhuis of the promotion team 'ChiAmsterdam', who asks whether he can bring up a point of order. Yen assents.

Kunay: The art budget has been under considerable pressure recently, because the extra budgets allocated for English-Mandarin translation costs are not sufficient.

Yen: Can't ChiAmsterdam use its own translators? The Han Group has just paid for a large screenwall and cannot submit additional expenses to the main office in Hong Kong.

Kunay: We are constantly understaffed. Six of our translators are currently pregnant and the Mandarin translations we get back from Poland are not of adequate quality.

Yen: Surely India can be a useful alternative?

– Lowe Percy of the Artists-Uni joins in the discussion –

Orgacom

Lowe: Hello

Kunay: Hi Lowe. What do you think?

Lowe: Our artists group just hired four Indian English-Mandarin translators. The Han Group's suppliers gave us a tidy sum for an artwork in the air space of the 4th Quadrant. Our programmers in India had told us they knew a good translation agency that also happened to be close to them physically, a luxury.

Kunay: What is the progress of your project, given the air-space restrictions that have just been imposed?

Yen: Air Space 4Q is Item 2 on the agenda. Let's do Item 2 first, since Kunay does not need to sit in on Point 1, about environmental standards.

Kunay: Convenient.

Yen: The Artists-Uni presented three designs to the Han Group suppliers. What was the reaction?

Lowe: Plan 2 has been approved, but there is still a great deal of discussion about the budget. The Han Group writes and talks about art the most, but in practice nothing happens. We have to work harder at selling the potential of art to generate positive attention, because in spite of our new veto position, the power balance is still off. The suppliers are also having difficulty accepting the plan because we vetoed their pagoda.

Yen: What does the borough council say?

Lowe: Two of our artists are in the new council, which is also against pagodas in the 4th Quadrant.

Yen: Lo of the Han Group's DGC is also against. The 4th Quadrant has been zoned for green tech.

Kunay: Ever since the Artists-Uni acquired the rights to Veto Public Space, the smaller Asian businesses are being told 'no' a lot. How is your relationship with them now?

Lowe: We gave a lecture yesterday to the SAP (Small-Asia Pact) about 'how to put together a briefing' and explained to them that a quiet area is definitely not a problem, but that they were selected to develop this area because they get the very best out of technology and the exterior space should reflect this. I said, 'Surely you don't want the Europeans to think you come from a village?'

Kunay: Oops . . . What was their reaction?

Lowe: Yeah, well, some of them were awfully quiet, but to most it made it clear that this was why no prod-ucts from the authenticity industry, like the pagoda, are being approved.

Kunay: I'm hearing noises that people find the public space too cold.

Lowe: Market research shows that high tech is a more significant factor in corporate selection than authenticity.

Kunay: Does market research define the applications of culture?

Orgacom

Lowe: We opted for this in order to generate a lot of positive press.

Kunay: But does it work? What do you artists think of this, internally?

Lowe: Most are used to it. They used to work in big workshops. There is one small group of account managers that tend to listen to the SAP, but that group is now working with the designers to find solutions for developing authentic products that don't look like they were designed by the authenticity industry. The initial results are remarkable, particularly in the area of green tech and plant design.

Kunay: I read about that in the paper. There is a risk that Zuidas art is being promoted too much, when many of the ambitions have yet to be fulfilled. This can lead to scepticism in the media and in other parties from which positive attention is needed.

Lowe: Yes, I've noticed the scepticism in the media. Perhaps we should go over our media plan one more time.

Zuidas Bankruptcy = The End of Art?

'A lack of allure' was one of the answers to the question of why project developers were coming out of the room without square footage.

When the auction for square footage at the Zuidas, aimed at international developers, was launched with great fanfare two years ago, punters were supposedly already standing in line to sign up.

Instead, the final result of the auction was far below the anticipated yield. Yesterday, the Zuidas NV public limited company officially applied for a suspension of payments. The consequences of a bankruptcy for other parties involved in the Zuidas are most visible in the cultural sector. A sector that is already under pressure at the moment.

From our correspondent Harre Hiemstra

'The Amsterdam Fund for the Arts is temporarily suspending activities, in order to consider how to proceed', said the chairman of the interim governing board, K. Koppers. The privatized Amsterdam Fund was one of the smaller shareholders in the Zuidas NV public limited company, and was responsible for art projects in the public and semi-private spaces of the Zuidas. In the wake of the failed Zuidas auction, all parties involved put in additional effort toward keeping art in the schedule of requirements. The idea was that the previously noted 'lack of allure' could be remedied with art (extra decoration and a socially conscious image). The Amsterdam Fund for the Arts invested a great deal and in so doing earned for its stakeholders not only the opportunity to realize the

Orgacom

'allure' of the Zuidas, but also a share of its debt of 330 million Local Euro.

A few years ago, things were going well for the Amsterdam Fund for the Arts, which was privatized in 2021. After a period of uncertainty as a result of the abolition of subsidies for culture, the resources of the Fund grew enormously in a few years' time, thanks to numerous donations by retired baby-boomers. 'We even had to be careful not to pay too much in taxes ourselves', said Koppers. 'That was why, in 2028, we decided to invest in the Zuidas, a project we had been involved in from the beginning … The idea was that by the time the baby-boom generation would no longer be able to contribute funds, we would be reaping the fruits of our investments in real estate.' The shrinking population and the surplus in office space have driven real estate prices to an all-time low, and many priva-

tized cultural organizations are now in trouble.

Rudy Barbon, a participating artist in the Funel project and an Amsterdam Fund shareholder, says that if the court decides, in the class-action suit against the former governing board of the Amsterdam Fund, that the Fund can pass the losses onto its shareholders, his one-man operation, Rubon, will go bankrupt. One-third of all shareholders of the Fund are cultural entrepreneurs who support cultural institutions with their incomes. Rudy: 'If the outcome of the class-action suit is that we have to pay, then not only will a large section of the larger cultural enterprises go bankrupt, but the support for the cultural infrastructure of the ROA [the partnership between the Province of North Holland and the Amsterdam Urban Area] will also disappear. The Urban Area does not want to spend any money on art, because it has to cut back on basic facilities because of the Zuidas fiasco.'

Even after the loss of provincial and municipal subsidies for the arts and the approval of the Second Report on Cultural Infrastructure in the Netherlands (TRNCI), little seemed to be amiss in culture land, thanks to the generous donations of the baby-boomers. Now, however, the cultural sector is witnessing the consequences of the new situation, and there is a new movement emerging, advocating a return to the era of government involvement. 'In the past people wanted to derive as much profit as possible from the new measures for tax write-offs for cultural donations, but now that things are not going so well, the government should foot the bill again. That's not how we do things', says H. Bakkel, chairman of the TRNCI.

A great deal depends on the previously mentioned class-action suit, in which an initial, indicative decision is expected on 18 March. The attorneys at Spong Limited are already making preparations for an appeal to the higher court in The Hague. Louis Spong: 'The impact of the class-action suit is very significant for the smaller parties. If we can immediately file for an appeal on the indicative decision with the high court, we can arrange for bridge credit with the insurers.' The insurers have already indicated they will settle with the smaller enterprises if the debt burden is reduced. For Rudy Barbon of Rubon, the settlement may come too late anyway: 'I make posters for museums. If the first indicative decision is negative for the stakeholders, my clients will cut back on their spending, and then I can forget about any new commissions.'

193

Artwork a pilgrimage shrine for hooligans
Transcript of AT5 news radio for
Tuesday 12 January 2030

Ferry:
On today's programme we have with us artist Lasse Halle.
Hello Halle, how are things going?

Halle:
Very well, why?

Ferry:
I understand that your artwork in the Zuidas has created
quite a lot of commotion in the city.

Halle:
That's true, but that's a good thing!

Ferry:
It might be helpful for the listeners at home or in the car if
you were to tell us what's happened.

Halle:
I made an artwork with football as its subject, because
football is universal and the project developer on whose
property I was allowed to create the artwork wanted something to do with football as well.

Ferry:
And then?

Halle:
My artwork is about hooligans and hooligan etiquette, which...

Ferry:
Football hooligans have an etiquette???

Halle:
 Yes, yes, they have their own ways of communicating with one another about where they're going to fight and they often look out for one another in their day-to-day lives, as well.

Ferry:
Give us an example?

Halle:
It's not easy to become a member of a hooligan brigade, but once you're an insider, everyone looks out for one another. Some of my fellow hooligans have helped younger guys get off [the party drug] Racco by taking them into their own homes when they'd run away from home.

Ferry:
But now on to the artwork. What does it look like?

Halle:
It's a very large football made of pigskin, tattooed with the symbols of the biggest hooligan brigades of the moment. Each symbol I chose is used by more than one club or hooligan brigade. It's a sort of alphabet of hooligan symbols.

Ferry:
I read in my personal newspaper that you first had the pigs tattooed in China, is that right?

Halle:
Yes, my boyfriend, the artist Wim Delvoye, has pigs tattooed in Chenjiatuo and then sells them for a lot of money to art collectors. We can't do that here because of animal rights, and you can't get a decent tattoo on a dead pig because the cuts have to heal.

Ferry:
Right... and now, these hooligans?

Halle:
The hooligans that were barred from the Arena recently had seen the Spits in the train from Schiphol that morning. My artwork was pictured on the front page because of the 'Fur for Animals' demonstrations. The football supporters thought that a riot was going on and so went to the Zuidas to see which club it was, because they thought that 'Fur for Animals' were supporters of some club or other as well.

Ferry:
And then they started fighting with the animal-rights activists, I understand from my newspaper.

Halle:
That's right, and now more and more clubs of hooligans are coming to the Zuidas because of my artwork. They really want to have their picture taken with it.

Ferry:
How does your client feel about this?

Halle:
He's let it be known that he is not happy with the attention of the hooligans and wants to move the artwork.

Ferry:
Where to?

Halle:
He's still discussing that with the city. The city partially funded the work, and because my boyfriend, Wim…

Ferry:
The one with the pig tattoo operation?

Halle:
Yes, our Art Farm… um, where was I?

Ferry:
The city…

Halle:
Oh yes, the city really wanted a work from us because Wim is famous and the Zuidas is a prestige project with international allure.

Ferry:
Then that's worked out very well: there have never been so many international hooligans at the Zuidas.

Halle:
The city's just released a report on the cultural sector about how there has to be more art that the ordinary public can relate to. Football supporters are the ordinary public too. The football clubs in Amsterdam have said they have no objection to the artwork, because it attracts attention to Amsterdam as a football town. Ajax does not want the ball near the Arena because it will become a meeting point for riots. The hooligans have told me they will not allow the ball to be moved.

Ferry:
Why not?

Halle:
They've declared the ball their monument and consider it their property.

Ferry:
How do other users of the space feel about this?

Halle:
The land belongs to the project developer so it doesn't matter how the other users feel. They were against the ball from the start anyway, because it's made from animal hides.

Ferry:
We have to move on to the rest of the show. Keep an eye on the front pages, people, this is going to get exciting...

And now 'Musica De Futebol', from Brazil.

Change of Address Form

Name: Steven and Lotte Dalfour
Former address
or postbox: Dr. Schaepmanstraat 48
Postal code and city: 2032 GK Haarlem

New address
or postbox: Zuiderdok 244 (blok 4)
Postal code and city: 1077 XZ Amsterdam
Effective date: 19.07.2030

Telephone: 020-32000382
VOid: 0500-2379900
VOid name: STEVLOT48
Mobile telephone: 06-19612314
E-mail address: -

Supplementary information:

At the WTC, take the south exit to Zuiderdok. Once outside,
you'll see an artwork of LED screens on the left; walk past
the artwork into the street with the green facing bricks, and
when you see a coloured plaza with little coloured buildings on the right, cross that plaza. The Zuiderdok is there.
Blok 4 is near the tall minaret by artist Giebema.

Orgacom

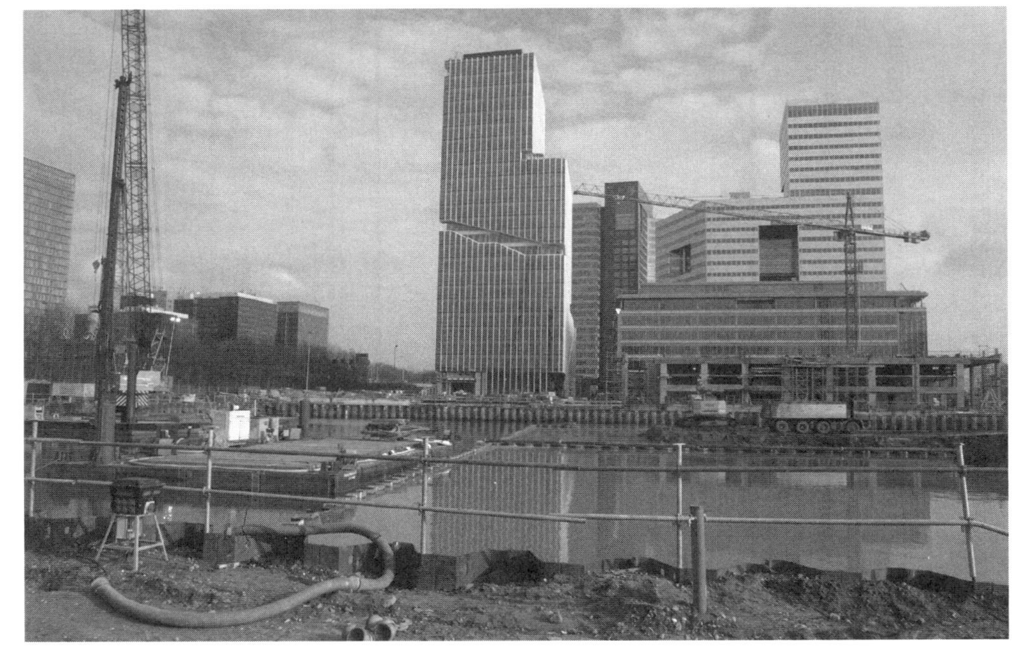

Dear parents,

I've taken the twins to the Zuidas. It's a nice day and this week they're having cultural activities for children up to age 12. The schools in the Zuidas are trying to use culture to compete with the schools in Brussels. Unfortunately Mark couldn't get the day off today. The children especially love an artwork that looks like a huge ice floe and changes shape under the influence of climate changes and variations in the weather. Most kids here use it as a playground and play hide-and-seek. All the intensive use makes it look pretty shabby, only two weeks after the inauguration. With all the offices there isn't much playing room for the kids, which is a problem for our school here as well. Mark and I may go look around in Brussels. We've also thought about Paris, but everything is so expensive there. I have to go, because I can't see the little one anymore.

Lots of love,
Gerda

Orgacom

Façade Signage

In many cases, if you, as a citizen, business or institution, wish to install signage on the façade of your building in the Zuidas (for instance an LCD screen or a billboard), you need a building permit. This is based on the concept of 'building' in the sense of the Housing Act. In a majority of cases, the installation of signage has to be considered 'building'. The question is then whether this can be considered *permit-exempt* building or not.

- In the residential section of the Zuidas you can never build without a permit; a building permit is always required there.
- Outside the residential section, the installation of façade signage is only permit-exempt if it is an alteration that is *not of a fundamental nature*, that is to say if it is a small, unlit piece of signage.
- If it is also an artwork, it also falls, since 1 January 2030, under the façade signage legislation, because prior to this date, the exceptions accorded to artworks were often abused.

An application form for a building permit can be downloaded from the site of the Ministry of Housing, Spatial Planning and the Environment. To qualify for the building permit, the signage must, among other things, follow the signage guidelines enforced in the municipality of Amsterdam Zuid-Oost.

More information? Contact the ROA office, Building Housing Habitat department, tel.: 020-5114400.

| | last updated on: 23-02-2030 |
| | |

Zuidas Again Battleground for Business Conflicts

Tuesday morning, somewhere on the Zuidas ring road   Local blog

10:29:09:2030

On the radio I hear that the series of conflicts between the heavy metal dealers Alkiet BV and Kazakh AS finally came to an end last night. Both parties announced they would jointly put up an artwork on the disputed piece of land located between the skyscrapers of the two companies at the Zuidas. 'The artwork will symbolize our new relationship and promote cooperation among our employees', said spokesperson H. Jansen of Alkiet BV. I'm on my way with Joop to the board meeting about the future of the Zuidas when, among a few telephone calls in the traffic jam, I get an odd text-message: 'Hacking attempt Zuidas account?'

I manage not to immediately step on the brake pedal to get more information, but my curiosity is piqued. During the board meeting my thoughts frequently stray: The Zuidas server hacked? What businesses might be affected? Luckily Joop and I have three hours of wireless access via the Gamma Mobile

Orgacom

hotel network, and we can find out how badly our network has been affected by the hacker.

As a starting point we have the IP address; this turns out, via http://www.dnsstuff.com, to be a Zuidas address: *Answer: 1.2.3.4 PTR record: a1-2-3-4.adsl3.zuidas.nl.* Without actual contact we can't find out any more information. Joop plucks up his courage and finds a mail server on port 25 that identifies itself as *220 jes-ni1.xyz.nl -- Server ESMTP (Sun Java System Messaging Server 6.2-2.29 (built Apr 28 2029)).* This identification is rather odd, because an nslookup of that name comes up with a different address, namely that of the company that lost the last pitch for our digital security, XYZ Maker. Might this ADSL address be a back door to their server farm? Joop called XYZ, who, once they stopped freaking out, also want to know what exactly is going on. We'll get the miscreant! We have an appointment with a police digital detective on Friday afternoon. I'm curious to see how that process will unfold.

Friday morning, Zuidas Police Station
Local blog

04:31:09:2030

During the conversation with XYZ it was decided that the Zuidas Bureau will file the complaint. Joop and I have an appointment with a digital detective. Because this is a break-in that involves the destruction of a structure, we have to go to the police station itself. The detective sits down and pulls up the programme we have to use to file the complaint on an antique PC. The questions the detective asks are not applicable to a business server. What virus scanner do we run, what brand of computer is it, etc. With great difficulty we try to turn the complaint into a conclusive story, but only his revolver keeps me from grabbing the keyboard and typing in the facts myself.

The guy tells us the case preparation department will deal with this on Saturday. They will look at the case with the Public Prosecutions Officer and decide whether it is worth the trouble. If it is, it will be then be coordinated onto the right department... So it might be a while. Stay tuned!

Orgacom

Thursday morning, home   Local blog
11:25:12:2030

I contacted the police again over a month ago. Unfortunately they said that it was once again a matter of waiting to see whether anything is going to be done. Should I hear anything, I'll keep you informed. By now I can well imagine that the majority of break-ins are not reported and that the chance of catching the culprits is therefore very slim. Unfortunately...

Monday morning, office   Local blog
16:29:12:2030

The hacking attempt that destroyed a large part of the Zuidas server structure turns out to be the work of an international company dealing in corporate information that has offices at the Zuidas itself. In an act of corporate espionage, they unwittingly trans-ferred a virus that was in their system, via the same server, to the Zuidas server. The fat's really in the fire now! The company in question, GMX Bedrijfsinfo, can expect a hefty class-action suit from the other compa-nies in the Zuidas, in which the accusation of corporate espionage is the least serious indictment. GMX's objective in the hacking operation was to obtain sensitive information about Petrol-Axis. The offices of Petrol-Axis were already the victim of physical break-ins six months ago, because they have a hard copy archive of their corporate data. The hacker, a 19-year-old visual artist from Gouwen, thought it was an assignment for the internal course Certified Ethical Hacker that GMX offered as part of its retraining programme. Because of this, the labour inspectorate and the PPP (public private partnership) agency are also getting involved in the conflicts. The Zuidas is gradually starting to look more like an arena than the Arena itself (Ajax-Feijenoord was too boring for words, again). Maybe our football clubs could use a retraining programme. :)

Orgacom

Invitation Zuidas Awards

Date and time: **6 December 2030 at 7 p.m.**
Place: **1ˢᵗ floor of the commercial Gallery
at the World Trade Center.**

The Zuidas Contemporary Art Prize is conceived and organized by ING ICA (Institute of Contemporary Art), with the support of the General Sponsor, the mobile telephone company Telfort, and the help of the commercial centre WTC and the Institute of Amsterdam Creativity.
First launched in connection to the 3ʳᵈ edition of the Creativity Awards in 2015, this event aims at supporting and bringing attention to contemporary artists and designers working together with companies in the Zuidas. Seven short-listed artists will exhibit their work and an international jury will award the prize.
The exhibition will offer a multiplicity of contemporary artworks including biological design, multinational co-productions, screenings, photography, painting, installation, sculpture, performance and text. Based on an extensive research, the Zuidas Contemporary Art Prize will also function as a tool in mapping the Amsterdam contemporary art scene, forging new relations between artists and audiences and encouraging discussions on new developments. The event also testifies to an increased social responsibility on the part of the General Sponsor, Telfort.

The ING ICA project leaders have short-listed the following artists for the Zuidas Contemporary Art Prize 2030: *Lang Yi, Leonard Vigo, Adella Lion, Nikolin Bulgari, Nikusha de Jong, Fatma Genco, Juka and Sidi Janssen.* ING ICA will also present a new project by last year's winner of the Zuidas Contemporary Art Prize, Suela Qost. The Zuidas Contemporary Art Prize will be awarded by an international jury, this year composed of Maria Sardani, Director of ASP (Artist Studio Program) in Milan, Adriaan Offenbach, International Artist and Guest Professor at Leipzich Academy in Germany, and Ivet Mady, member of the curating team SINC (Sticky If Not Cohesive) from Zagreb.

The Zuidas Contemporary Art Prize is made possible through the sponsorship of the General Sponsor, Telfort, as well as the support of the WTC commercial centre. ING ICA's program is supported by our Program Partner, the European Cultural Foundation, and also enjoys the support of the Stedelijk Museum Amsterdam and the 'Moving Borders' NGO. For more information on ING's programmes please visit our website: www.ing.nl/cultuur

Verso of invitation

209

Recto of invitation

Residents of Zuidas Get Artists as Present

Artist Suela Qost, winner of last year's Zuidas Contemporary Art Prize, is now a member of the jury for this year's Prize. Suela Qost won the prize for the concept of 'giving' an artist to individual residents of the Zuidas. The concept was based on the criticism that the end users of the Zuidas facilities, up to that point, had never been included in aesthetic and artistic decisions about art in public space. The artists that were given to the inhabitants developed art projects together with or for specific individuals. Some of the art projects that resulted from this concept have already been completed; others are so utopian that they will never be realised except in the minds of the persons that have collaborated with the artists who developed the ideas.

Which concept will win this year's Prize? What idea will be realised with the € 50,000 the winner takes home? Will it be *Lang Yi*'s poetic cancellation of shadows in the Zuidas, *Leonard Vigo*'s successful interpretation of Zuidas political power structures, *Adella Lion*'s new time piece for the Zuidas, focusing on the perception of time by office workers, *Nikolin Bulgar*'s bombastic destruction of polished surfaces, *Nikusha de Jong*'s new transport machines, *Fatma Genco*'s mobile restaurant with refugee cooks or *Juka and Sidi Janssen*'s frontal lobotomy project, which researches mistakes made by powerful figures?

This year's theme was 'How can we present an "entertaining" project which is critical at the same time?' The art world has a tendency to regard the question of art being entertaining as backward. However, does 'entertaining' always have to mean 'light', 'simplistic', 'not serious'? What if the entertainment value comes from darkness, poetry, satire or black humour? A great many artists sent in their responses and all these are on display in the Zuidas Design Museum from 6 through 23 December 2030. Opening times are Tuesday to Sunday 10:00 a.m. to 7 p.m., Zuiderpark 23, Zuidas.

Child Drowns at the Zuidas in Artistic Water Feature

A four-year-old girl, Emmy Wang, drowned last night in the artistic water feature on the Zuidas-plein.

The child, who was playing with an older sister and some neighbourhood children on the plaza, had climbed onto the rim of the basin and presumably slipped, was knocked unconscious and subsequently drowned. 'I couldn't find her anywhere and I thought she'd gone home', said the older Wang daughter. The Wangs are now holding Amsterdam liable for the death of their daughter, but the fact that the land upon which the water feature is built is partly owned by the company Arc Entertainment NV, as well as the question of whether the artist or the arbitrator is also liable for flaws in the design make the case legally complex.

When the Wangs signed up for a new home at the Zuidas, their reason was a cosmopolitan setting from which travel to Brussels (his work) and London City (her work) was easy. International two-income couples chose the Zuidas as their 'residency'. As once was the case on the Amsterdam Islands, however, the young, ambitious couples had children, and the Zuidas was not built for that purpose. The art projects that were put up at the time in an innovative partnership involving the city, project developers and artists, like the rest of the Zuidas, did not take children into account.

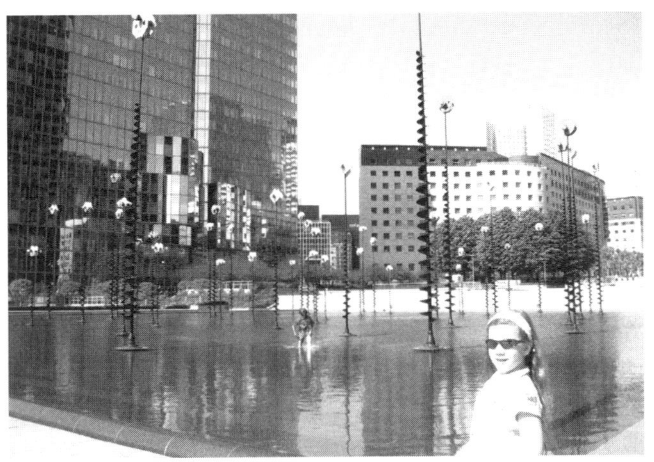

The water in the water feature, according to the land registry, lies in public space, and the city is liable for this. The rim from which the child slipped, according to the land registry, is situated on land belonging to Arc Entertainment NV. The artist, François Dey, has a foundation that is liable for the design. The city and the project developer of Arc Entertainment NV had engaged an art arbitrator to plan the water feature on 'left-over space' between various facilities and to supervise its construction. The contractor that did the construction work, in consultation with the arbitrator, decided to set the rim at an angle different from what was indicated in the artist's drawings. We took this case to several legal consultants.

Orgacom

The civil court in Amsterdam
SUMMONS IN A CIVIL CASE   CASE No.: 777-6655

Johannes Maria WANG

V.

ARC ENTERTAINMENT NV

TO: <u>**ARC ENTERTAINMENT NV**</u>
Doornepad 46
1832 AH Amsterdam

YOU ARE HEREBY SUMMONED and required to serve
upon PLAINTIFF'S ATTORNEY,
mr. Q.A.G. Masius
Essenlaan 43
1095 AX Amsterdam

An answer to the complaint which is herewith served
upon you, within TEN (10) days after service of this
summons upon you, exclusive of the day of service.
If you fail to do so, judgment by default will be taken
against you for the relief demanded in the complaint.
You must also file your answer with the Clerk of this
Court within a reasonable period of time after service

Jody Peter Van Heegen
2 February 2030
(clerk)

STATEMENTS OF THE CASE

Facts

1. The daughter of 'Johannes Maria Wang', 'Emmy II Wang' (hereafter 'Walker'), injured herself and subsequently expired while playing upon an unprotected object that was placed upon the premises of 'Arc Entertainment N.V.' (hereafter 'Arc').

2. The object (an artwork by the artist 'François Dey') has a height of five (5) metres and a length of three (3) metres. It consists of a metal construction that rises from a ditch filled with water. Although the object is very high and broad, the object is protected neither by a fence or a security guard.

3. A kindergarten called 'Tamagotchi-Childcare, Entertainment and Learning Facilities N.V.' (hereafter 'Tamagotchi') is located next to Arc at Stravinskylaan 1999. Tamagotchi has repeatedly asked Arc to repair the fence between the two premises, as children continually try to escape from Tamagotchi.

4. Plaintiff states that Arc should have exercised particular care due to the placement of a dangerous, unmonitored and unprotected object on their premises, as the Arc premises are located next to a kindergarten.
A proper fence is also lacking between the Arc premises and the premises of Tamagotchi (despite several requests made by Tamagotchi to Arc concerning this). This structural neglect by Arc of the dangerous situation entails a greater presumption of liability.

5. Therefore, plaintiff states that Arc created a situation that can be concluded to be dangerous. Arc therefore is responsible for an unlawful act as stated in 1:162 BW(oud)/ A:6789 CW. Based on this this article of the civil code, plaintiff demands payment of immaterial damages. Those damages amount to EUR 20.431,67. (**exhibit 1**).

6. In support of this claim, plaintiff refers to the existing jurisprudence regarding this matter.
(**exhibits 2 through 8**)

7. Arc has so far failed to respond to the claim for payment of immaterial damages. Plaintiff refers to the letters sent on 8 June 2029 and 24 November 2029.

Conclusion

8. It is clear that Arc has wronged plaintiff by creating a dangerous situation that was unprotected and unguarded. Therefore Arc must pay damages in the amount of EUR 20.431,67. This claim is based on the articles 1:162 BW(oud)/ A:6789 CW of the civil code.

THEREFORE

Plaintiff requests the court to stipulate:

1. That Arc be ordered to pay EUR 20.431,67. This payment should be made within 14 days.

2. That Arc be ordered to pay all additional costs connected with this case. The additional costs amount to EUR 928,40 incl. VAT.

The costs of the clerk are EUR 97,60.

Clerk

____

This case is submitted by mr. Q.A.G. Masius, de MASIUS & ZHANG ADVOCATEN, Postbus 567, 2019 AD Amsterdam

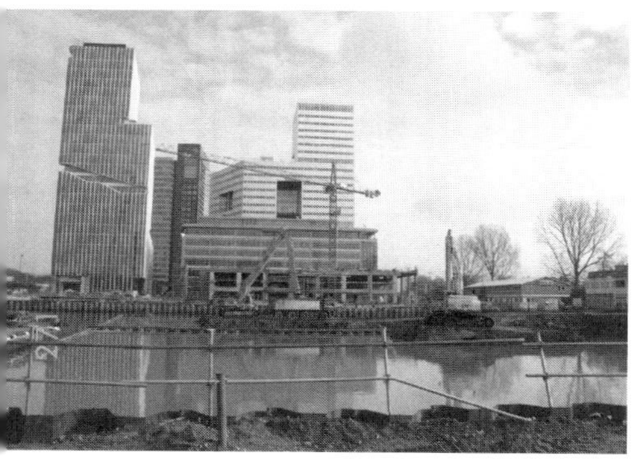

BAVO

The Dutch Neoliberal City and the Cultural Activist as the Last of the Idealists

A Top European Location *and* a Breeding Ground for New Art Forms

Amsterdam-Zuidas is a new urban development in Amsterdam entirely targeted at international top players. This is made clear by the brochures in which the words 'top' and 'international' come up again and again. One could see the Zuidas development as a playground for the new European elite of managers, lawyers, consultants and advertising agencies. It is a combination of 'top of the range' office buildings, luxury apartments, green and sports facilities and even its own design museum and theatre complex. Underneath this top district, an immense transport hub will be constructed, guaranteeing its connection to such transport links as the A10 motorway, the metro and the Dutch Railways and HSL high-speed rail networks. This will immediately make the Amsterdam-Zuidas station the fifth-largest in the Netherlands.[1]

It might seem surprising that the construction of a city district with such a one-dimensional composition is possible at a time when large sections of Dutch cities are being turned upside-down in a veritable crusade against a unilateral socio-economic profile. Whereas poor neighbourhoods are having strict distribution schemes imposed on them in order to create a 'good mix' – and thus a housing differentiation is being organized by stimulating the influx of middle and higher incomes – the Zuidas will no doubt become the most monolithic neighbourhood in the Netherlands. The Zuidas is an enclave within Amsterdam, entirely intended for the top segment of society. It is therefore difficult not to conclude that some urban planning rules and arguments clearly do not apply for the higher strata of society, and that in the area of urban development, a double standard is being applied.[2]

It has become a tradition in the Netherlands, for integral urban developments, to include the cultural and/or culture-historical dimension in an early stage of the planning process.[3] This is also the case for the Zuidas development. In this instance, the Zuidas Project Bureau has invited cultural actors to actively participate in the conceptualization of the development of an artistic climate in the area. As the Zuidas Project Bureau formulated it '... we want an inspirational and lively artistic climate in the Zuidas. When you say "Zuidas" a few years from now, we want people to think of art.'[4] This has led, among other things, to the 2003 founding of the Virtual Museum

Zuidas, a foundation consisting of prominent figures in the Dutch cultural world.[5] Their ambitions include turning the Zuidas into 'a kind of museum', 'a place within which new art forms can be created'.[6] This foundation has launched various initiatives, including a plan for a design museum and arts centre as well as a programme aimed at safeguarding the integral, architectural qualities of the area.

The overly optimistic, constructive institution of the Virtual Museum is not the only response of cultural actors to the open invitation of the Zuidas Project Bureau. The obscene, elitist character of the Zuidas development has also re-ignited the 'good old' debate about the social role of art and culture. Some intuitively sense the questionable nature of the new alliance between capital and culture, between the real estate sector and art, and bluntly assert that cultural actors should keep far away from involvement with such dubious societal players and practices. Think for instance of Hinrich Sachs, who recently argued that artists 'should not want to play any role' in urban project developments like the Zuidas.[7] Others, like the Logo Parc initiative, instead take up the challenge of finding out how art can undermine such urban developments from the inside out. There is an effort to find, in other words, ways for artists to accept the invitation to take part while preserving their critical position or autonomy.[8]

This essay sides with the second group when it comes to ambition, but with the first when it comes to scepticism. It argues that cultural forces must fully accept the mandate they have been given, and take the attendant symbolic and financial power as well as the room for negotiation extremely seriously. If culture today is increasingly 'internalized' by government authorities, project developers and investors as a factor that can determine the success of a development – and for this reason is asked 'to play a role in the process' – then it must fully endorse this and pursue its cultural agenda with a determination and consistency the other parties often have not intended.

A crucial element of this internal resistance is a proper insight into the forces cultural actors have to deal with, as well as the nature and logic of the planning process in which art is asked to participate. The first and longest section of this essay, indeed, consists of an analysis of the political-economic and ideological processes behind urban-design developments like the Zuidas. From this analysis, a counter-strategy is outlined. To the cultural actors who want to keep far away from such developments, and dismiss them as discussions external to artistic practice, we can only say that those who do not first work through the determinative conditions of their own production lose the right to pontificate about cultural engagement. In such a case, the sempiternal complaints about the misuse of art as the 'wallpaper' of economic development – whereby the critical intentions of the artistic sector are continually neutralized – are merely an empty gesture.

Neoliberal Planning ...

An oft-heard justification for the development of Amsterdam-Zuidas is that this kind of monolithic, antisocial urban development is the logical consequence of a situation in which the real estate sector and financial capital have been given free rein. This is supposedly the result of the rapid dismantling and retrenching of the Dutch state in the wake of the Purple Coalition debacle in the nineteen-nineties – manifested in the area of spatial planning by the abandonment of 'bloated' government planning. In short, the unabashed development of the Zuidas into a new work and residential ghetto for the top segment of society is supposedly a symptom of the unstoppable rise of a neoliberal policy based on the *laissez faire laissez passez* principle or, what amounts to the same thing, the idea that 'the market regulates itself'.

Nothing could be further from the truth. The government authorities involved – in this case the city of Amsterdam and the Dutch state – are two of the most passionate promoters and champions of Amsterdam-Zuidas![9] The development not only fits in perfectly with Amsterdam's efforts over many years to establish itself as a top international city – think for instance of the recent 'Amsterdam Topstad' campaign[10] – it is also, for the state, one of six 'key projects' intended to put the Netherlands on the international map.[11] What's more, Zuidas-Amsterdam is the largest of these key projects, involving a state investment of 653 million Euro.

How can we explain this fusion of a retrenching government with a hyperactive role – often as client, investor, entrepreneur and customer all at the same time? Of course, the thesis of this 'retrenching government' has not been made up out of thin air. As in business, it is fashionable these days, at various government levels, to sharply redefine the 'core business'. Instead of trying to be good at everything, government institutions too are being guided by the idea that investments should be strictly limited to sectors and/or activities that contribute to the top position of a city, region or country. Anything that does not meet this criterion must be inexorably passed off to lower levels of government or put on the back burner. The fact that the government is now copying the health norms of business is in itself a telling characteristic of the rise of neoliberal ideology in more and more spheres of society.

The results of this 'business revision' by the state can be read in the recent *Nota Ruimte* (the Dutch government report on spatial planning), with the suggestive subtitle *Ruimte voor ontwikkeling* ('space for development'). In it, without a shred of embarrassment, it is argued that the national government, in the area of spatial planning, should only concern itself with what it calls the 'Main Spatial Structure'. This refers to the most important 'assets' of the Netherlands, the economic magnets, the sectors in which the Netherlands can compete on a global scale. Think of the Port of Rotterdam and of Schiphol Airport, but also, in the future, of the Zuidas. The state sees its core task primarily in the intensive (economic) development, possibly in consultation with the relevant partners, of these 'mainports'. The rest of its former jurisdictions are being devolved to lower levels of government – the cities, regions, provinces – or to the market. Along with its intensive involvement in the Main Spatial Structure, it is still committed to the monitoring of basic spatial quality. This entails a number of minimum standards or floors for such basic concerns as security, water management or the environment.

The active role of this retrenched government should not be underestimated and is evidenced by the frequently raging debates waged in its wake. The focus is always which projects deserve the label of 'national importance' and therefore can be assured of sorely needed state funding. In early 2006, for instance, when the distribution of FES (Economic Structural Reinforcement Fund) surpluses was discussed, there was a great deal of controversy about the Zuiderzee train link to the north of the country. In the television programme *Nova*, this link was scrapped from the list of issues of top economic importance by Professor Albert Pols – to the great displeasure of the united northern provinces.[12] Even the superficial theorizing about the 'competitive position of CBDs' (central business districts) by someone like Pieter Tordoir has to be seen in this context: it is nothing less than an attempt to underscore the international relevance of the Zuidas and to elevate it to a national issue.[13]

So when this retrenching government is brought up, we have to be very precise. Rather than a total eclipse – the 'death of planning' critics are so fond of proclaiming – we are witnessing a selective retrenchment. Even as it is 'outsourcing' or divesting itself of certain sets of tasks and responsibilities, it is strengthening its role in relation to other matters. In short, while the government, in relation to certain areas and sectors, is planning from the top down more than ever before, it is doing so with a specific agenda: to shore up the international competitive position of the Netherlands. The Amsterdam-Zuidas project is clearly part of this ambition.[14] In the *Nota Ruimte*, the state justifies its commitment to the Zuidas in terms of increasing the diversity and economic foundation of the 'Noordvleugel' (the 'North Wing' of the Randstad, the urban conglomeration in the west of the Netherlands, which includes Amsterdam, Rotterdam, Utrecht and the Hague) – one of the key economic areas of the Netherlands and, as such, part of the Main Spatial Structure. It sees this as an element of providing top-flight metropolitan business locations around Schiphol Airport, especially for international operating corporations. In this, the state aims to fulfil the demands of multinationals in terms of agglomeration advantages, logistics, knowledge institutions and manpower.[15]

The Zuidas development is thus the showcase for 'urban planning in the era of neoliberalism': a spatial planning policy that operates according to the ethos of the market and has fully adopted its objectives. In this the government has not only reformed itself according to the norms that operate in business, it has also made the ambitions of the market – creating competitive advantages, exploiting 'strong sectors', outdoing the competition, etc. – its own. It is clear, in any event, that socially motivated spatial planning objectives have been purged from its set of tasks and transferred either to lower administrative levels or to the market. From this we can only conclude that the institution and safeguarding of spatial planning equitability is no longer seen as an essential cornerstone of good national spatial planning policy.[16]

... and its Democratic Face

This neoliberal sea change in spatial planning policy is naturally not publicized as such by the government – or at least not exclusively so. Planning 'according to market standards' is sold as a great step forward in the democratization of spatial planning desired by all of society. In the *Nota Ruimte*, for example, under the heading 'Government Management Philosophy', we can read that the government humbly admits having neither the wisdom nor the solutions for the countless spatial planning controversies, and that it primarily wants to ensure that others, better suited to this task, can shoulder their responsibilities.[17] In this regard it openly admits that in the past it has too often meddled unnecessarily in local issues and in so doing ignored democratic decision making.[18]

Presenting its recent, neoliberal make-over as its contribution to the popular ideal of an entrepreneurial society in which market partners in consultation with social partners are given the chance to organize their own habitat is undoubtedly strategically motivated. Through the mobilization of all kinds of societal forces – encouraged to take advantage of the opportunities presented by a city or region –

the government is securing a broad base of support. Winning this support would be far more difficult if it were done in the name of a hard-nosed economic agenda, or the outsourcing of its social responsibilities. As always with ideological justifications, and certainly when 'democracy' is trotted out, we have to be extremely alert and ask ourselves just what these opportunities are, as well as for whom these opportunities are intended.

To start with the first ('what are these opportunities?') we can refer to the observation of social geographer Erik Swyngedouw on the role of the government within the neoliberal development of the Zuidas. He argues that '... contrary to what its ideology holds dear, conservative liberalism has always maintained a very unique and intimate relationship with state intervention ... Planners and local authorities adopt a more proactive and entrepreneurial approach aimed at identifying market opportunities and urging private investors to exploit them.'[19] In short, when the government talks about creating and taking advantage of opportunities, it primarily means economic opportunities. Viewed from this perspective, democracy fits perfectly, of course, in its neoliberal agenda.

From the necessity of this proactive attitude, we can deduce, in any event, that the ideal of an entrepreneurial, democratic city is anything but problem-free. Why, after all, should the government have to stimulate its partners to 'take advantage of opportunities', if it were not for the fact that the city is not as naturally entrepreneurial as is usually presumed? Or at least not as enterprising in the sense meant by the powers that be: in terms of the economic exploitation of niches. Before the city can live up to its expectations as an entrepreneurial city, it must therefore first – not to say constantly – be encouraged to take up this specific sort of entrepreneurial practices. This even applies to market players. It is a rule of spatial economics, for instance, that market players have a tendency to 'under-invest' in facilities in which other parties, be they private or public, might derive an advantage. Think of road infrastructure, public space, schools or research institutions. Government authorities have to expend an unusually large amount of energy to get market players to dig into their own pockets to invest in this so-called 'grey area'. The burden of proof is more often than not placed on the government authorities, who have to prove to their partners that certain investments will generate significant returns, as well as provide guarantees to that effect, such as a sizable preliminary investment as well as the shouldering of potential financial risk.[20]

In regard to the second question ('opportunities, for whom?') it does not take much to see that, while there is of course a formal equality, certain opportunities – and here we are primarily speaking of the opportunities that actually matter, such as the implementation of a project like Amsterdam-Zuidas – can only be exploited if one has the financial as well as knowledge capital needed to carry out the exploitation. The fact that everyone has an equal right to claim the democratic playing field, to shape the city, and so on, therefore does not mean that everyone possesses the means to do so. It is clear that large real estate corporations can enjoy a vastly disproportionate portion of the democratic right to 'take advantage of opportunities'. In short, we encounter here one of the most cunning tricks of the neoliberal ideology of the entrepreneurial city: the presentation of individuals and businesses as equivalent entities. The two are seen as equally autonomous forces that, in satisfying their own desires and interests, make creative use of the 'opportunities' contained in the urban arena.

Aside from the issue of unequal means, the problem is also that citizens, unlike businesses, often do not necessarily have an entrepreneurial or exploitative relationship with their city. It is this non-economic relationship – driven by different values: ecological, moral, even political – that is not tolerated within the neoliberal form of urban development. In the latter, all stakeholders (including the government) are reduced to 'merely' one of the discussion partners who must be prepared to negotiate their desires in a transparent, economic negotiating process. A protectionist government policy in favour of vulnerable sections of society – which, driven by democratic ideals, offers them certain privileges in the negotiations – is of course entirely out of the question. Within the negotiation process, the only idealism allowed is the calculation of mutual interests. What is denied here is, again, the unequal balance of power – or sometimes even the relationship of dependence – that exists among the various discussion partners at the negotiating table.

Is the government then not allowed to adjust the course of this process of negotiation at all? It does, but then only in the choices made by the social forces to the extent that these can have a positive spin-off for the economy, or if the competitiveness of the latter comes into play. Here we face a paradoxical situation in which it is the very spatial planning policy based on the radically democratic character of the urban production process that is constantly active in ensuring that the urban players use their democratic rights properly, or use them at all. In this the national government is copying the (neoliberal) definition of democracy as propagated by the United States for decades: democracy as the right of free choice, which you are guaranteed as long as you make the right choices. Or to put it another way, the arena of forces is given the chance to play a part in shaping the city on the condition that it do so as an entrepreneur and cause no damage to the urban economy.

All this lends nuance, of course, to the popular thesis of the end of the 'malleable' society, city or even human being. The new, market-driven operations of the government also demand a massive change in thinking on the part of the social partners. With the retrenchment of the government – however selective – these partners have to shoulder a lot more responsibilities and take the initiative in the economic arena. All this being said, the role of the policy maker remains fairly tradi-tional in this regard. The government takes on the role of the prophet of the new reality of a creative, self-entrepreneurial city and works tirelessly to educate the social partners to act accordingly. Urban policy makers are thus busy pointing out 'opportunities' to the market players, urging social partners to communi-cate their desires and getting them to the point of starting to develop certain areas of the city. In this way, under the guise of development planning and in the name of the public good, spatial planning policy makers are preparing the urban area for its colonization by the market.[21]

After 'Red for Green', Now 'Red for Culture' too

Although all of this might seem of little concern to many cultural actors, this is nevertheless the dubious framework within which artists, designers and architects today – in initiatives such as the Dutch government's Space & Culture Action Programme – are invited to contribute to the development of the city.[22] From an early stage of important project developments, they are asked to join the coalition of government authorities and project developers. The cultural legion is not only asked to shoulder its responsibility as keeper of the aesthetic and symbolic quality of the public space, but also to take advantage of the apparently unique opportunity to make its mark, at an early stage, on a future piece of central urban domain. In short, whether they like it or not, cultural forces are immersed up to their neck in the neoliberal planning processes with a democratic face described above. And, we argue, the further artists wish to keep away from such processes, the greater their complicity in them. This is particularly true of the cultural actors that are active within Amsterdam-Zuidas.

The central question is thus how we should interpret this alliance between culture and big business. How, for instance, to explain the privileged position of the cultural actors within a development like the Zuidas, which after all primarily serves the interests of the real estate sector? How to explain that, of all the social partners, government authorities count on the cultural forces to democratize the city? This seems to indicate that cultural forces are seen as ideal allies in the neoliberal planning process. Furthermore, the question also arises whether the cultural forces are capable of making a development like Amsterdam-Zuidas – which in reality is a vulgar marketing strategy, tarted up with a democratic flavouring – transcend itself? Should they want this at all? And if so, how can cultural actors bring this about?

Let us begin with the first cluster of questions, relating to the new alliance between government authorities, market partners and cultural actors. This alliance can seem unconventional or even progressive. Where else in the world do artists get a chance to exchange ideas with property magnates about a brand-new city centre? This seems already less so when we assess it against the backdrop of the current tendency to present culture or cultural history as an indispensable asset for a strong city or region. Aside from creating a so-called creative city, it is also considered crucial for creating an attractive location climate for multinational corporations. The most often cited justification for this is that the employees of (international) companies, because of their high levels of education, set particularly high standards for their living environment. Factors such as spatial quality, a diversity of cultural venues, a rich history, a tolerant social climate, etc., are deciding factors in convincing this elite to commit to a city.

This 'promotion' of culture must be situated against the age-old process of internalization by the market – as well as by its political appendage – of what are called 'externalities'. In the last several decades, it was primarily the environment that was in the spotlight as an essential externality of capitalism. A broadly supported social movement decried the fact that although the environment was one of the determinative conditions of the economy – as a reservoir of resources, as a dumping ground for its waste, as a habitat for its workers, and so forth – the market pays nothing for it. What's more, the negative effects of this exploitation – pollution, depletion, loss of quality of life – often have to be borne by local communities or the state. After years of struggle by green movements in particular, this externality is now increasingly internalized. Businesses are being required to pay for their use of nature, or to invest in its regeneration or clean-up. Environmental impact is now fully accounted for in the costs of project developments as well. Think, for instance, of the 'red for green' arrangement – heavily promoted by the Dutch government – whereby the maintenance or creation of green space is funded by linking it to so-called red functions such as housing, commercial estates and traffic infrastructure.[23]

In fact, culture or cultural history – think of the recent hype about cultural planning – is undergoing the same fate as the environment: it too is being fully adopted as a necessary determinative condition in spatial developments. For years it was considered a nice extra – when it was considered at all. Today, on the contrary, the presence of a rich cultural history or a fertile cultural climate, for the reasons outlined above, is seen as an indispensable added value for the success of a spatial planning development. The market and the government in fact attempt to integrate this explicitly in the city's planning. It is in this light that we must understand the ambition of the Zuidas Project Bureau to excel both in the area of popular culture venues – by using popular theatre guru Joop van den Ende as an ambassador and standard-bearer of the development – as well as in the more difficult quest for 'new art forms' – a commission laid at the door of the Virtual Museum Zuidas.

Whether cultural forces should be happy with its internalization as a market factor – apart from the issue of whether it is at all possible to plan anything as fragile and obscure as a 'fertile cultural climate' – remains very much to be seen. In the first place, it reduces their specific activity to the object of a market deal and therefore to a form of capital: that is, cultural capital. Analogous to the 'red for green' arrangements, the economic colonization of the last 'uncapitalized' spaces in the city is exchanged or traded for generous compensations to the cultural sector, so that we can rightly speak of a 'red for culture' arrangement. The hand being extended to the cultural sector is also clearly motivated by a fear that if the Zuidas development is left entirely up to the government and the real estate sector – if the Zuidas Project Bureau leaves it up to itself, in other words – it will remain deprived of the exciting malfunctions and frictions that are so essential today in seducing the highly demanding, internationally operating high-income earner. Philosopher Slavoj Žižek once described the latter as a yuppie who has his financial affairs well in order, but who still cultivates an alternative, anti-capitalist aura.[24] A project development exclusively targeted to these groups cannot avoid incorporating this aura in its plans. The Zuidas Project Bureau clearly believes that no one can better stimulate such an image than the cultural actors. These cultural actors are subsequently expected to dress up an intrinsically capitalist development in an anti-capitalist, 'critical' package.

The Cultural Sector as the Only Hope for Amsterdam-Zuidas?

The transfer of tasks to the cultural forces, however, goes much further than the demand to produce an elusive urban quality so crucial to the success of urban developments. We can also see this invitation extended to the cultural sector to 'jump into the process' as a solution to the crisis of legitimacy looming for a spatial planning that has been reduced to mere project development – with government authorities increasingly running their cities like a business. For what is left, within such an outlook, of their political task, their role as defender of the public interest? The answer, of course, is precious little. Spatial planning policy has today regressed into facilitating the interests of private real estate groups and investors or the outlining of a global strategy for fierce competition with other, often neighbouring cities.

The prominent position accorded to culture within neoliberal planning must be understood as a compensation for the political sector giving up its political task. We can see this as an example of what is known in psychoanalysis as 'transference'.[25] The latter can be described as a trick to resolve an internal crisis – for instance the perceived impossibility of doing anything – by passing it on to someone else. A typical example of this is a socially

240

inhibited, timid person who consistently associates with more extrovert personalities, because the directness of the latter obviates the need for him to express himself. This transference relationship takes place, of course, on the unspoken condition that the Other, the object of transference, continues to play his part. Well, the division of tasks among the neoliberal, 'entrepreneurial' government and cultural actors – as enshrined in the Space and Culture Action Programme – is equally characterized by this sort of transference. The cultural forces, for instance, are expected to politicize the little public space left to us and assign it critical value. In this way, the government fobs off onto the cultural forces what it itself considers impossible: that is, doing anything— within current global conditions – other than cater to the needs of big business.

In short, with the neoliberalization of planning, the only way the government still acts as the keeper of the public interest and social justice lies in allocating a budget for art and culture. To put it another way, its only political act consists of creating opportunities for others to do something in which it no longer believes. This can take the form of the allocation of a sum of money, the necessary infrastructure or even know-how to cultural actors. In this way, the general lack of faith in the possibility of a radically democratic city is compensated by ascribing magical powers (and big budgets) to cultural projects that enthusiastically and – from the entrepreneur's standpoint – even naïvely focus on reconquering the urban public space or the allocation of a place to excluded groups. Art and culture are elevated to the alternative stage upon which things that do not easily fit into the interests of the market are still possible. If today's neoliberal government, in spite of its superficial blather about democracy, still possesses any idealism, it is an 'outsourced' idealism. It has neatly transferred its faith in politics to the cultural sector and even expects a political act from this quarter.

This same transference is also at work within the Zuidas development. Cultural forces are given the task of proving that the mega real estate development is more than the sum of the private interests of a handful of globally operating financial institutions. The cultural forces, for instance, are expected to vouchsafe different, non-market-driven values like beauty, reflection, engagement or spatial quality in an otherwise completely generic development. Here too, the affair will last as long as the cultural actor – the privileged partner of the project developers – keeps playing his or her role as a 'simulator' of a political consciousness.

In this way, the cultural sector is trapped in what Slavoj Žižek calls 'interpassivity'. The demand to generate permanent friction within

BAVO

the well-oiled machinery of the entrepreneurial city is aimed at preventing problematic situations arising at the political level – it must divert political debate toward discussions of culture's value in life. Precisely because of this, the cultural actor cannot, under any circumstances, step out of his role of a 'freshly disturbing' force. The problem is thus that the transference of the political task to the cultural level is merely grist for the mill of the depoliticization of planning within neoliberalism. The torrent of discussions about how far street art can go, how confrontational it can be in relation to its client, and so forth, must be situated against the backdrop of this problem. These questions are quite capable of unleashing a battle within the holy alliance of the entrepreneurial planning machine, but then on the condition that the cultural sector be prepared to let culture become the stage of this battle. It can do this, for instance, by putting the partnership between developers and cultural forces on the line, by stretching the rules of the game of their amorous relationship with the client to further its own agenda or – to borrow a notion of Boris Groys – by claiming equal aesthetic rights in the area of the design of the spatial environment.[26]

Conclusion: Culture as the Continuation of Politics by Other Means

The question that arises is therefore not so much how cultural forces can adopt a critical role *in* the process – which is what is assigned to them by government authorities or development corporations – but in fact how they can subject this process *itself* to a thorough critical analysis. This raises issues such as the undemocratic character of urban developments, the transformation of the city into a consumer commodity, spatial planning as an extension of the market, and so forth. To adequately tackle these issues, an intermediary position is needed, whereby the cultural actor has both feet in the process, but at the same time is not part of it – an 'extimate' position, in other words.

For an answer to this question we can take inspiration from Slavoj Žižek and his contention that in the present post-ideological era, in which every ideal is negotiable and is subjected to the demands of flexibility, a policy maker with an ethical sensibility has become the exception.[27] This is a person for whom flexibility belongs to the economic sphere and is not relevant to issues related to the public interest. It is precisely the appearance of such a person 'with a backbone' that has become so traumatic today. Think of the controversy surrounding the Dutch soldier who refused to take part in the Dutch peace-keeping mission in Afghanistan. Although he justified his refusal by arguing that the Dutch army was not adequately prepared, he nevertheless made explicit what everyone already knew: that the mission is part of a new wave of imperialism.

This discussion is highly relevant to a development like Amsterdam-Zuidas. The latter, after all, is the excrescence of the current culture of flexibility, which increasingly colonizes the sphere of the ideal. Think of the government's flexible handling, within the Zuidas, of its traditional task as the defender of the public interest. The latter has been 'translated' without too many scruples in terms of project development. Think also of the flexibility in relation to the individual agenda being demanded within the Zuidas of all social and market partners involved – and this regardless of rank, from project developers to environmental associations, heritage societies and artists. Within this atmosphere, it is considered inevitable that everyone sacrifice some of his or her own agenda points in the name of the common interest – and the smooth progression of the process – and be prepared to negotiate on questions of principle as a matter of course.[28]

If we follow Žižek's suggestion, then the person who obstinately sticks to his or her guns – and keeps these demands outside any economic negotiation – could hold up this process for a brief moment and therefore create a space in which the terms of this negotiation *itself* are called into question. Although this person will most likely be portrayed as a spoilsport in a political process that has already degenerated into a flexible negotiating process, he or she will nevertheless come to embody what is known in political philosophy as 'the political'.[29] This designates the moment at which the prevailing definition of what is considered politics in a given context is called into question. Within the discussion about the Zuidas this would be the moment at which the definition, considered unimpeachable, of politics as 'an economic negotiation among individual interests and desires' itself becomes the subject of political debate. Well then, if the cultural actor, as presented above, is the figure to whom all the idealism of society has been transferred and who is trumpeted as the last keeper of the public interest, is he or she not in an ideal position to provoke such a political moment – or better, such a moment of the political?

The traumatic, and therefore effective, aspect of such a position was illustrated by the recent television appearance by Dutch landscape architect Adriaan Geuze in a documentary about the shrinking of the Groene Hart – the 'Green Heart', a large area of natural beauty and agricultural land in the middle of the Randstad urban conglomeration in the west of the Netherlands.[30] He strenuously protested against the surreptitious yet systematic disappearance of the Groene Hart, as all kinds of interest groups have been taking bites out of it for years. Not only is this leading to a rapid fragmentation of the Groene Hart, but this increasing 'fragmentation' only leads to its very existence being increasingly called into question – for why hold on to the Groene Hart if it is only a fragmented, inconsistent pile of 'greenery'? In the face of these 'societal developments', Geuze made an impassioned and uncompromising appeal for the integral preservation of the Groene Hart. We need hardly explain that Geuze, with this inflexible attitude, attracted the fury of the entire right-minded planning community. One counter-criticism often expressed by his interlocutors was that he ignored the 'inevitable' societal trends that were leading to the dismantling of the Groene Hart. For instance, Joost Schrijnen – director of spatial planning for the Province of South Holland – flatly stated that Geuze 'had a romanticized picture in his head'. Others faulted him for his fixation on the aspect of 'landscape quality' and disputed whether spatial planning can be redirected to achieve this. Melanie Schultz van Haegen – at that time Junior Minister for Transport and

Water Management – resolutely argued that it was not her job to 'beautify the country' and that she focused solely on 'proper management of spatial developments'. Ultimately, it was Wim Derksen – director of the Netherlands Institute for Spatial Research – who made the clearest admission of guilt, in his response to Geuze's criticism that the institute's study on the Groene Hart had accorded too much importance to the space demands of existing forces, allowing them to take over even more of the Groene Hart. Derksen had no answer to Geuze's criticism except to confess that 'in this Dutch political and Dutch planning culture' he had 'given up on the Groene Hart'.

The remarkable thing about this incident is that Geuze intervened in the debate about the Groene Hart from his specific position as a landscape architect, that is to say, as an expert in the domain of landscape quality. He alluded, for instance, to the important Dutch movement of landscape painting that specialized in the unique quality of the light and the sky in the Groene Hart, but also to ecological factors such as the greenhouse effect and water management, and the deterioration of the quality of life for residents of the Randstad as a result of the loss of what might fulfil a function analogous to that of Central Park in New York. In that sense Geuze did the impossible:

he broke through the transference relationship in which today's designers are often trapped. Within Dutch spatial planning, transformed into a negotiating process of 'give and take', he took on the role of an uncompromising idealist who did not hesitate, in the pursuit of his interests – which he elevated to the order of the sacrosanct and therefore public interest – to question even the space requirements of society. No wonder, then, that Geuze was vilified. He had violated, after all, the prevailing dogma of Dutch planning, as set out in the *Nota Ruimte* – a tenet of which is that 'accommodating space claims' contributes to a democratization of space production.

We argue that cultural actors should adopt an equally unshakeable position with respect to their own expertise, whether ascribed to them by others or not. If they are now being presented as the only ones who can bring about the necessary fertile artistic climate or the alternative spatial quality of an urban development, they should do this with the same idealism and the same uncompromising attitude as Geuze. They should declare these issues 'sacrosanct' at the outset of any economic negotiation. The cultural sector should approach its brief to democratize the planning processes in the same way that Geuze did with securing the quality of the Dutch landscape. It must do this with a tenacity that will quickly compel its partners to put their cards on the table about their genuine desire for a democratic urban production. Only in this way can the cultural sector politicize the production of space – where the government refuses to do so – by posing the uncomfortable question about the utility and benefit of the current neoliberal trend in spatial planning, and call its protagonists on the way in which, in the name of democracy, it makes the arena of social forces complicit in developments like the Zuidas. In short, the cultural actors have to take very seriously the role thrust upon them by a government that only dares to perform its political role through culture, and reformulate their own practice as the continuation of politics by other means.

Notes
1. For more information and data, see
www.vrom.nl/pagina.html?id=8309 and
www.zuidas.nl/smartsite.dws?id=2
2. See for example the *Tegenlicht* documentary
'Planner's blight: de strategie van het gummetje',
www.vpro.nl/programma/tegenlicht/
afleveringen/22966523/items/22153505/
in which André Thomsen (professor of real estate and
housing management) criticizes the current restructuring
of neighbourhoods in large and medium-sized cities for

BAVO

being mainly driven by the profit-seeking of the corporations and the dubious demographic policy of city
authorities. In his view, this is based on a market outlook
whereby the problem is not the housing stock in the so-
called problem areas, but the residents.
3. See for example the 'Actieprogramma Ruimte en
Cultuur' ('Space and Culture Action Programme')
launched by the Ministry of Education, Culture and
Welfare in June 2005,
www.minocw.nl/cultuur/publicaties/
4. See www.virtueel-museum.nl/
5. More specifically, Simon den Hartog (former director of
the Rietveld Academie) was appointed as supervisor. The
website of the Virtual Museum features this text: 'Den
Hartog put together a programming council and
developed a vision with a practical, implementable plan
for the realization of this artistic climate. Based on this
vision, the Virtual Museum Zuidas foundation was
officially founded in 2003. The Zuidas area itself is
viewed as a kind of museum. A constantly changing space
in which art has a place and within which new art forms
can be created. The Zuidas Virtual Musem is an umbrella
label for temporary and permanent activities, an
exhibition and exchange centre, visible as well as more
invisible projects in the Zuidas.'
www.virtueel-museum.nl/ (See also Henk de Vroom's
article elsewhere in this volume.)
6. See www.virtueel-museum.nl/index.html
7. Curator/artist Hinrich Sachs made this observation
during a symposium at the Jan van Eyck Academie (19
April 2006) about the role of design in the development
of Amsterdam-Zuidas.
8. Think of the 'Logo Parc' initiative, a research project of
the Jan van Eyck Academie. (See also Daniel van der
Velden's article elsewhere in this volume.)
9. The state is the initiator and co-financial backer of the
necessary adaptation of the main infrastructure, in

The Dutch Neoliberal City and the Cultural Activist...

particular. The city of Amsterdam is in charge of planning
and implementation: cf Ministries of Housing, Spatial
Planning and the Environment, of Agriculture, Nature and
Food Quality, of Transport and Water Management and
of Economic Affairs, *Nota ruimte. Ruimte voor ontwikkeling*,
2006, p. 44; www.zuidas.nl/smartsite.dws?id=570.
In addition, the city and the state are also partners in the
development corporation Zuidas NV, which serves as the
coordinator of the Zuidas projects. Other partners include
ABN-Amro, ING, Fortis, Rabobank, Bank Nederlandse
Gemeenten.
10. This is a joint venture with the business sector to put
the city and the region on the international map. The city
executive's contribution is 51 million Euro.
11. *Nota ruimte. Ruimte voor ontwikkeling*, op. cit., p. 44
(see note 9). All the key projects involve developments in
and around the high-speed rail stations. For more
information about the Zuidas as a key project,
see www.vrom.nl/pagina.html?id=8309
12. On the *Nova-DenHaag Vandaag* television programme,
23 May 2006.
13. Pieter Tordoir, 'The economic pentagon: central
business districts in the global economy: Consequences
for the Zuidas development', in Willem Salet and Stan
Majoor (eds.) *Amsterdam Zuidas. European Space*
(Rotterdam: 010 Publishers, 2005), pp. 99-122.
14. Looming in the background are negative reports
noting that the Netherlands is dropping ever further out
the international top rankings. Whereas the Netherlands
still occupied fourth place on the World Economic Forum's
list in 2000, by 2005 it had been relegated to 12th place.
15. *Nota ruimte. Ruimte voor ontwikkeling*, op. cit., p. 31
(see note 9).
16. See also Netherlands Institute for Spatial Research, *Ex
ante toets Nota Ruimte* (Rotterdam: NAi Publishers, 2004),
p. 10. In this publication, it argues that of the four
traditional values that can steer a spatial planning policy –

social equitability, financial economics, sustainability and spatial quality – the current planning regime has clearly opted for the second.

17. Ibidem.

18. Ibidem.

19. Erik Swyngedouw, 'A new urbanity? The ambiguous politics of large-scale urban development projects in European cities', in: Salet and Majoor (eds.), op. cit., pp. 61-79 (see note 13). Think also of the statement by the Netherlands Institute for Spatial Research that current planning 'is characterized by an offensive approach, in which stimulation, development and design take precedence. In this way, governments can attempt, together with social organizations, businesses and citizens, *to exploit the opportunities present in a given region as fully as possible.*' (italics by the author) Netherlands Institute for Spatial Research, *Ontwikkelingsplanologie. Lessen uit de praktijk* (Rotterdam: NAi Publishers, 2003).

20. The Netherlands Institute for Spatial Research also wonders, rightly, whether it is at all the task of the government to help finance such things as office parks (*Ex ante toets Nota Ruimte*, op. cit., p. 11, see note 16). It wonders whether the government should compensate for market failures that are actually the responsibility of the private sector, not the public sector.

21. It is disconcerting to observe how cultural actors often take on a similar role. Think of the cultural initiative Welcome in my backyard! (WiMBY!) by the architecture history agency Crimson in Hoogvliet. WiMBY! set out to document the potential for redevelopment of the problem community through innovative proposals. With the 'test factory' project (campus Hoogvliet), for instance, the initiative tried to reconnect employment opportunities in the community to the activity in the Port of Rotterdam, which had turned Hoogvliet, as a result of mass techno-logical developments and outsourcing to low-wage

The Dutch Neoliberal City and the Cultural Activist...

countries, from a dynamic working-class community into a socio-economic wasteland. WiMBY! proposed setting up an information and knowledge centre where the many unemployed residents of Hoogvliet could be trained according to the new requirements of the port enterprises. By highlighting this golden opportunity, WiMBY! is attempting to lure market players into investing in the sustainability of the community. In short, we are faced with an uncomfortable situation in which cultural actors, of all people, are operating as investment scouts, encouraging businesses to use the community as a reservoir for manpower.

22. See note 3.

23. Think for example of project developer AM Wonen, which set up a special subsidiary called 'Groen door Rood' ('green through red'). The market demand for exclusive, spacious homes in a green landscape is promoted, in this construct, as a sustainable development (see www.nederlandmooi.nl/content_ fr.php?pageCode=4.4.3).

Similar constructs are also the order of the day in relation to monuments of cultural and historical value, the restoration of which is financed, for instance, by building a commercial estate in the vicinity.

24. Interview with Slavoj Žižek, 'I am a Fighting Atheist', by Doug Henwood, February 2002, bad.eserver.org/issues/2002/59/zizek.html

25. For an elaboration of this theme of the cultural actor elevated to the subject supposed to undermine the existing order, see BAVO, 'The Spectre of the Avant-garde: Contemporary Re-Assertions of the Programme of Subversion in Cultural Production', in *Andere Sinema*, no. 176, pp. 42-61.

26. This promotion of culture is also often paired with a humanitarian discourse about culture. In this, culture (beauty, history, creativity, reflection, etc.) becomes a basic human right – alongside basic values such as

BAVO

security, quality of life, environmental quality and so on.
In this elevation of culture to a 'fundamental human right',
a depoliticization of culture is of course carried out.
Cf. the Boris Groys' essay 'The Politics of Equal Aesthetic
Rights' in: BAVO, *Cultural Activism Today: the Art of Over-
Identification* (Rotterdam: Episode Publishers, 2007).
27. See Slavoj Žižek, *Organs without Bodies*
(London/New York: Routledge, 2004).
28. This is also the core of Žižek's notion of 'post-politics'.
See Slavoj Žižek, *Pleidooi voor tolerantie* (Amsterdam:
Boom 1998), pp. 25-28.
29. A key reference work for the understanding of this
notion is Jacques Rancière, *Disagreement: Politics and
Philosophy* (Minnesota: University of Minnesota Press,
1998).
30. See 'New Orleans in de Polder. De eenmansoorlog
van een landschapsarchitect', first broadcast on
Nederland 3, 26 March 2006 (see www.vpro.nl/
programma/tegenlicht/afleveringen/27615611/).

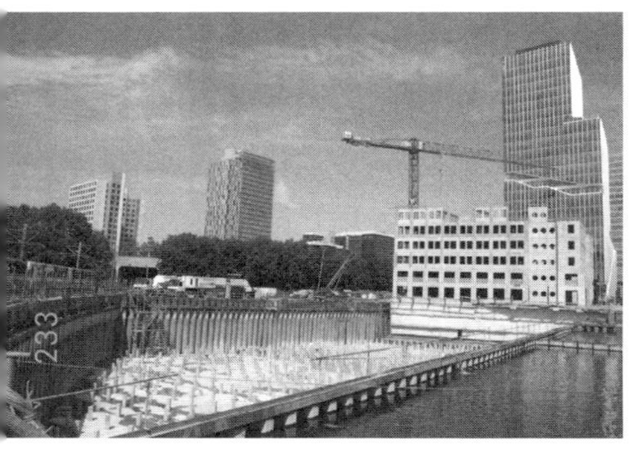
233

Daniel van der Velden

Logo Parc: a Model

When a prestigious business district in the making invites artists and 'creative industries' to add to its profile and even influence its public space, what politics are at stake? It is an opportunity for the ambitions of the individual artists involved, but to what effect? Can they, in effect, disagree with it? And what does it tell us about the reality of culture in present day up-market city quarters? Logo Parc proposes a strategy that claims the model as a site for disagreement about Amsterdam-Zuidas.

The project Logo Parc might seem a work of science fiction, but it is a work of 'science passion'; the illusory aspect, the fiction, has been replaced by the life force of 'passion'. The topic is that of the Zuidas, the international business district of Amsterdam.

The Zuidas is a public-private development that forms the Netherlands' highest bid in the international office space market. As will be apparent from other articles in this book, art and design play an important role in its development. The question at stake, however, is what role? I don't believe it will be possible to conceive of something like a definitive, conclusive essay on the Zuidas. The Zuidas, to a certain extent, is to today's Amsterdam what the Bijlmermeer was in the nineteen-seventies, except its politics and economics are different.

The Bijlmermeer, as most of us know, is considered a 'failed' experiment in large-scale housing that came about through the direct implementation and application of utopian ideas about society and human behaviour, eternalized in reinforced concrete. The Zuidas, on the other hand, bears some hallmarks of an opposite, but equally vulnerable utopia. One that centres on not the social and behavioural aspects of urban space but on its economical and aesthetical factors. Its matching material, here, would not have to be concrete, but glass. The commissioned pieces and projects of art and design which accompany large developments like the Bijlmermeer and the Zuidas thus, I would imagine, kind of automatically align themselves with the politics and economics which called them into action. They cannot do anything else than that.

By means of analogy: Flies and mosquitos are circulating around the head of a walking elephant like tiny helicopters. They are annoying the elephant, but they are dependent on it as much as on its general direction of movement. Where the elephant is ultimately going, to what goal it is proceeding, is not determined by insects and is literally none of their business – they will simply have to go there too if they want to remain in its ecosystem.

Artists and designers, to some extent, are like those flies and mosquitos, with the exception that they can reflect on their own role and position. They can, so to speak, worry about what they cannot change.

Let us pause once and wonder where the elephant that is the Zuidas is going if not in any direction we've given it. The direction that the Zuidas is going is determined by its value. Not the amount of Euros that its material reality of glass and marble and plastics and carpet and security cameras and boardrooms and cables and antennas and car parks would be worth were it to be disassembled and sold off. Rather, this is about the area's value as the return on investment once the material, social and financial the Zuidas is fully operational.

The principal utopian element in the Zuidas is not to be found in its 'realistic' public-private schemes and aesthetical-economic paradigms of 'wine-and-dine urbanism'. The utopian element is to be found in the assumptions which are made, and the methods which are applied, as to how to establish, sustain and increase such value in the (temporary) absence of return on investment. In these methods, the Zuidas, like the Bijlmermeer, relies on some kind of imagined social contract. In the Bijlmermeer of the nineteen-seventies it was the belief that people would lead happy and

Daniel van der Velden

orderly lives in their gargantuan hexagonal living quarters amidst seas of green, faraway from the noise of the city and even the whole idea of automotive vehicles (in reality the elevated motorways and parking garages became a principal source of Bijlmermeer terror). In the first decade of the twenty-first century the belief is that the same people – but tanned, better dressed, and more trained in the art of fusion cuisine and sushi – will lead happy and orderly lives amidst the international head offices of multiple multinational financial corporations.

This brings a question to the fore that is equally urgent for citizens as well as for artists and designers who engage with the Zuidas or are commissioned to do so. That question is to what extent they politically comply with the regime of the Zuidas. The regime of the Zuidas has it that the potential dissent that may result from the uneven division of power, income and labour conditions is reshaped into a fashionably dressed consent demonstrated by the contributions which artists and designers make to the area. To be sure, such a potential antagonism and conflict is there because the Zuidas, from its makeshift and improvised master plan to its execution amidst the grey slabs of Buitenveldert, presents a radical break with the surrounding urban conditions. Although the Zuidas is not 'gated', its radically public and sudden transition from polyvalent urban wastelands and residential areas on both sides of the A10 motorway into a heterotopia for global business and finance does constitute a kind of virtual wall – perhaps we could imagine it as one made of marble. As a corporate resort, the Zuidas concentrates economic power so that it perfectly articulates that those who can afford to work or live there are the ones who 'have'.

This entails the potential conflict with those who 'have not' – those involved in cleaning the offices, those who cannot find a place to live in Amsterdam's overpriced and perverted housing market while the Zuidas boasts soccer fields worth of vacant office space, those who are underprivileged or simply those who no longer wish to passively watch the increasingly abstract and de-socialized theatre of corporate capital, hedge funds and mergers and acquisitions setting its own course. This last group may even involve workers at the Zuidas. Recently, ABN-Amro bank's employees even organized a rarely seen public manifestation against the acquisition and break-up of their company by Fortis, Royal Bank of Scotland and Banco Santander.

Artists and designers are, thus, potentially in the position to say 'no' to the Zuidas. But they don't do that. On the contrary, the aesthetic lure they add to it transforms it into a 'maybe' and then into a 'yes'. Are artists and designers then, perhaps, lured to 'cash in' on

Daniel van der Velden

a Zuidas assignment? Absolutely not. Their contribution has very little to do with 'corporate art' (as in corporate sculptures by celebrated artists like Alexander Calder and Montserrat Soto), primarily because their pay check is not raised by the presence of the corporate. They are not part of the cycle of return on investment but are brought in, so it seems, to soften, socialize or aestheticize the potential conflict between those who have and those who have not.

In short, artists and designers cannot propose or realize 'another world' here. They can funkify the edges of heterotopia and that's about it, really. But there is one image, more than ever, that both dictates and symbolizes the proposed route to go for the Zuidas. (Metaphorically, the route that the elephant will take.) That image is immaterial. That image is the computer-generated, 3-dimensional mirror of the Zuidas as used by developers to sell the area as a non-material image of future value. That image constitutes the aesthetics of an 'opening bid' in the cycle of return on investment. Unrecognized as a piece of art, the future model is where speculative value is visualized.

Using computer-generated images, a world is designed that is 'almost there'. It leads one to think that the task formerly assigned to social utopias and hyper-impossible city models — the proposition of alternatives by constituting 'not-yet' future spaces, and note that the Bijlmermeer was the rare materialization of such a space – has fundamentally shifted to that of promoting real estate value. A large part of that utopian image of real estate is only a façade. Behind the façade, structurally, the inside consists of repetitious, identical open plan floors of reinforced concrete. In principle, the worth of this 'bare space' is not higher than that of any other space constructed in a similar way. It is its speculative value that counts. The tenants' and developers' return on investment on the basis of belief in, and so-called 'willingness to pay' for, a fictional entity called the Zuidas.

In the slipstream of the development of this structural plan of identical insides and varying fronts, artists and designers are commissioned to 'add flavour'. The way these interventions are supposed to function is exactly the opposite of that of the real estate developer's computer-generated future dream. While the latter is supposed to deliver a valuable promise, thus constituting an imaginary bridge between present and future, a public art or design piece at the Zuidas cannot propose such a future. It must create a 'now'. This is the position that artists and designers working with and inside real estate developments have forced themselves into.

But can the added value of these art and design practices – called upon long after principal decisions have been made – be applied to act politically at the Zuidas, which means realizing dissent with it? I do not see political action itself as diplomacy or negotiation, but as the formation of an identity based on the choice for something, therefore disapproving of something else. This may have many effects in practice, including negotiation, but it is eventually about sustaining an irresolvable disagreement.

This position is impossible at the Zuidas if artists and designers see the admittedly complex reality of development as a kind of natural state of affairs. In fact, even if art and design are allowed and stimulated to insert 'smart' friction and tensions into the already finished programme – of which the core values cannot be contested – they may have to first and foremost attempt to ask public questions about their cause and effect in a system that rests on the (silent) consensus around the values created and sustained by development. Tackling this therefore demands a Houdini act that takes the designer back to where dreams and nightmares were first designed: the virtual 3D model of urban space at the beginning of the cycle for return on investment.

'Discursive Surface',
three-dimensional model

Design team: Gon Zifroni, Daniel van der Velden, Matthijs van Leeuwen, Katja Gretzinger, Matteo Poli, Jan van Eyck Academie Maastricht

The Zuidas 3-D model 'Discursive Surface' is situated at the crossroads of analysis and nightmare. In part it consists of stripping down the Zuidas; ridding its architecture of surface, exposing the skeletons.

This gesture suggests that the speculative capital of real estate is in fact literally a speculation; a veil that hides the vast empty – structurally identical – areas of concrete, open plan space inside.

The Zuidas is now surrounded by a marble wall (a prison of class), on which graffiti tags are placed that form the names of people – thinkers, politicians, architects – who are relevant by making the topic of public space into a discursive surface proper.

The octopus inside the Zuidas is globalization; its tentacles, marked with the fading colours of nation states, are conceived as concrete pipes that lead to Singapore, Dubai, London, Hong Kong and New York. Inside these concrete pipes there is only darkness.

265

Daniel van der Velden

At the Zuidas the hegemony of class elite is sustained by the massive presence of banks and law firms. We are not talking about a 'nobility', but about a class that was largely 'created' (we would be tempted to say 'designed') by neoliberalism. We can describe this class as the generation that got the first benefits from capital accumulation, in effect the advent of the yuppie as commemorated by Robert Longo in his 1981 work *Men in the Cities*. The web site 'Art of the Eighties' states: 'The figure in this work seems to be falling, or even dancing, but also may be helplessly contorted by forces beyond his control.' Longo's piece was incorporated in the 3D model.

The glass façades of buildings are taken down, so that not their outside image but their inner structure remains. Please note that the so-called palaces of business and finance, and the living quarters of the poor - the social housing estates that will eventually be demolished to make room for more Zuidas - are thus shown to be, as structures, identical. Therefore it becomes possible to 'see through' the Zuidas, not only through its rhetoric, but also through its 'fictitious wealth', as David Harvey calls it.

Advertising architecture, the privately owned 'street furniture', has been emptied out. They, too, have become hollow frameworks. The frameworks are rendered red and placed in the same point grid as the follies, pavilions of Parc de la Villette in Paris, by architect Bernard Tschumi. That is to say, the highly rhetorical pavilions of this park, that were called in the French media by their double meaning 'les folies de Mitterrand', bring us to make the subconscious suggestion that after years of learning from La Villette, literally all we got were these lousy billboards.

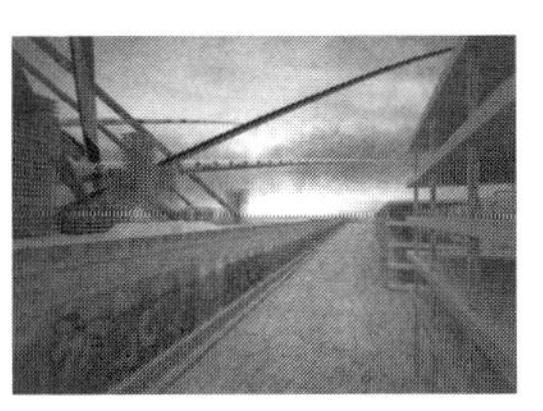
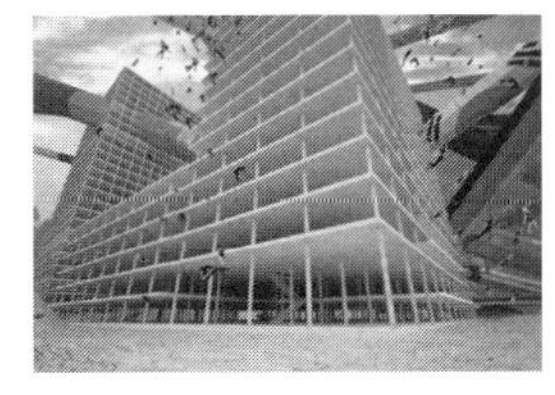
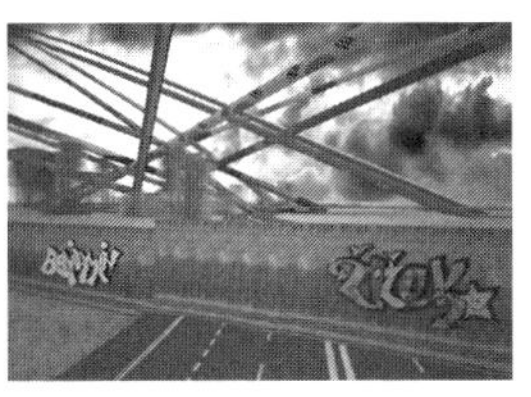
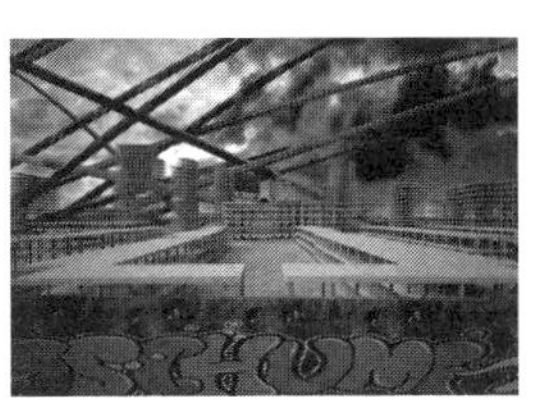

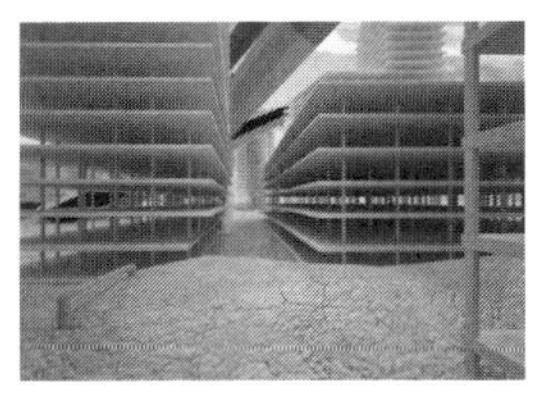
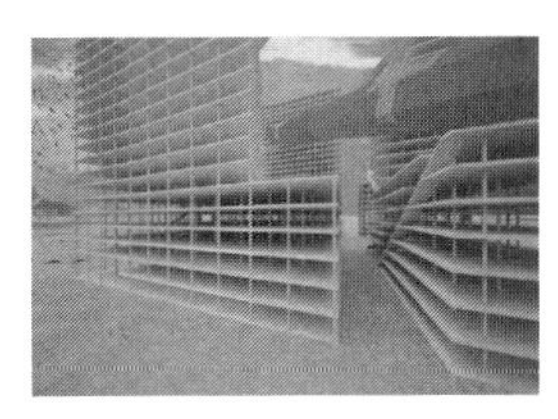
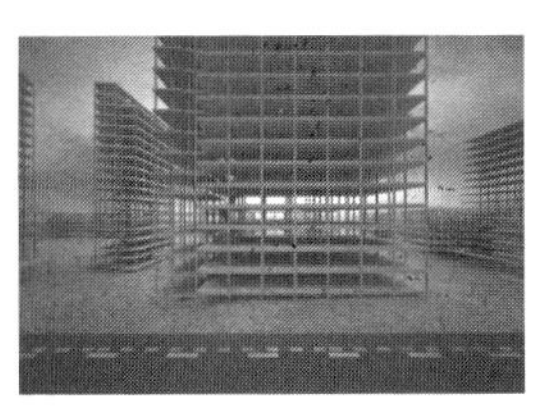
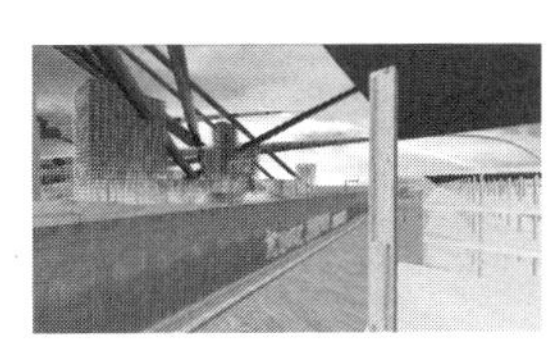
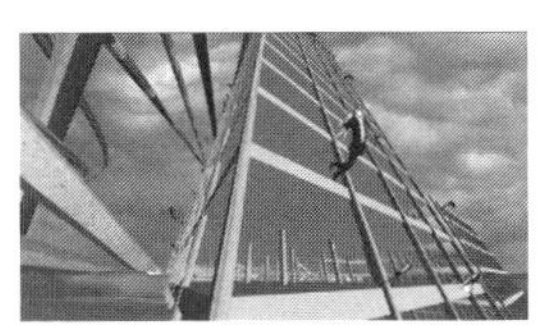
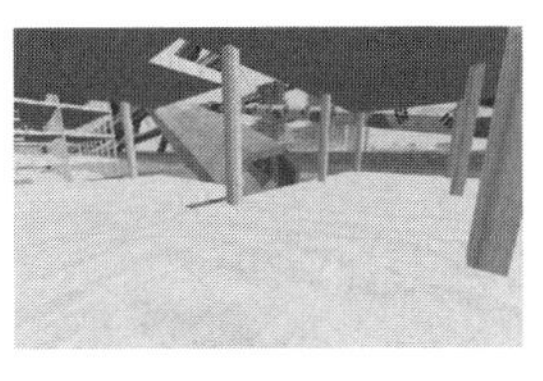

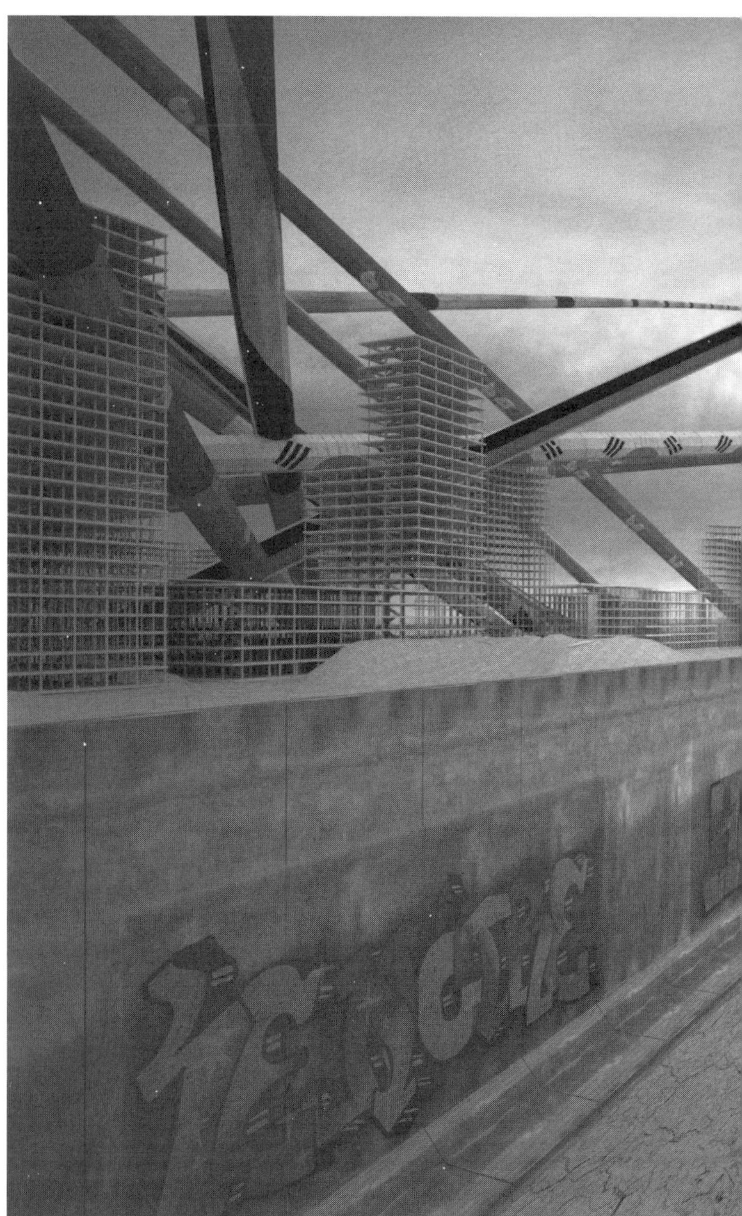

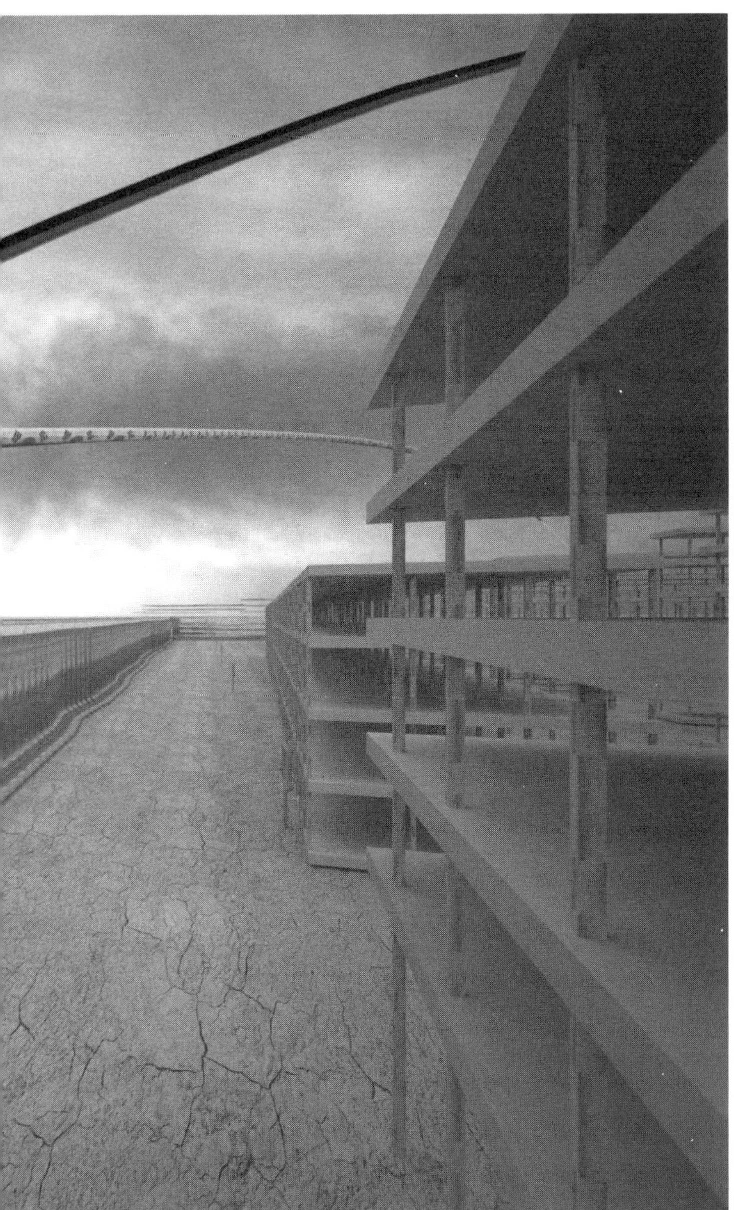

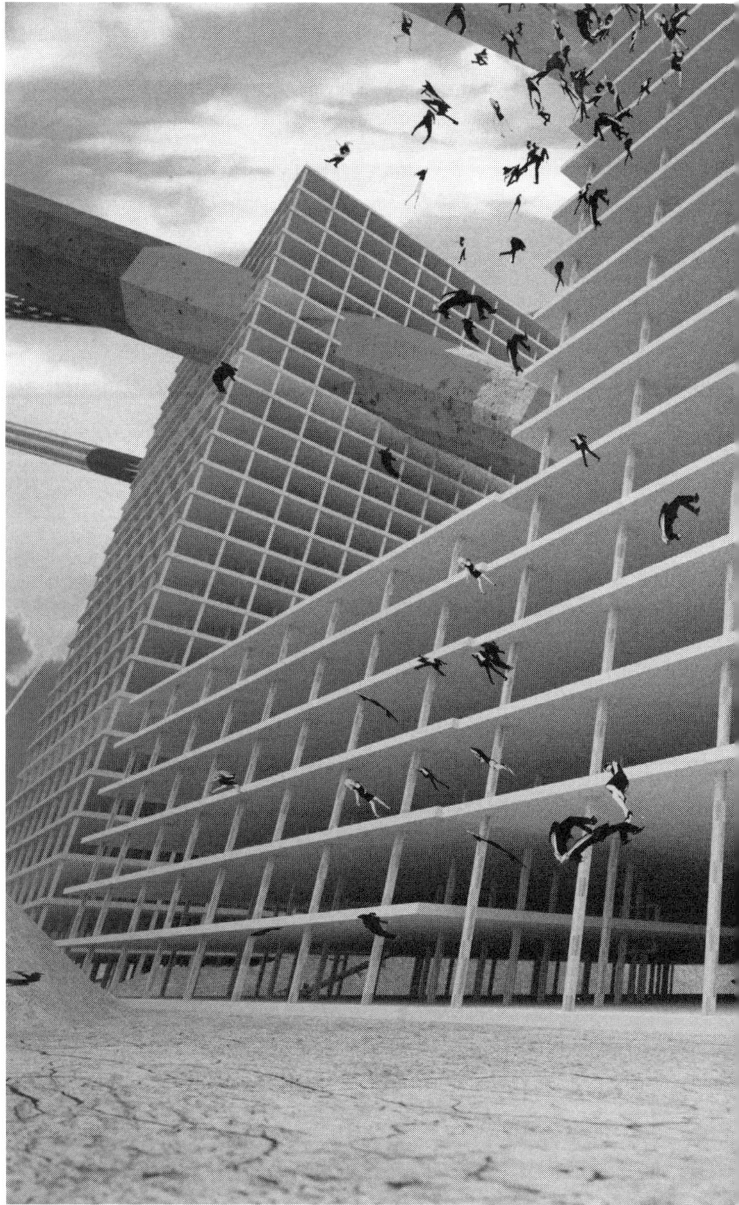

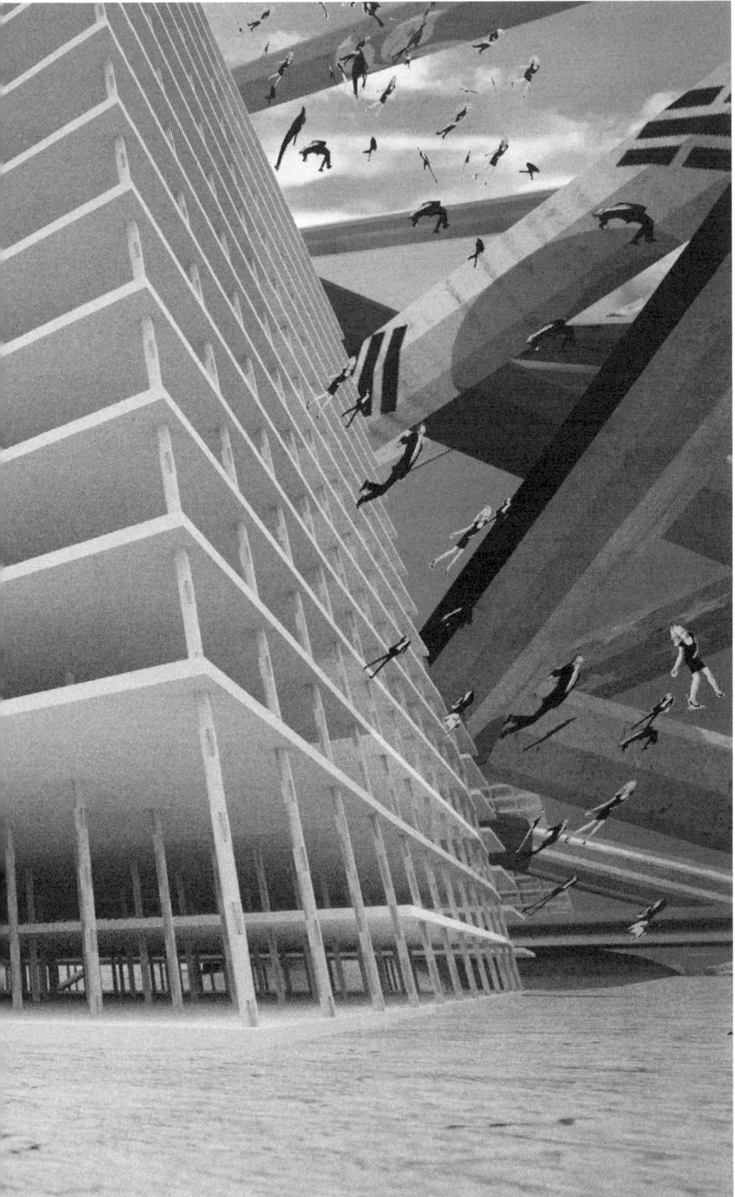

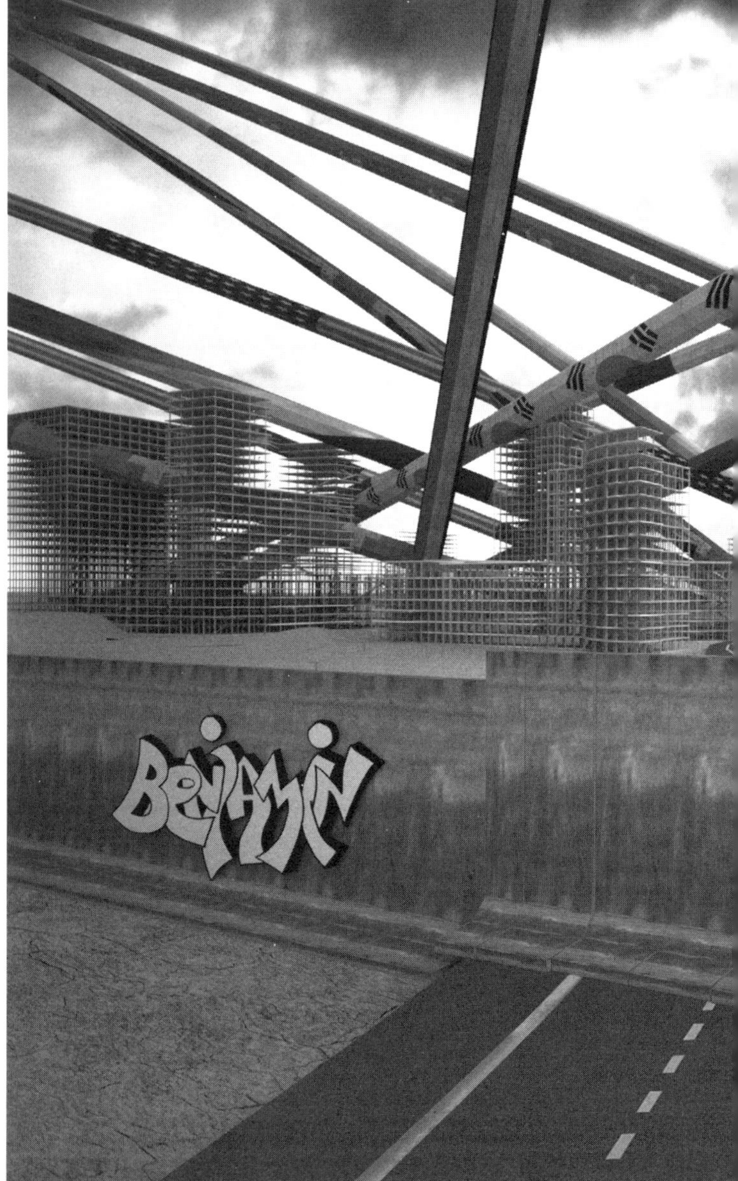

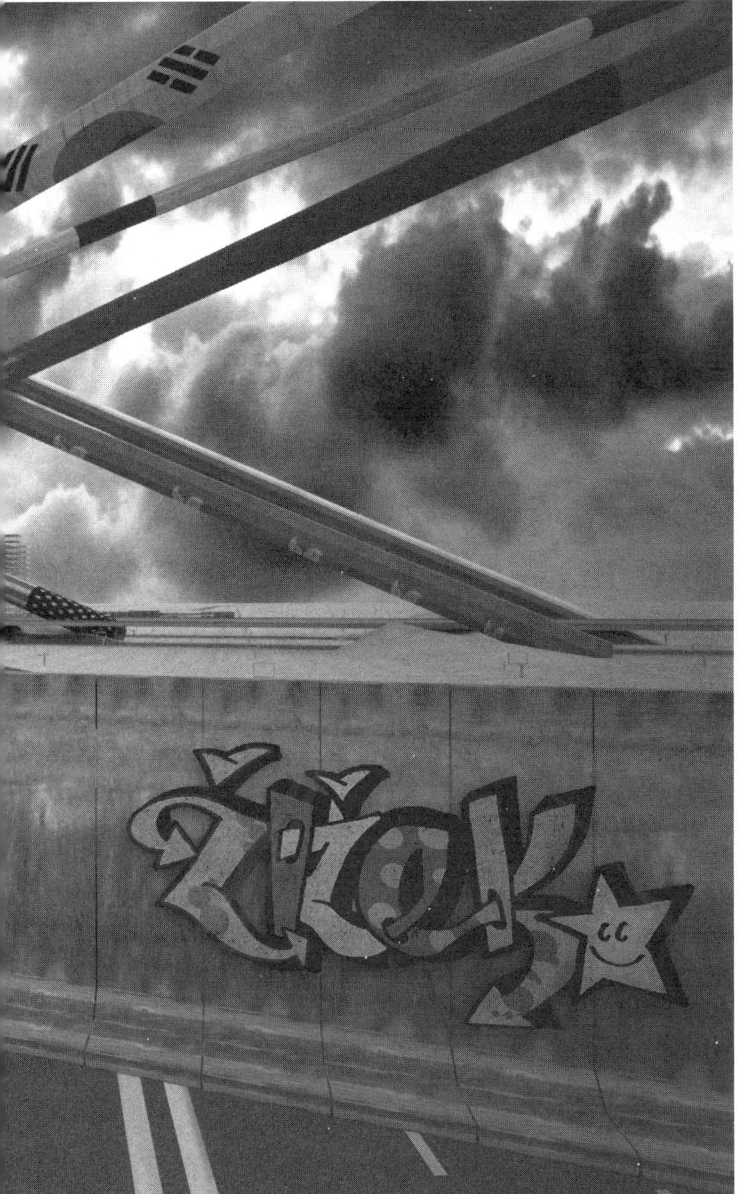

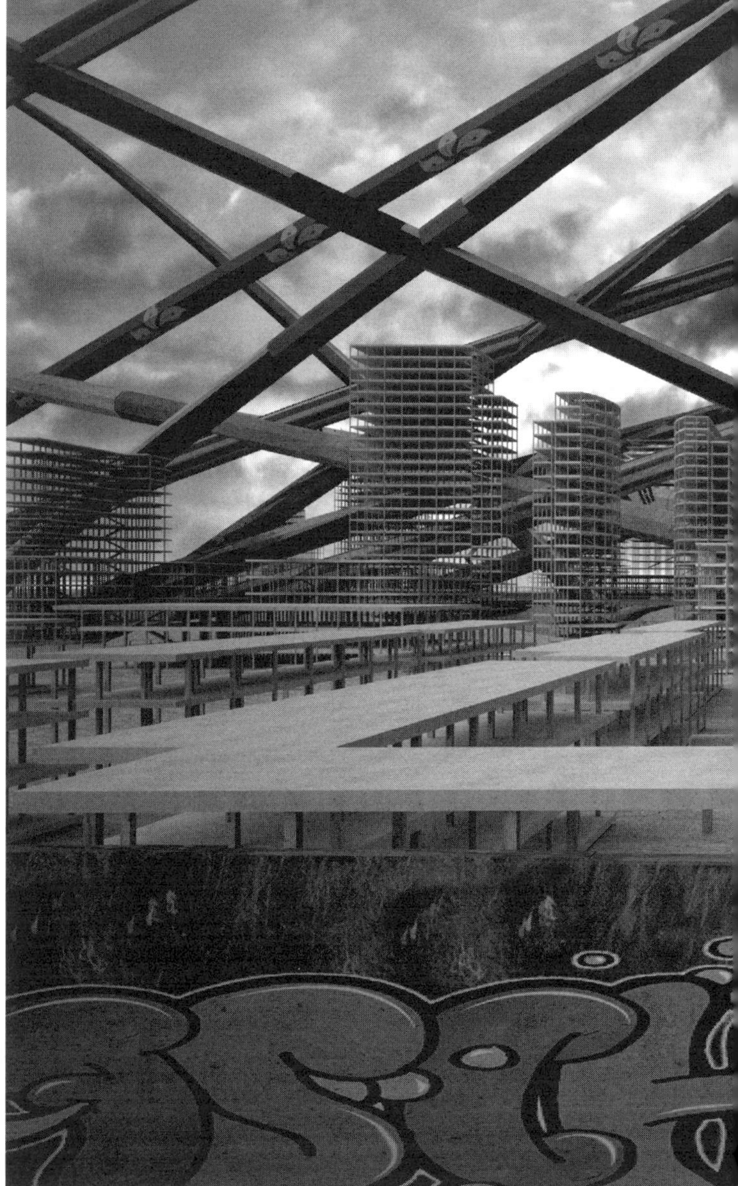

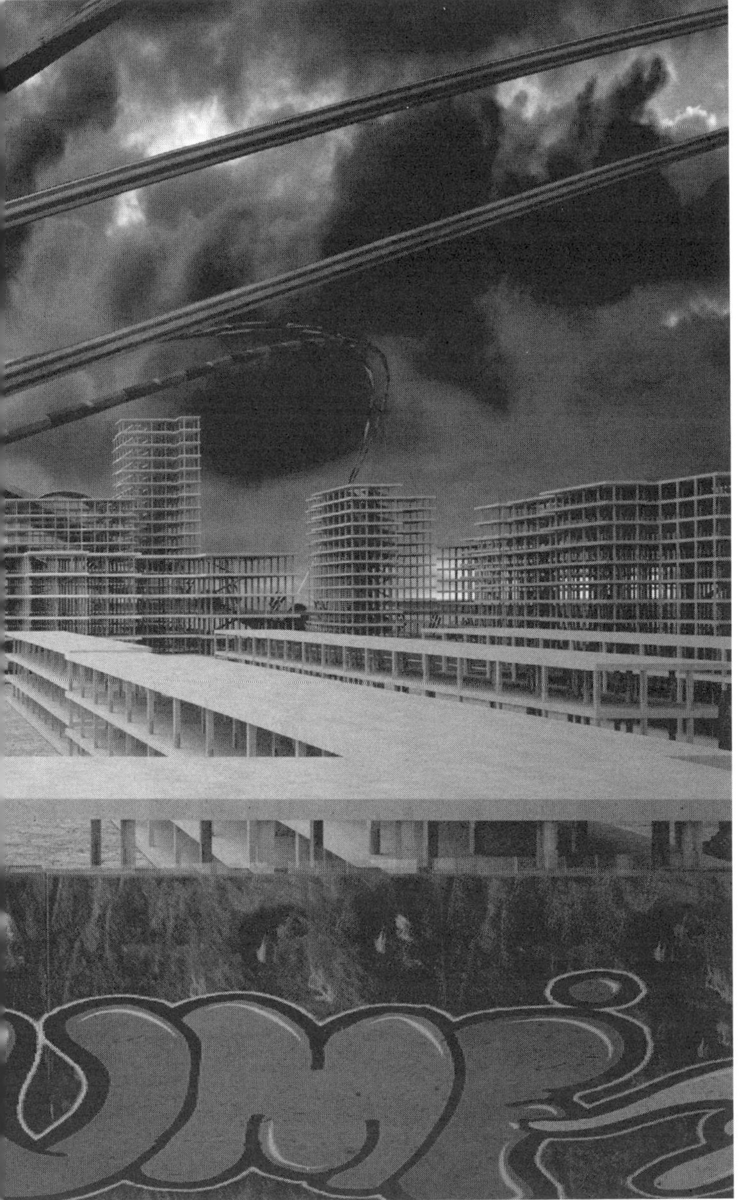

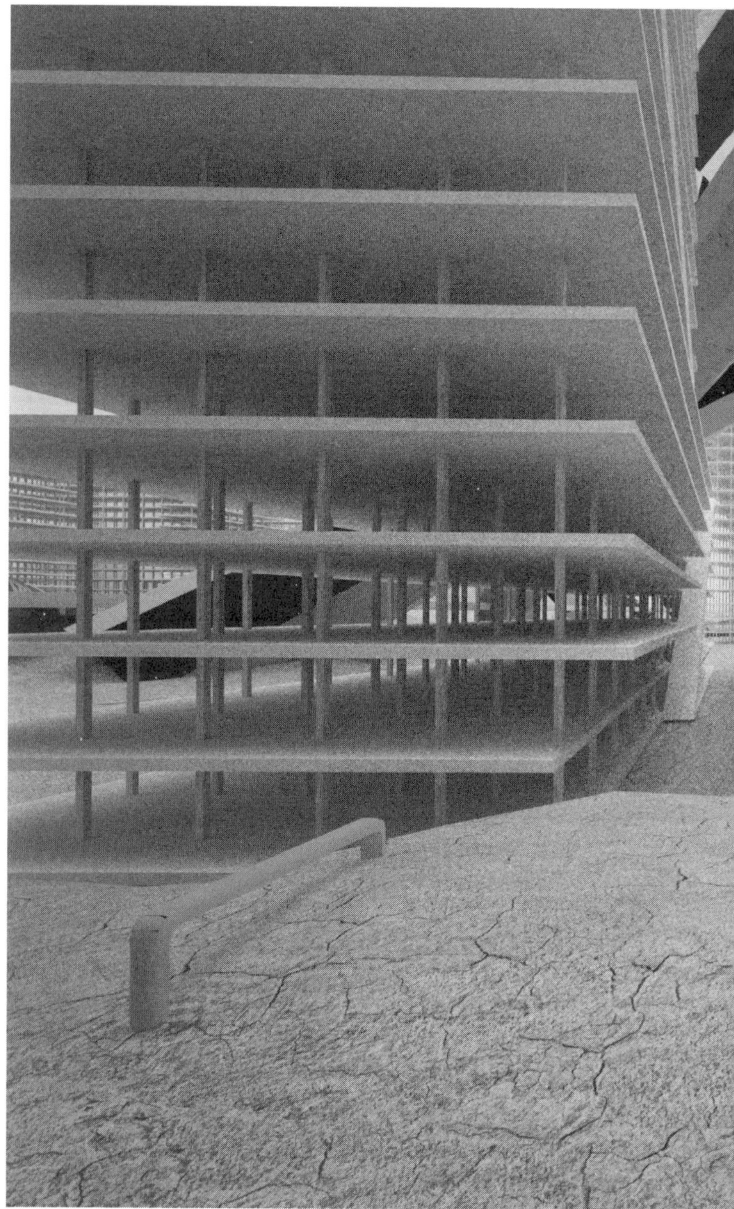

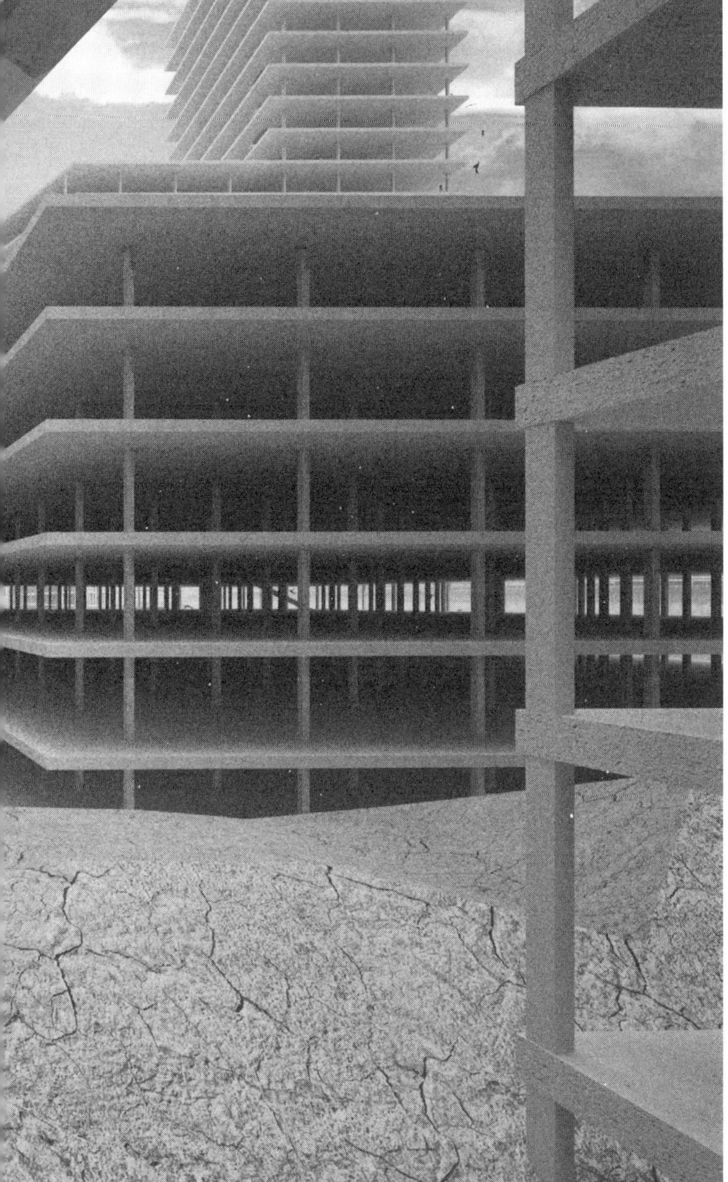

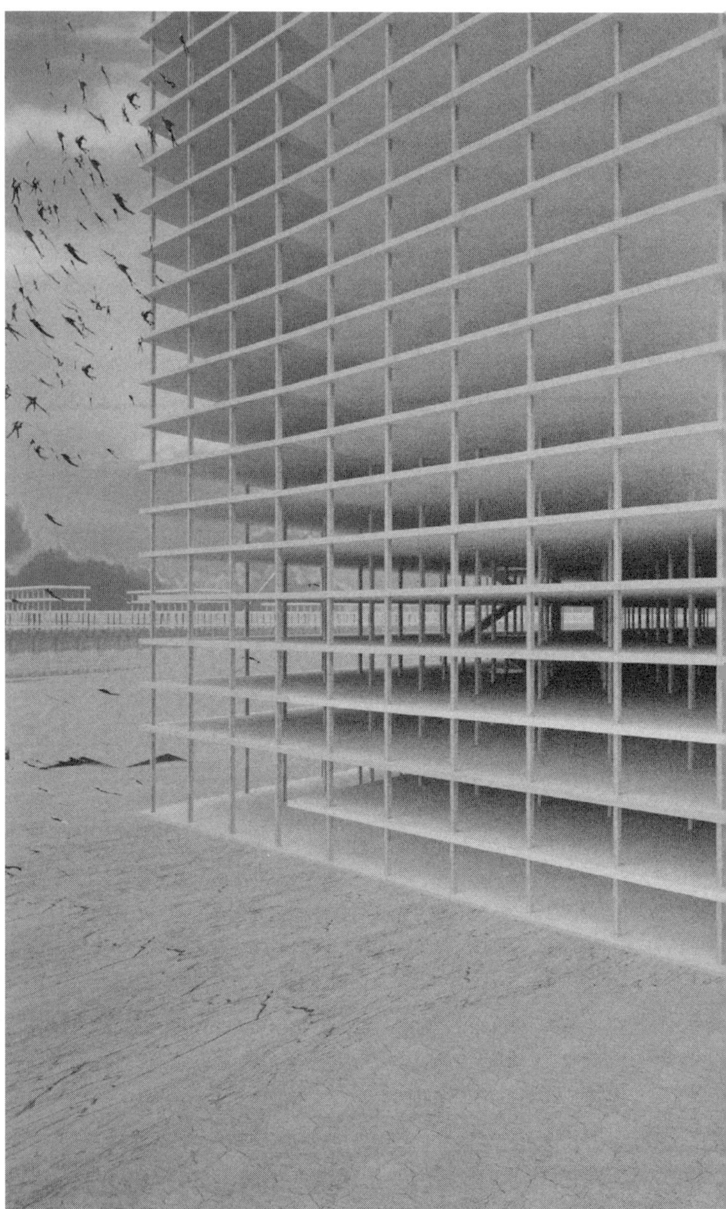

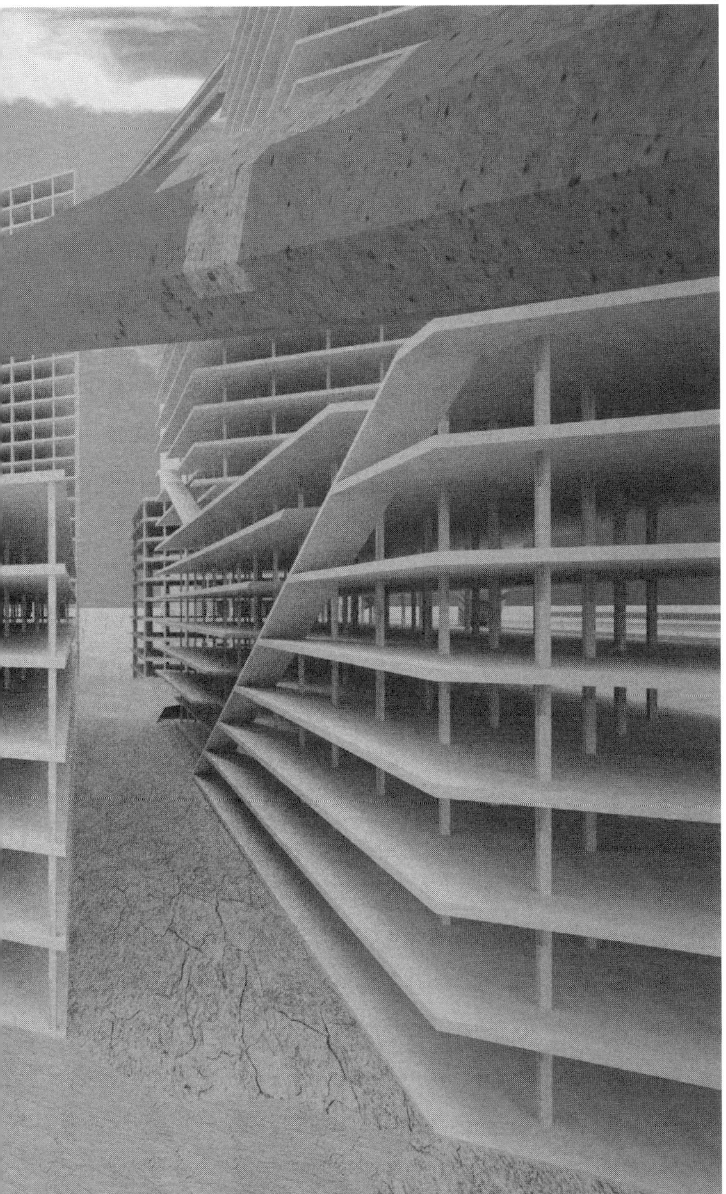

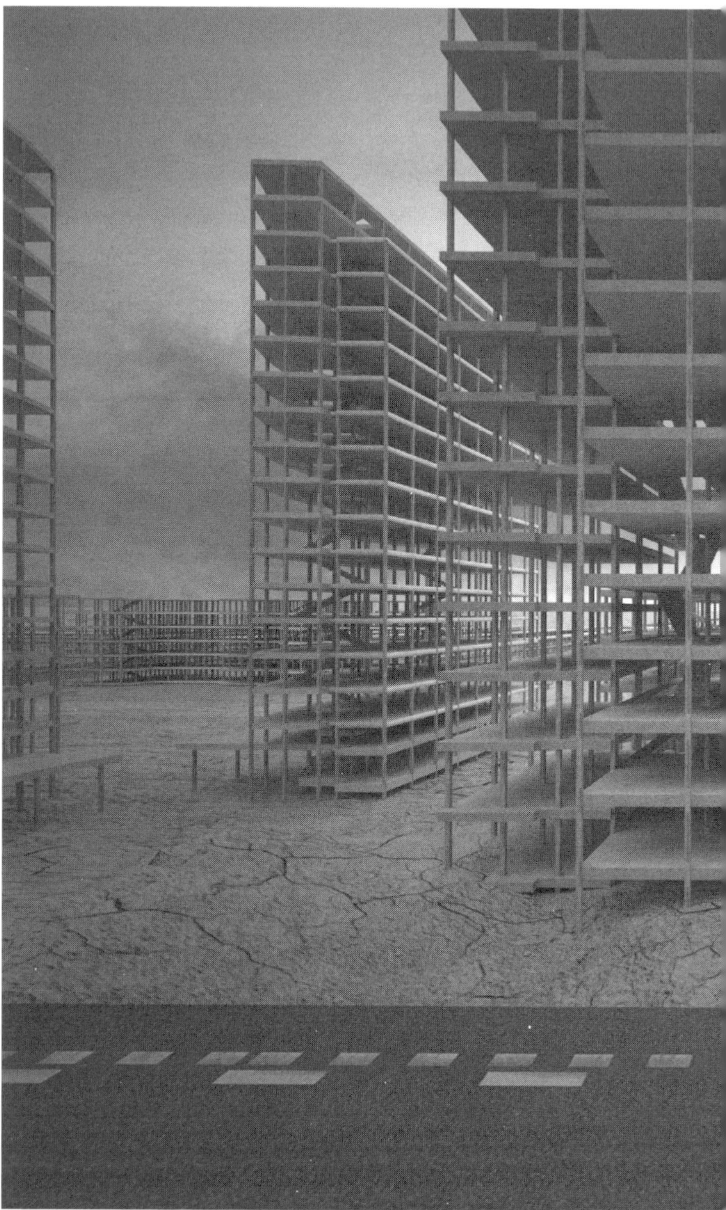

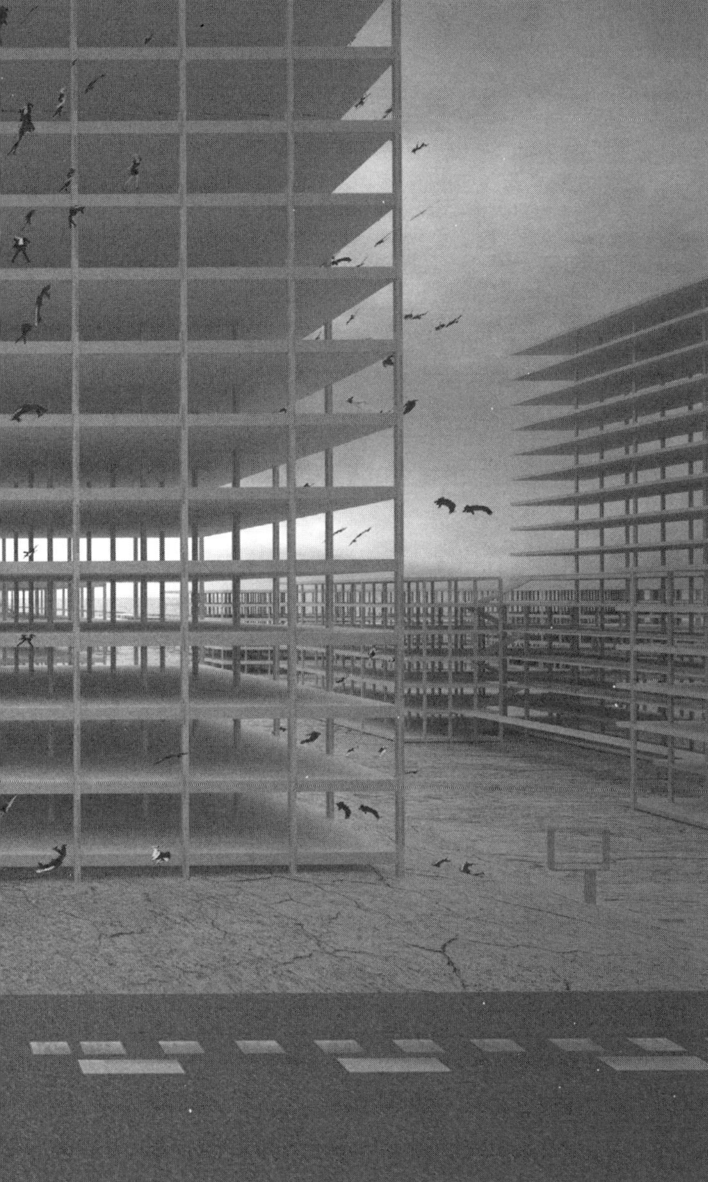

Daniel van der Velden

Public Art and Power

If we want to examine the possibility of art in public space, capable to unlock the political, we may have to consider how public art practices came into being. They did not start from good intentions. The commemorative statue is much more like how it began. A heroic knight on horseback, commemorating a so-called 'good cause' in direct service of the ruling elite: that long forgotten, but basic typology for public art, the statue, is a direct representation of power.

As the state lost interest in a direct representation of its rulers (if only because every so many years they were elected anew), and art lost interest in depiction, consequently embracing abstraction, the visual languages of power and art began to diverge. The 'public art' that became an obligatory companion of building projects (in the Netherlands) had little or nothing to do with expressing interests of power, but was not contesting them either.

Think of enormous industrial or architectural shapes on wind-infested piazzas. Abstraction had been embraced not as an exclusive vanguard but as an everyday language for art. 'Hello' became a stainless steel angular object near a newly built school; 'Goodbye' became an armed concrete geometrical intervention in the central hall of a residency for the demented elderly, and so on. This was simply the proper language used by artists to express themselves in public. The 'liberation' – or political moment – lay in the past. That was when art liberated itself from figuration and hence from making portraits of power. Again, it is important to distinguish this development from forms of 'corporate art', which has artists create landmark works mostly for banks and trade centres – an exceptionally well-paid form of commissioned practice that seems more related to logo design, and positions corporations rather as art collectors.

When state and market began to converge in the nineteen-eighties, conditions became increasingly hard for abstract art in public space and its regime of absolute political neutrality. There is, of course, no final proof for this, but we could imagine these colossal abstract structures with their good intentions as visual metaphors – symbols that is – for the supposed bureaucracy and inefficiency of the nation state and its practices. In fact, the Bijlmermeer contained a few such sculptures and what is more, the project as a whole may qualify architecturally as a social sculpture which failed as a utopia.

In response (not so much to the Bijlmermeer as to the general condition of European political economy in the second half of the twentieth century), the suggestion was that the

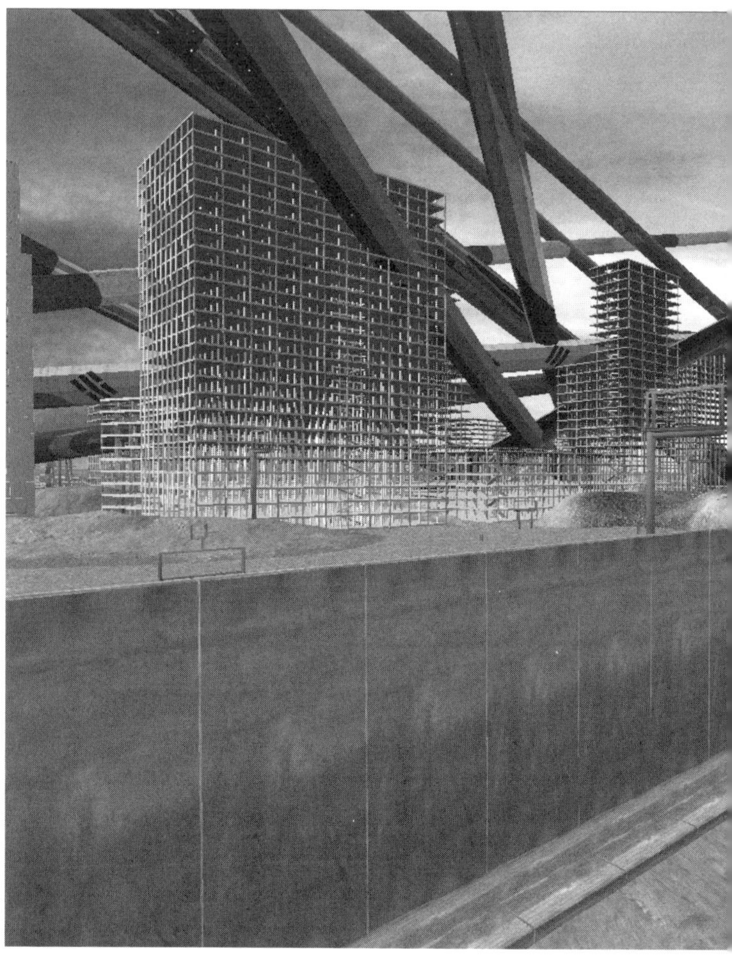

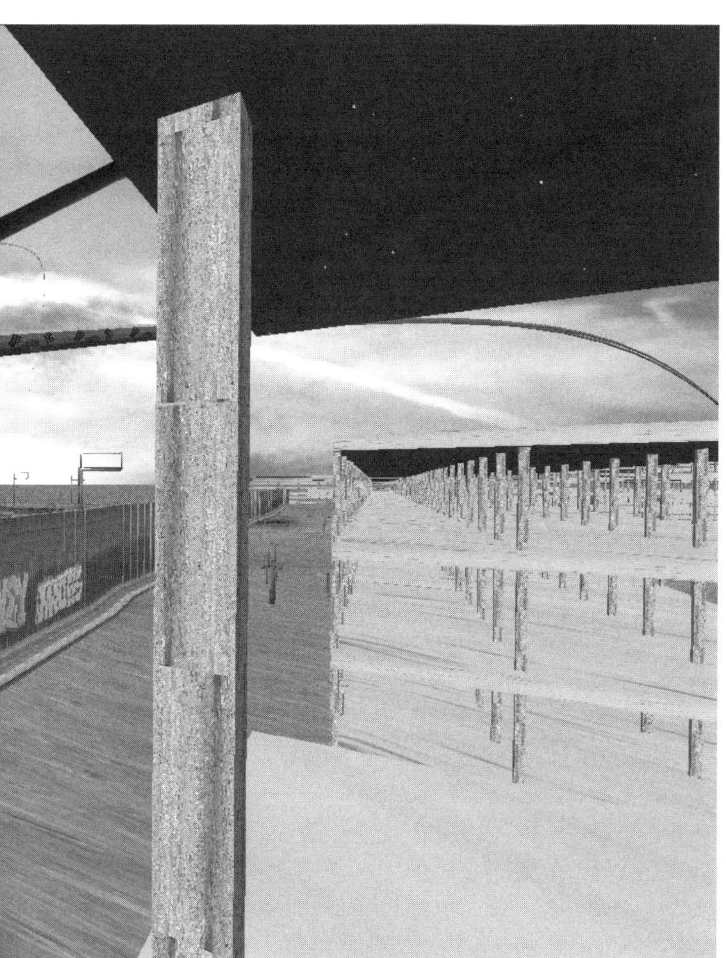

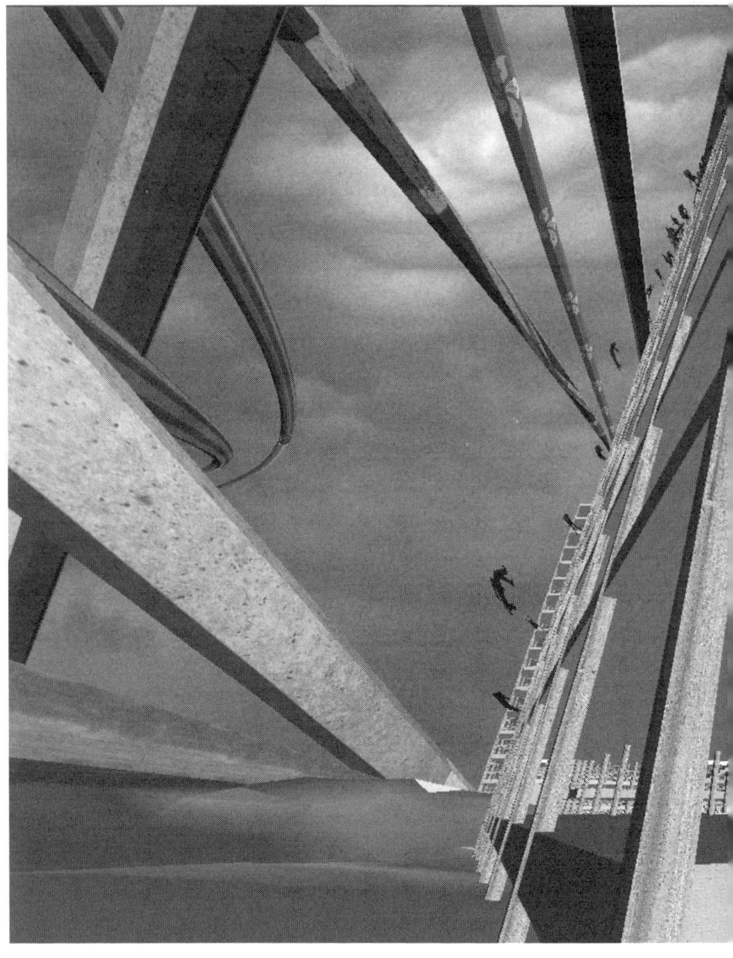

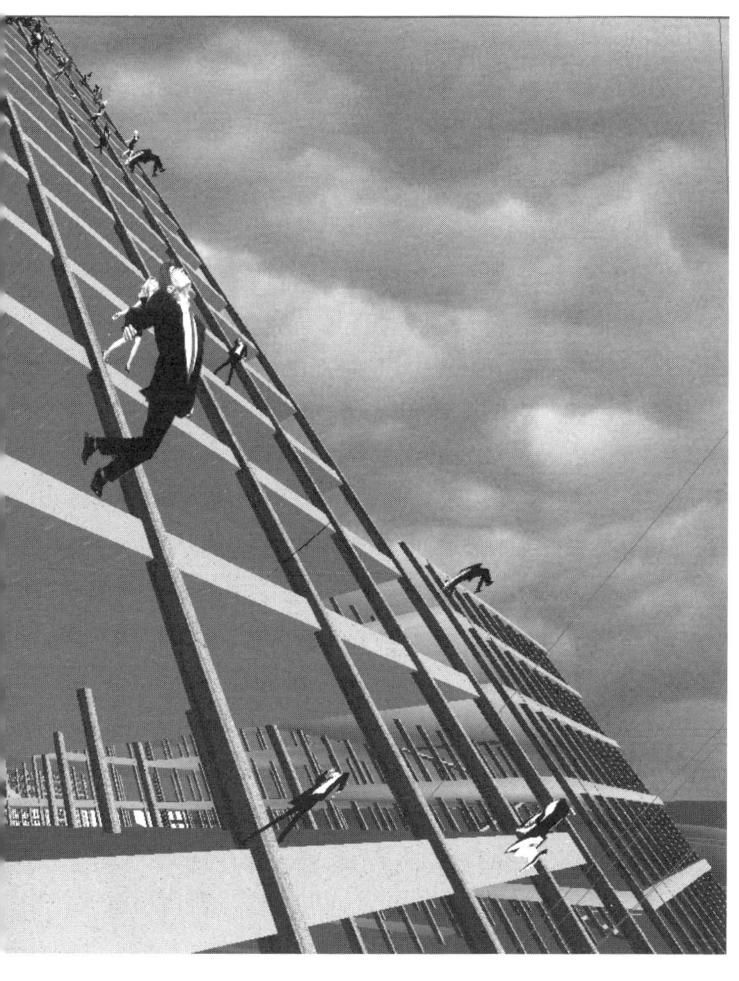

288

welfare state was an inert giant predestined to erect irrelevant and ineffective social policies. This suggestion – quasi-legitimized by grotesque examples from former Eastern European attempts at total planning – propelled the neoliberal project as it was carried out by Ronald Reagan and Margaret Thatcher, in the Netherlands under the leadership of Ruud Lubbers and Wim Kok. Neoliberalization governed privatizing state enterprises and liberalizing state regulations; partially to lighten tax burdens and stimulate economic growth, to the effect that new inequalities and class differences were created. By positing that various services hitherto maintained for the good of all have to become profitable businesses, neoliberalist thought no doubt deeply affected the level, accessibility and affordability of public sector services. Additionally, by reducing its own autonomy, the state obliged itself to seek continuous agreement and collaboration with market forces, which, as the indispensable source of money, thus gained increasing control over the symbolic dimension of the public-private partnership.

The state became 'state +', as social geographer Erik Swyngedouw calls it: state and market rather than state or market. We are still addressing public art here, in particular the strange Dutch rule that has it that 1% of the building budget must be spent on it. While the official commissioning agent for public projects remained the state, it was from that moment on presupposed that it acts in collaboration with private interests. The partnership between state bodies and commercial enterprises, between public and private, became a new paradigm in an era of and-and choices and win-win situations. Everyone involved in the public-private development process became each other's 'partner'. The reassuring sound of the word partner supposes that there is nothing to disagree about other than household matters, hence disregarding the possibility that behind the scenes, commissioners and artists might actually defend different positions and represent different interests.

In reality, artists working in public space, their commissioning bodies and their various partners often do not agree. But they express their doubts and second thoughts about the consensual treadmill of their joint ventures in private, not in public. In the apparent absence of disagreement, much public art becomes disguised boredom. The task of the work of art becomes to distract, which itself may take the shape of pseudo-revolt.

As an aside, there exists a powerful current in public art that seeks to attach itself to the notion of 'sites'; places that have distinct identities and histories, excavating their 'repressed' narratives. Those places are not just square

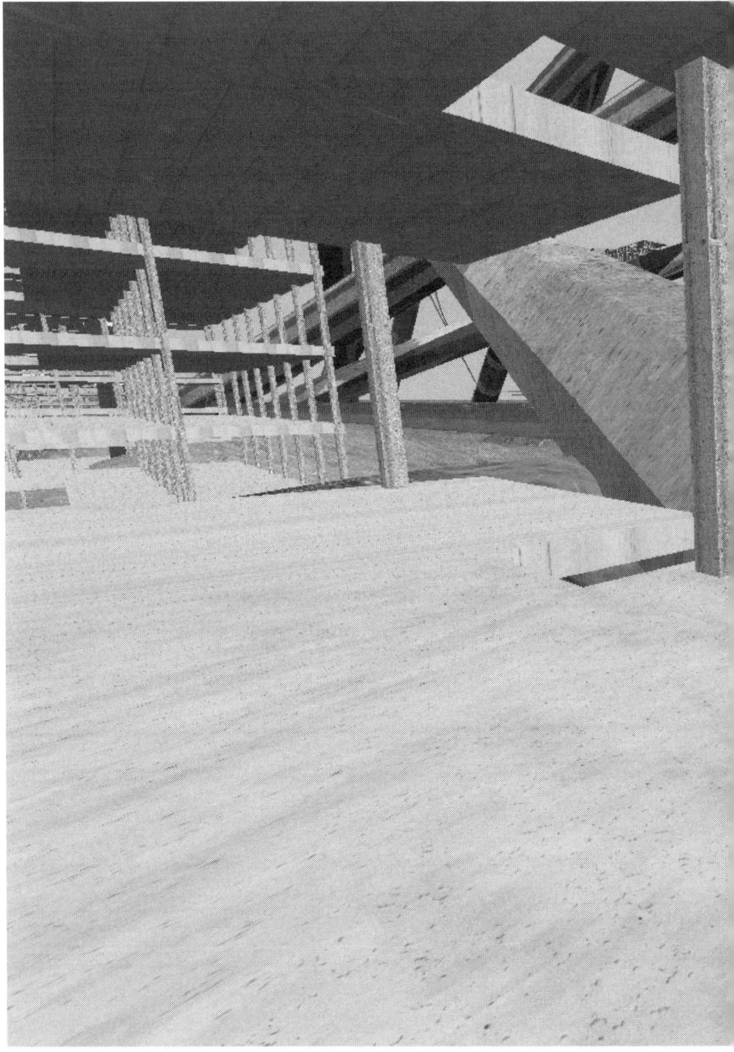

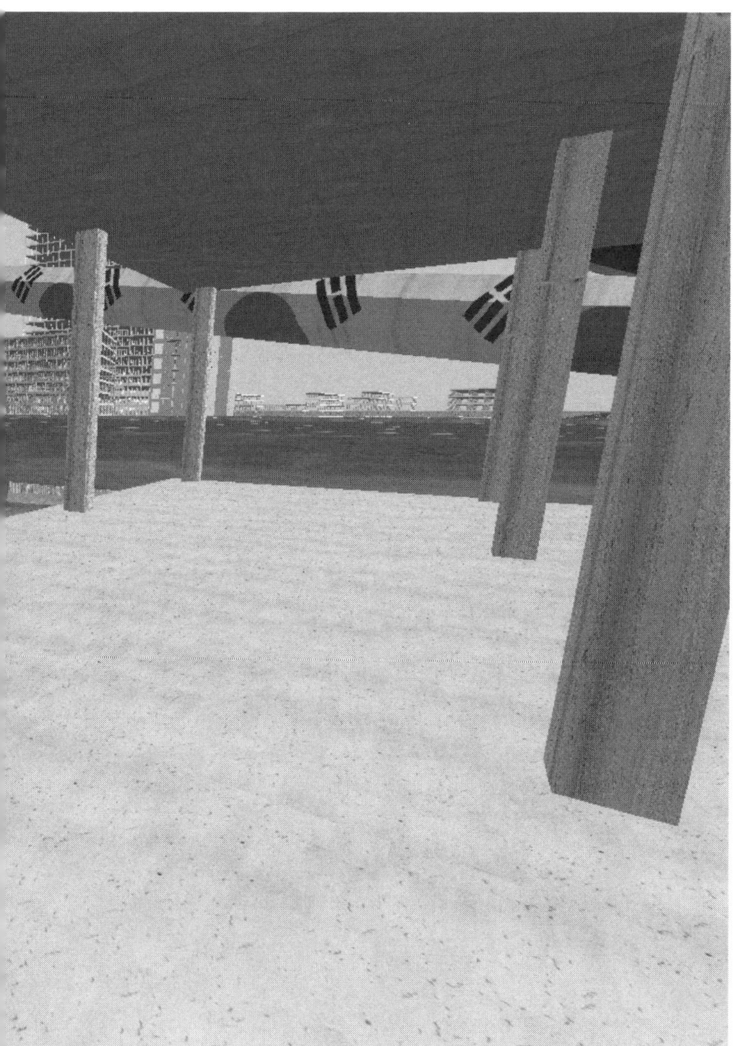

Daniel van der Velden

meters to project images upon. They might contain hidden antagonisms as their main characteristic.

For example, the public projections that artist Krysztof Wodiczko did on buildings in Tijuana (Mexico) and Hiroshima (Japan) tie themselves deeply to hidden and unspoken local problems – often even locked within people – which they bring to the fore. In the case of Tijuana, it is the border crossing between Mexico and the U.S. In the case of Hiroshima, it is the impact that the A-bomb had on the different generations living there, formulated through a series of interviews where also the families of former Korean slave labourers were included. The way Wodiczko chose to remember it has nothing to do with creating a gigantic imposing statue about pain inflicted to one people – it thus refuses to commemorate the disaster in a consensual way. Yet it doesn't lose track of a more universal and symbolic realm.

Due respect to Wodiczko, both Hiroshima and Tijuana are recognized trauma sites. How does the notion of 'site' work at Amsterdam's Zuidas – if anything a place that seems to harbour no traumas at all?

In Advance of Disagreement

The Zuidas came into being (more or less spontaneously, unplanned, at first) in the late nineteen-nineties, and is still in the process of being built. In that process the Zuidas is both 'present', 'actual' and 'not-yet'. It is simultaneously a built reality and a project under semi-eternal construction, a situation smartly used to make up for its current shortcomings and promotion of future virtues.

The Zuidas represents Amsterdam's main hotspot in the global marketplace of business and finance – which is imagined as a borderless space of connectivity. It is not to be held accountable for its actions by democratic politics and, conversely, we as citizens cannot democratically elect the CEOs of the companies that have chosen the Zuidas as their prime Northern European business location. On the other hand, the 'value' of the Zuidas directly relies on such (by definition trans-national) decisions. On an earlier occasion we have described to what extent Zuidas is de-localized from its surroundings, for example by its proximity to the motorway, to high speed train transportation and to Schiphol Airport.

In the partnership between the Zuidas's stakeholders, including banks, project developers and the city of Amsterdam, meticulous attention has been given to 'public space', yet only in the sense of its material qualities. Dutch

Daniel van der Velden

author Camiel van Winkel, in the essay 'Zeit-geist as Lacuna', refers to the quizzical phrase 'high-quality design of the open space' appearing in the Zuidas master plan, where 'the standard of quality must be extremely high' and there will be 'public space of a quality not yet seen in the Netherlands'.

He wonders what that word 'quality' stands for. The problem is not just that the meaning of 'quality' can never be presupposed – as Van Winkel notes in his conclusion – but that 'quality' also serves as a tool to suppress disa-greement. Objections against 'quality' proper were deemed impossible and unreasonable and unimaginable for any opponent to make.

The main tenants at the Zuidas are banks and law firms, sectors which have grown tremendously in the past two decades or so and got cramped in their former canal-based palaces of seventeenth century-style prestige getting disconnected from their increasingly globalized playing fields because of the sheer time it takes to travel from Keizersgracht to the United Arab Emirates via Schiphol Airport. The Zuidas presents itself as the solution to those old barriers. It is located at the centre of every-thing, characterized solely by its connections. It offers itself completely to the network and, as such, is really an urban version of web 2.0 (with the exception that the 'user generated content' has to be brought in by artists and designers). In effect, as a result there are literally thousands of lawyers and bankers working at the Zuidas who, as the affluent upper echelon, until 5 p.m. represent the utmost of decision making power in the Netherlands, and after 5 p.m. represent the utmost of spending power in the Netherlands. The game is to keep them there after 5 p.m. and have them live their whole lives at the Zuidas, while providing them with direct connections to Dubai, Singapore, Frankfurt, London and New York – a global hub, rather than an Amsterdam suburb. The site of the Zuidas is then defined by the presence of those who travel, but may choose not to because they can find competitive alternatives where they live. The parallel desire on the part of the local authority and its 'partners', to create both a 'perpetuum mobile' of real estate value centred around increasingly trans-national decision making processes, and a vibrant new city quarter with a true social value in the form of its 'excellent' public space, brings about the Zuidas as the hallmark of a new, entirely systemic and planned form of neoliberalism that presents facilities solely benefiting the elite as if they belong to the essentials of urban fabric: fitness, wellness, sushi and dry cleaning facilities as proof of a city for all classes.

The trauma and tragedy of the Zuidas is that the real potentiality of a radical coexistence of economics and public space is not played out to the extreme, but frozen in a sacred

consensus of 'partners', where the scary consequences of an urban heterotopia of business
and finance are prevented from their full actu-
alization. A similar consensus has, in other
contexts, been called 'post-political'. Artists
and designers are the agents of that softening
process; they add to the Zuidas the very touch
of disorder and friction that makes it accept-
able. Trauma is not the same as drama and of
course, Zuidas as a built form is merely the
messenger of a text that was written elsewhere.
To say that under the agreement at the Zuidas
public art becomes consensual does not mean
that this art is 'bad', while it should be 'good';
not at all (that would be as meaningless a
category as 'quality' – see Van Winkel). But it
does mean that public art practice at the
Zuidas, the post-planning 'cherry on the cake',
needs to show a blind eye to the political
context of the place (therefore reading it inten-
tionally uncritically, not recognizing the
trauma) for the sole purpose of its own realization. In other words, public art paradoxically is
now again the statue of the ruler – by seeming
to be the opposite of that statue, by seeming
'free'.

We claim that at the Zuidas, no public work
of art that is truly critical of the Zuidas can or
may be realized. But it may be unrealized. It
may be a model. With Logo Parc, we've made
the computer-generated 3-D model a site for
such a discourse.

Strip to the Bone

'Quality': Zuidas rightly asserts that we have become too polite to object to it. Hence the visual practices and creative forces of art and design, called in to render the notion of 'quality' tangible, are also extremely polite forces. Ultimately the utopia of the Zuidas is its 'ambition' or 'allure' – but what else is going to realize such goals than difference-by-façade? Since the development is based on return on investment, it is about ways to imagine certain stacked concrete floors at the Zuidas as more valuable than other such, structurally identical, floors located elsewhere. We can imagine the Zuidas stripped down to a bare essence of naked concrete structure, where there is no longer a value difference between the financial and legal high-rise and the post-war social housing estates in its immediate surroundings. This vision is expressed in the Logo Parc model.

What we had asked ourselves in the beginning is whether dissent with the Zuidas can be translated into a public work of art or a piece of design to be realized there. This can be called a political act. The answer is that such a piece can probably not be realized on commission, but that it can be unrealized, i.e. proposed as a model and have its non-actualization stand in the same space between

Daniel van der Velden

present and future as the 3D model used by developers to secure future value.

Here we can go one step further and say that although public art – within the limitations of previously discussed parameters and 'Dutch circumstances' – seems to be liberated from the obligation to create imposing statues that service the ruling elite, it is in fact often still doing that. Only the way in which has changed.

Its paradigm is now reversed: every public piece of art that is not openly contesting the post-political condition under which it is commissioned, is supporting that condition. It is advancing the supposed agreement and consensus to the point where there will be no longer be any peaceful ways to articulate the difference.

Logo Park: a Model

References
Erik Swyngedouw, lecture, Jan van Eyck Academie,
Maastricht, November 3, 2006
Camiel van Winkel, 'Zeitgeist as Lacuna', in: *Archis*, no.12,
1997
Daniel van der Velden, Katja Gretzinger, Matthijs van
Leeuwen, Matteo Poli, Gon Zifroni, 'Logo Parc – Post
Public Space', in: *Open – Hybrid Space*, no. 11, 2006
David Harvey, *A Brief History of Neoliberalism* (Oxford:
Oxford University Press, 2005)

Logo Parc was created by Daniel van der Velden, Gon
Zifroni, Matthijs van Leeuwen, Katja Gretzinger and
Matteo Poli, as a research project at the Jan van Eyck
Academie in Maastricht commissioned by the Research
Group Art and Public Space, Gerrit Rietveld Academie/
Universiteit van Amsterdam, and Premsela: Platform for
Dutch Design. It started in the beginning of 2006 and was
definitely unfinished in 2007.

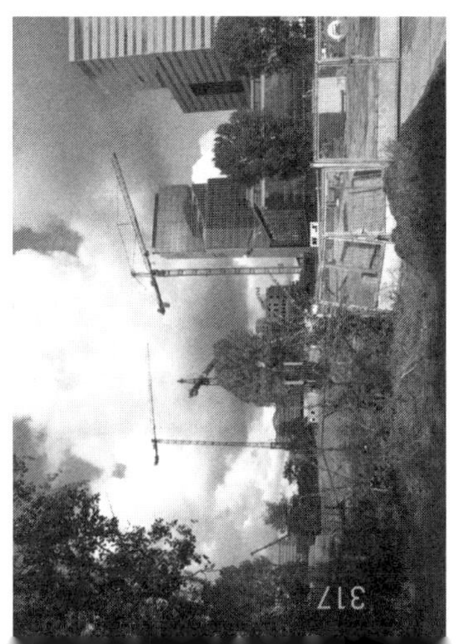
317

Henk de Vroom

Space for Art at the Zuidas

Imagine it's 2040 and you're looking at Amsterdam's Zuidas with Google Earth. What kind of art do you see? In 2040, the Zuidas does not feature art objects that seem to have crash-landed there like comets. What you do glimpse amid the sleek, towering commercial buildings are mysterious spaces so full of adventure, crafted with such refinement and care, that you zoom in for a closer look and are seduced into wandering from one artistic site to the next. For among the buildings, streets, shops and theatres runs a ribbon of such oases, places of freedom and imagination, inextricably bound with the city.

This Google Earth vision of the future may seem like a dream sequence out of *Alice in Wonderland*, but serious work has been going on for six years to turn that dream into reality. For the city, banks and developers are not simply building a new financial, commercial and legal business district along with apartments and theatres at the Zuidas. Plazas designed by artists are also being built and sites intended for art and culture are being created.

Henk de Vroom

302

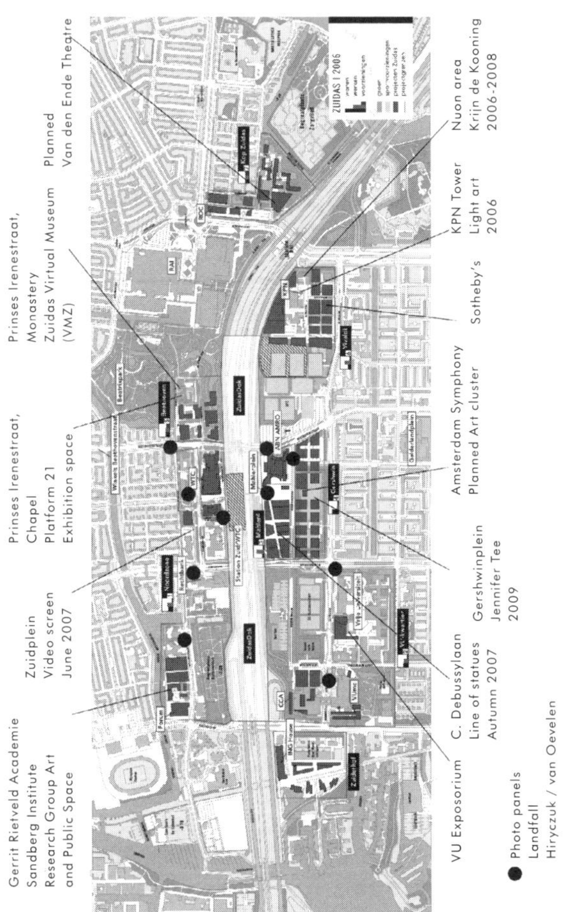

Art and Culture on the Zuidas Amsterdam
2007 – 2008

While the Virtual Museum Zuidas, the foundation responsible for art and culture at the Zuidas, considers the entire area-in-progress a living and constantly evolving museum, the laws and rules that operate at the Zuidas are different from those within the secure walls of a museum. In a museum, the point is to present autonomous works of art away from a disruptive environment. Art at the Zuidas, especially the public space designed by artists, is created to have a function as well. It coincides with the space in which people meet, stroll and find recreation and entertainment. At the same time it creates a free zone in which 'autonomous imagination', the work of the artist, defines appearances and which the spirit and passion of the artist inhabit. This turns this public space designed by artists, inextricably connected to its urban design and planning, into a mysterious and exciting world. A different world, in which everyday life temporarily fades and the strict rules of work can be momentarily suspended.

For in spite of the function factor, as much a complication as an enrichment, art at the Zuidas, just as in a museum, has to embellish life, elicit amazement, surprise and admiration, serve as a foothold for imagination and unexpected possibilities. Art at the Zuidas, just like art in a museum, should have depth and stimulate reflection. In addition, however, it must be substantively and physically connected to its surroundings. What's more, it must be understandable for all, without apology.

The level of ambitions may be comparable to those of a museum, but the conditions inherent in a construction project, set to cost billions and span decades, in which art is created are fundamentally different. These conditions are defined to a significant extent by time and money; plans evolve amid constantly changing conditions and require patience and endurance. The number of parties involved also differs. The builders and planners from the city and national governments, the private investors, the project developers, the established businesses and educational institutions, the artists, designers and architects, the residents and the legions of workers, everyone is taking part in reflections, observations and decisions. This is vital. If art is to be taken seriously and claim its place for the long term, it must elicit the interest and command the respect of those who are in daily contact with it.

This article is about the art policy at the Zuidas and outlines the process of the last several years, during which its vision has been formed and tested in practice. This vision has also grown, and this growth process is of essential importance. Art that participates in building the city is not about high-minded theories or the pursuit of trends that are by definition ephemeral. It is about creating high-quality physical spaces that suit the area and will still matter not just 40 years from now, when the area is completed, but 200 years from now as well. In order to achieve this, this art must take advantage of the specific conditions of the area; it must grow along with the process, establish itself in the reality of the built environment – without making compromises. Developing such a policy attuned to a single area requires time, flexibility, creativity and endurance. It is an extremely fascinating and exciting process, because its outcome cannot be predicted.

Setup and Organization

The art policy for the Zuidas is based on the plan developed by Simon den Hartog, the former director of the Gerrit Rietveld Academie in late 2000 and early 2001 at the request of the Zuidas Project Bureau in its incarnation at the time, when it was the city's delegated commissioning agency. The project bureau now operates as the project management unit of the new NV Zuidas public limited company, under the name Zuidas Amsterdam. Since 2007, the city, the national government and private investors have been operating jointly within Zuidas Amsterdam, with Elco Brinkman as its president-commissioner.

From the start, it was clear that the planners and builders, in order to make the Zuidas a fully fledged urban area, also had ambitions for a cultural climate. Art and culture would imbue the area with character and identity, improve its quality of life and create an informal atmosphere, which would allow people to form an attachment to it. To work out the requested plan, Den Hartog set up a programming council, bringing together people not only with expertise in the field of art in public space but also competent in organizing exhibitions and special events. The programming council made a tour of the country, visiting museums, businesses, foundations and meeting with other experts, including Sjarel Ex (then the director of the Centraal Museum in Utrecht, now the director of the Museum Boijmans Van Beuningen in Rotterdam), Pi de Bruijn (an architect, at the time urban design supervisor for the Zuidas), Jan Wijle (head of the departments for art in the public space and architecture at the Stroom Foundation in The Hague), the Foundation Art and Public Space (SKOR), the Amsterdam Fund for the Arts (AFK), and the Art and Business Foundation, as well as visual artists like Joep van Lieshout and Krijn de Koning and architects like Jeroen van Schooten.

These meetings with experts highlighted the importance of a two-track policy: alongside permanent art in public space, temporary and supporting art projects had to be organized. After all, with only art in public space —

however essential it may be – a sustainable, complete and inspirational art climate cannot be created. In order to achieve the latter, it is imperative to embed art in the public space – which is by definition static – in an active, artistic environment and in a cultural programme that encompasses both the incubation period – the 40-year process during which construction will take place – and the permanent situation and the life that will follow.

That cultural programme will be filled in with art and culture specifically tailored to the Zuidas, in order to avoid competing with existing activities in the rest of the city. At the Zuidas, activities that entail an enrichment for the area itself as well as for the cultural climate of Amsterdam and its environs can flourish. With this non-competitive principle in mind, two areas of attention were identified during this initial period. Rein van der Lugt, the former director of the Groninger Museum, advised bringing the design community, which was in full development and had not yet put down roots, to the Zuidas. In addition, the Zuidas would do well to get the fickle new media on its side. The plans were set out in November 2001 in the Vision on Visual Art at the Zuidas.

The concept of 'participating in the construction along with the architecture' as a unique form of art in public space also dates from this initial period. The premise was that art should

Henk de Vroom

be an essential element of the area's development. Too often, art in public space is merely
the cherry on top of the cake, and artists are
brought into planning at such a late stage that
they can only serve as decorators and object
makers, or they are expected to produce so-
called interactive art, as a palliative measure,
to redirect failed social processes. At the
Zuidas, on the contrary, the ambition is to
connect art and culture, by means of structural
interventions, to the urban design, the architecture and the public space. Artists from the
Netherlands and abroad are to be invited at
an early stage to contribute to specific
elements of the Zuidas, in order to think about
a substantive contribution to the planning from
the very beginning – a premise that carries on
the tradition of 'total urban planning' that has
been established in Amsterdam. The works of
art created in this process are new, unique and
specially made for the Zuidas. This calls for
artists who are capable of operating independently within such a process. The objective
is two-fold: to enrich a newly constructed city
with art that is an integral element of it as well
as to contribute to the development of the
artist, of art in general and of art in public
space.

Once the Vision on Visual Art at the Zuidas
was approved, Simon den Hartog was
appointed visual art supervisor by the
Amsterdam city authorities. The supervisor

advises the city and the project's management about the establishment and promotion of an attractive and inspirational artistic climate and is also the central contact for all the initiative leaders and planners involved in visual art activities at the Zuidas. As the supervisor cannot operate alone, the foundation Virtual Museum Zuidas (VMZ) was created out of the programming council in 2003. In order that the foundation be firmly embedded in the development process of the Zuidas, its governing board includes prominent partners from the business community, the borough authorities of ZuiderAmstel, Zuidas Amsterdam and Dutch art institutions.

Ambitions

After six years of work at the Zuidas, the importance of the most lasting contribution to the future of the area – that artists should play a part in the construction of the city – has not diminished. The idea is that the art should not function as a parallel world to the tower blocks. In 2040, when the Zuidas city is complete, there will be six or seven sites that will stand out from the rest, both in their appearance and in their significance. These sites will particularize the urban context and give it a unique face. To use a metaphor, if the buildings are the trees in the jungle, the works of art are the beasts that live in that jungle. Without the one,

Henk de Vroom

the other cannot come to life. Unique art that engages in a harmonious and adventurous symbiosis with the city: that should be the goal.

In order to reach the desired level of ambitions, several interrelated criteria apply. As previously mentioned, in 'participatory construction' the **autonomous imagination** of the artist is of paramount importance. Just as in a museum, art at the Zuidas should be a mirror held up to our civilization, in which values such as freedom, beauty, reflection and tolerance find expression. In the process they must appeal to the conceptual, collective memory, and perhaps build on the past or look forward to the future. Unlike in the temporary projects, to which complete artistic freedom applies, imagination in the 'participatory construction' projects is bound by certain rules. The permanent artistic contributions cannot be tied to a particular period; they must be based on universal values and build on a tradition of art and public space.

The second criterion is the importance of **durability**. The art is inextricably connected to its environment, but even if the buildings are obsolete and perhaps are replaced or given a facelift, even if the city is torn down around it, art should essentially last for eternity. After all, it nestles in our collective memory, defines the image of an area and of a city, assures recognizability and identity.

Imagination and durability must be matched by **craftsmanship** and the art of creating, an aspect that has been rather neglected in the last few years. The material interpretation of imagination at the Zuidas will have to meet strict standards. The final product must stimulate the senses and be skilfully made. This takes time: to conduct tests, to look for the right concrete structure or for durable materials. It also takes money. All too often, there is hardly any money available for the high-quality, durable implementation of what is in principle a brilliant concept. At the Zuidas, the money is there. This creates the unique opportunity to stimulate and breathe new life into the art of creating, as well as intellectual depth.

The same principle applies for the art as for the architecture: striving for **top quality**. The artists who have been invited to contribute have earned their stripes in one way or another, are conversant with the latest developments and meet international standards.

The final criterion is **flexibility**. Those who cannot work with others, those that are unable, in the course of the construction period, to respond to the evolution of the built environment and the demands of functionality and durability have no place here.

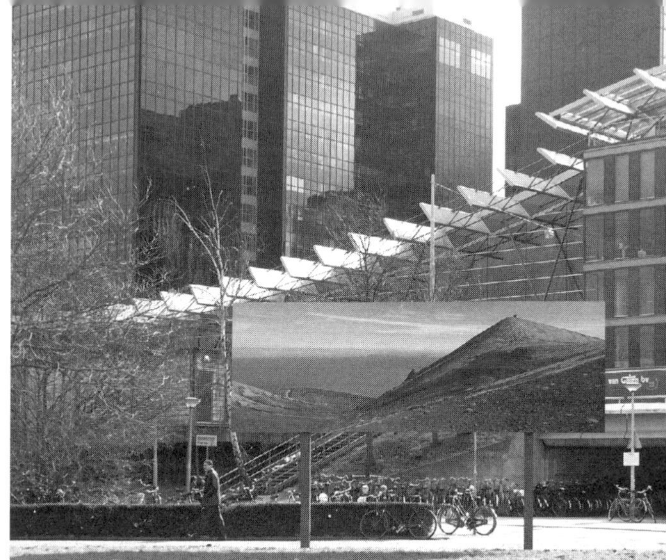

Elodie Hiryczuk and Sjoerd van Oevelen, *Landfall* 2005,
Minervaplantsoen, one of the ten billboards
on the Zuidas

Temporary Projects

Not all the plans from the Vision on Visual
Art at the Zuidas have become reality. All the
parties were convinced of the importance of
the two-track policy, but the economic tide
turned. As a result of the declining economic
situation, ambitions for the Zuidas had to be
adjusted and the funding allocated for visual
art was also cut back. This spelled the end to
several initiatives already underway for events
and temporary projects. A new set of priorities
emerged, in which art in the public space
remained the focus.

Another reality also made itself felt. In that initial period, the attitude of the various players at the Zuidas toward art differed significantly. It took a great deal of time for the gaps in outlooks of the various parties to narrow and for the needed support to be created. In addition, it was a while before buildings began to rise out of the tabula rasa and users took over the area and in so doing began to form the basic requirements of any art policy: a podium and an audience. Working methods also changed over the years. The small, programming council, operating part-

Bik Van der Pol, Mobile Exhibition and Exchange Centre, 2003 (model)

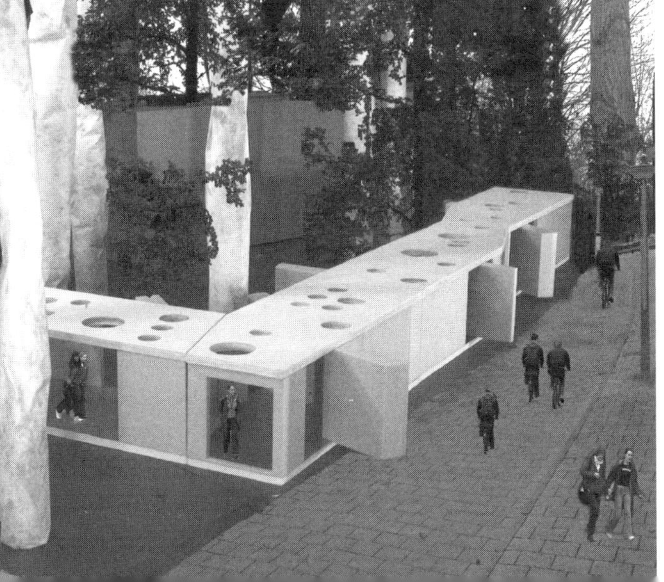

time, was expanded with external project curators. These curators are responsible for the content and organization of a specific project and have access to an extensive international network in the art, tailored to the project.

Although the temporary projects, special events and initiatives, in particular, have had to endure budget cutbacks, with all the consequence this entails, there have nonetheless been successes in this domain in the past several years. The temporary (two-year) art project *Landfall* by the artist duo Elodie Hiryczuk and Sjoerd van Oevelen, which investigates how a natural landscape and an urban landscape of comparable size to the Zuidas are experienced physically and in the imagination, attracted a great deal of positive attention and was therefore extended.

The initiative 'Platform 21' was set up, a platform for the twenty-first century in which design, fashion and creativity come together. Originally (in 2003) the VMZ had commissioned Bik Van der Pol to design a mobile exhibition and exchange centre, which was to serve as an intermediary art institute for the VMZ's visual art activities. Ultimately, it was decided to set up an exhibition space in the nearby chapel of the former St Nicholas monastery, under the name Platform 21. Free Spaces for Artists in Residence were also inaugurated and housed in the monastery. Here, ideas and plans are hatched in complete freedom, and research and reflection take place, in order to nurture the exhibition and conceptual climate.

Another significant accomplishment is the establishment of the Research Group Art and Public Space. This Research Group, established by a partnership of the VMZ, the Gerrit Rietveld Academie, the Sandberg Institute, the Foundation Art and Public Space (SKOR) and the Universiteit van Amsterdam, has taken on the role of gadfly and conducts research on the cultural development of the Zuidas as well as waging debates about it in the symposia it organizes.

The Virtual Zoom, a multi-year photography project, is also up and running. Each year, two to four photographers nominated by a curator are invited to record the Zuidas-in-progress in their own way. Foam, Amsterdam's photography museum, has agreed to take over, preserve and exhibit the growing collection. In the process, in the midst of the crucible of commercial forces and the thundering advance of the construction process, space has been built in, by means of a small number of temporary projects, for reflection, openness, debate, humour and critique.

Now that the economic tide has turned, economic activity has picked up and the Zuidas has entered a new phase with the wind in its sails, the programme of temporary projects has been resumed. This includes work on a regular series of events based on specific themes or locations. From this event structure, featuring a broad programme of music, theatre, symposia and debates, a net of temporary activities will be spread across the Zuidas. For the importance of temporary projects continues to be acknowledged, and the lack of a supporting cultural climate has left its toll over the last several years. Because of a lack of public events, for instance, the hoped-for stream of interested visitors and tourists has so far been a mere trickle. And if innovative projects are to be created, a range of experiments and trial projects remains imperative, if only to nurture the intellect.

Art in the Public Space

It is clear that artists, in projects like those for the Zuidas, cannot reach their objectives on their own. If they want to achieve a unique performance within such large-scale processes and shepherd their design intact to the finish line, they must, just like architects, work with feasible designs and collaborate with a team that includes people from municipal departments and the engineering, design and construction disciplines, as well as financial experts. The idea is not simply to come up with and erect a sculpture in the public space: the artist must also be able to lead and work with such a team. For in the philosophy of 'partici-patory construction' it is the artist who deter-mines what a section of the public space will look like. He or she provides artistic direction throughout the design process. The other parties follow his or her directions, produce test models, drawings and calculations, think about feasibility. This has consequences for the budgets. We are no longer dealing with erecting a sculpture in the public space and budgets around 200,000 Euro; financial expenditures for art have increased by a factor of 10. A plaza for which an artist is the main designer, for instance, now costs about 2 million Euro. This is not due to delusions of grandeur or American-style bombast. The setting in which the artist works demands this larger scale; his or her work must relate to the buildings and the public space, and the facili-ties in the public space must relate to the art installation. This has an impact on the budget.

It goes without saying that in order to achieve the desired quality and attract the necessary funding, it is necessary to join forces. The point is to create the art we want to have, without cutting corners or fiddling with dimen-sions or quality. In order to achieve this, other sources of funding have to be tapped besides the VMZ. It also goes without saying that such a process takes time – four to eight years on average – as long as a construction process,

Henk de Vroom

longer than we have hitherto been accustomed to for art in public space.

In order to preserve the autonomy of the artists, a good client relationship is necessary, as well as a system that monitors and safeguards quality in the course of the process. If the artist is not supported by the commissioning client throughout the project, if the process is not managed from A to Z, the likelihood of success is nil. The commissioning client of a work of art is the investing party, or the joint parties, possibly with the addition of outside donors. In practice, this usually involves a partnership of several parties and is then dubbed the 'commissioning team'. In this case, the VMZ is the delegated commissioning client for the artists on behalf of the commissioning team.

The visual art supervisor and the artistic manager for art and public space of the VMZ stand above the parties and can therefore bring them together, seek out solutions where needed and operate strategically. They monitor artistic content and quality throughout the process and guide and advise the artist during planning and execution. The Zuidas Amsterdam project manager is responsible for the progress of the total process. Final decisions are made by the Zuidas Amsterdam Board of Commissioners, which takes the recommendations of the urban design supervisor, public space supervisor and art supervisor into account. The recommendations of the supervisors are based on the presentations of the various design phases and discussions of the designs with the artists.

By now, years of investment and patience are bearing fruit and the first results are emerging. In the Vivaldi sector, artist Krijn de Koning is working on the transformation of the Nuon site.[1] This area, which until now had escaped the notice of the planners and builders, is being transformed by De Koning into the eastern gate of the Zuidas, featuring two multi-coloured transformer sheds placed one on top of the other, a public transport folly,

Krijn de Koning, design Nuon site, eastside, 2007 (montage)

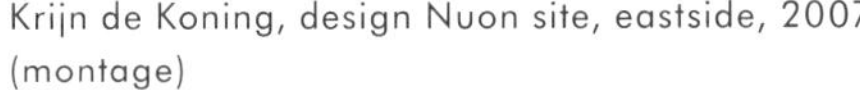

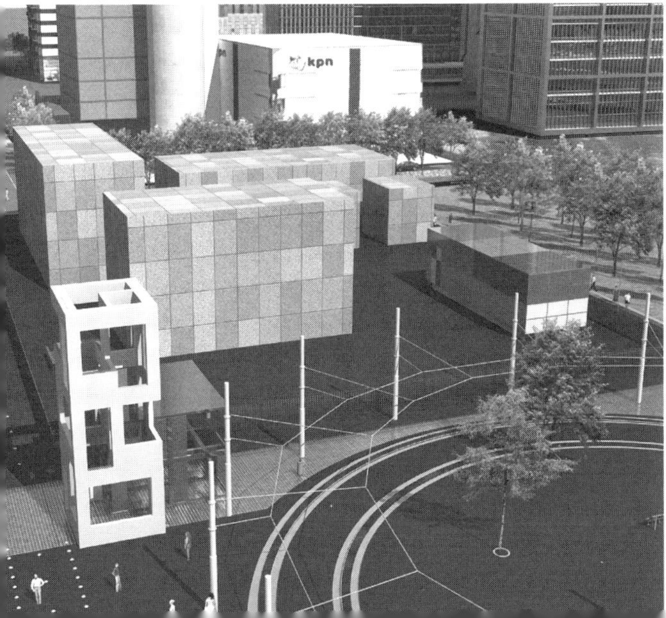

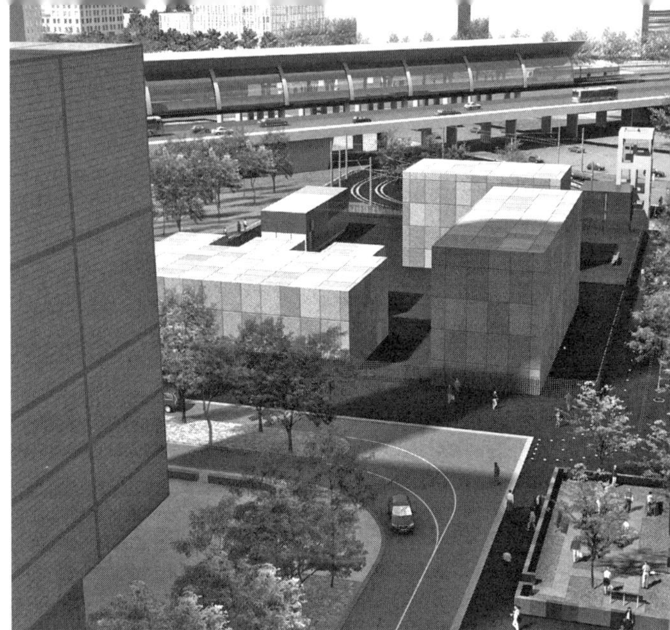

Krijn de Koning, design Nuon site, westside, 2007
(montage)

a park and an expansive, open plaza. Part of the plan has already been implemented, and it is already clear that private domain and public space have been turned into a single area, that art and setting are merging. The rest will be completed in phases: the plaza and the park will follow in 2008 and the folly will be built in 2009, along with the new tram stop.

Four artists – Giny Vos, Germaine Kruip, Nicky Zwaan and Johan Vonk – are currently making preliminary designs for light-installation art on the KPN transmission tower. The project is due to be completed in early 2009.

On 22 November 2007, a new cultural axis lined with temporary sculptures by international artists was inaugurated. For this form of sculpture exhibition, the VMZ entered into a partnership with the Dutch Association of Corporate Art Collections (VBCN). Every two years, a new curator will be appointed to put together a new collection. Art historian Ernst van der Hoeven was appointed to make the

LED Screen CASZuidas, 2007

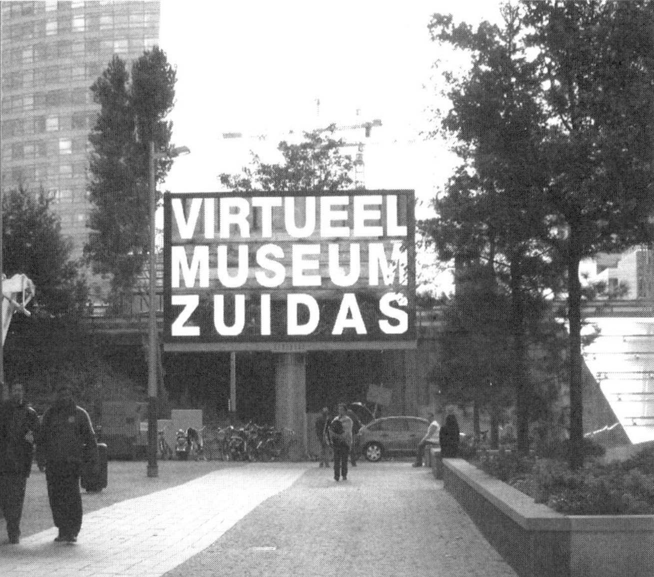

first selection. He chose from among the corporate collections works by artists Rob Voerman, Ewerdt Hilgemann, Charlie Roberts, Frank Bruggeman, Tony Cragg, Henk Visch, Sjoerd Buisman, Thomas Ruff, Julika Rudelius, Fernando Sánchez Castillo and Lukasz Skapski. The participating corporations are ABN-Amro, Aegon, Akzo Nobel, Rabo Bouwfonds, Fortis, ING, KPN, Rabobank and SNS Reaal.

In mid-2007 a large, semi-permanent video screen was installed on the Zuidplein. The LED screen originated from the concept 'Het kunstwerk als podium' ('The artwork as stage'), a project that was developed in 2003 for the Zuidplein by Tom van Gestel (SKOR) and Henk de Vroom (VMZ). They departed from their original idea of a static work of public art and, instead, decided to conceive of the artwork as a stage in itself.

The Zuidplein is located in the central business district of the Zuidas and functions both as a meeting place and an intersection where people cross paths on their way to and from work or meetings. From the outset of the project the aim has been to broadcast a provocative programme that will attract local, national and international interest with the help of state-of-the-art LED technology. The program is innovative in nature and its content is made up of 80 percent art and 20 percent announcements and commercials. A new curator will be responsible for each new season of programming. The project took four years to complete, due to extensive research in the areas of technology, feasibility and financing, as well as negotiations with the display suppliers, cultural organizations and artists, calls for EU tenders, construction permits, decision-making procedures and final approvals.

At the initiative of the VMZ and in partnership with SKOR, CASZuidas (Contemporary Art Screen Zuidas. Moving Images In Public Space) has been set up for the programming of the video screen, which will serve as an exclusive and provocative podium for visual art in the public space of the Zuidplein. Since 5 October 2007, every day from 6 a.m. to midnight, CASZuidas has been showing work by renowned Dutch and international artists as well as promising young talents. Spectators can call a toll-free telephone number to hear the soundtrack of a film on a mobile phone or headset. In addition, CASZuidas is already working with initiatives such as PARK4DTV and NIMk (Amsterdam), Impakt (Utrecht), Argos (Brussels) and TankTV (London), and it will provide space for art and cultural events such as the Holland Festival. The programme is put together by curator Jan Schuijren. This ambitious focus on art on a video screen makes CASZuidas not only unique in the Netherlands, but in the entire world.

Henk de Vroom

In the newspaper *NRC Handelsblad* Reinier Kist writes about CASZ: 'What does a video screen do to a plaza? As long as it is not intrusive, it turns it into a living room. The redesign of the Zuidplein, completed three years ago, was already a success, because the architects, in spite of the office blocks towering alongside and the adjacent train station and motorway, had managed to make the plaza an intimate place. People hang out here, reading a book or a newspaper on the rim of a tree container, strolling past terraces. The only thing it was missing to make it really welcoming, the object that most evokes a sense of home for modern man, was a television set. CASZuidas is

Jennifer Tee, in collaboration with Richard Niessen and Joost Vermeulen, *Oeverloos verlangen* 2007, design Gershwinplein (montage)

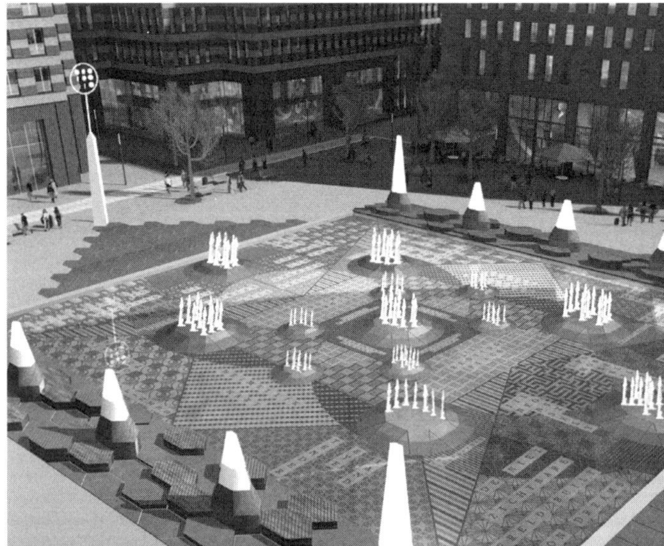

intended as an escape from the whims of the day. "Video art allows you to look at your environment in a different way," says Jan Schuijren, the screen's programmer. "In that sense it can be an enrichment in comparison to visual culture on television, which currently consists almost exclusively of reality shows."[2]

For the Gershwinplein with its water basin measuring 45 by 45 metres, artist Jennifer Tee, in collaboration with Richard Niessen and Joost Vermeulen and the advisory team, has produced a preliminary design.

The definitive design had been scheduled for autumn 2008, whereupon implementation would begin, with completion to coincide with that of the buildings around the plaza, in 2009. At the moment (autumn 2007), the further development of the plaza is at a standstill. The reason is that a new visual quality plan is being formulated by the new Zuidas urban design supervisor, bOb Van Reeth, who took over in late April 2007, and by Zuidas public space supervisor Paul van Beek, who began work in August 2007. In the view of these supervisors, Jennifer Tee's design does not fit in with the new visual quality plan being developed. The question is why that is. And how a design process that has been worked on for so long can be halted. For Jennifer Tee's preliminary design has the potential to accommodate new visions on visual quality in the next design phase.

Henk de Vroom

One answer might be that it is already known that the Gershwinplein, in the new visual quality plan, is seen as part of a greater whole dubbed the Minerva axis. The sequence of the existing plazas – Minervaplein, Zuidplein, Stationsplein, Mahlerplein and Gershwinplein – which will be lined with iconic architecture that will define the area's aspect, can represent an advance in quality, durable construction at the Zuidas. But this does not have to mean that integrated art in the public space of the Minerva axis is impossible. Jean Tinguely's fountains in Basel and the water plazas by Yaacov and Takis at La Défense in Paris demonstrate that it can be done. At La Défense

Jean Tinguely, *Fasnachtsbrunnen* (in winter), Basel, 1981

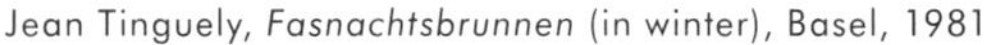

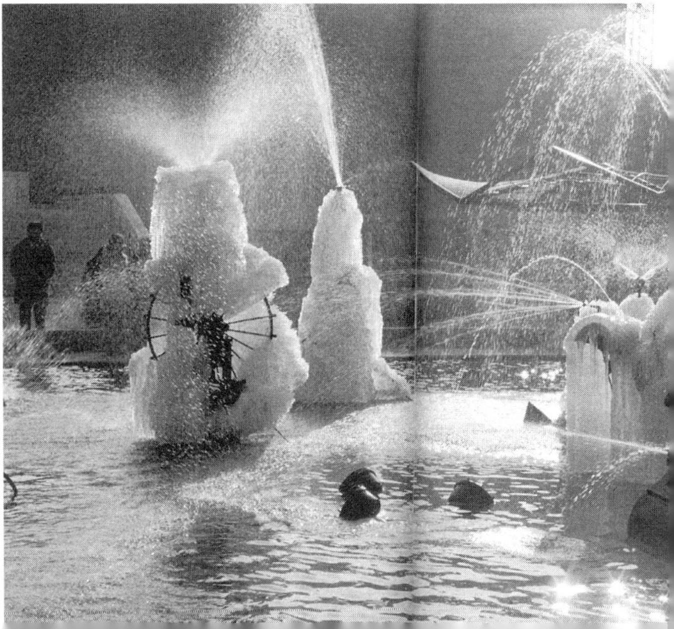

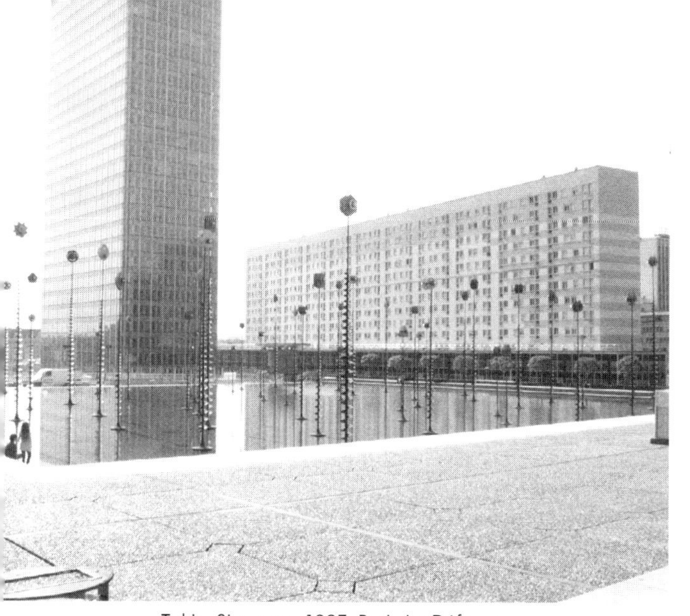

Takis, *Signeaux*, 1987, Paris La Défense

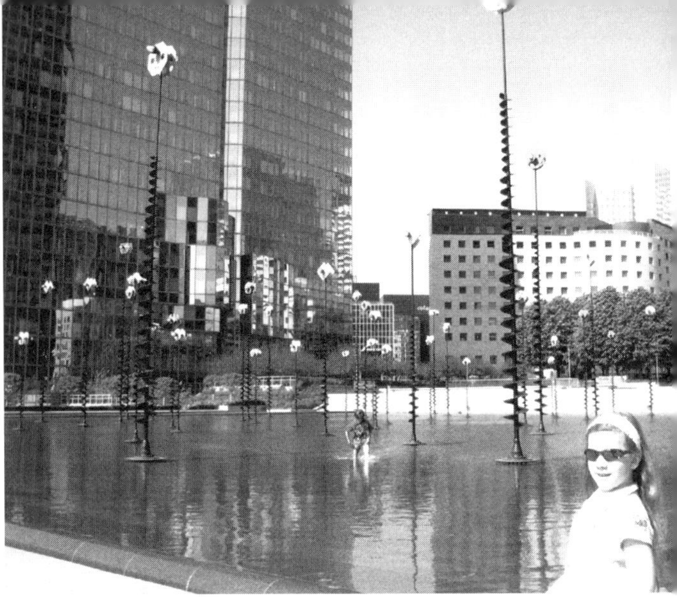

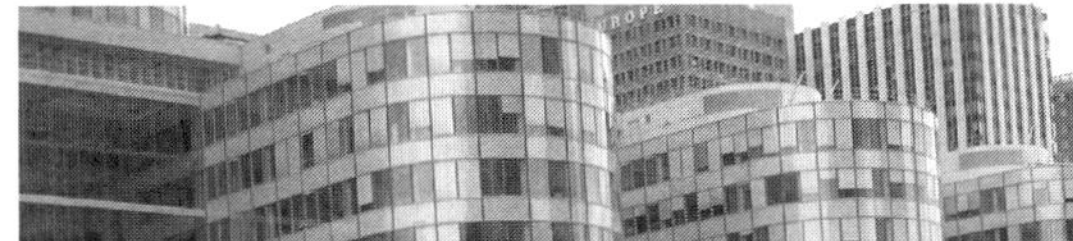

Takis, *Signeaux*, 1987, Paris La Défense

Yaacov Agam, *Fountain*, 1987, Paris La Défense

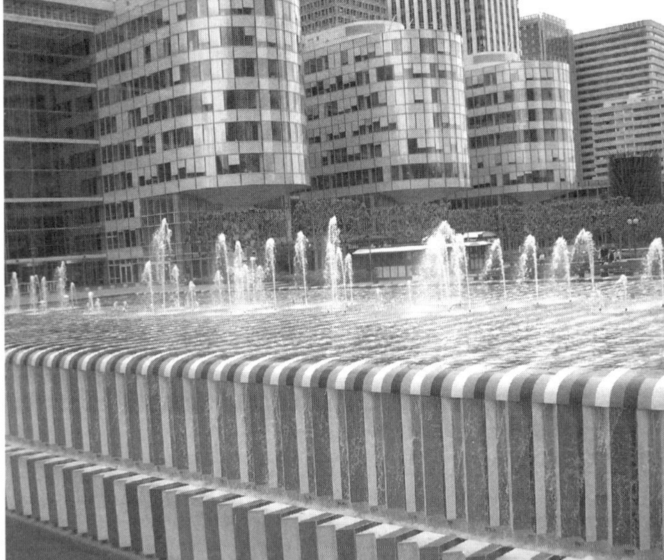

in particular, it is clear that in a large-scale public space lined by iconic buildings, integrated art and even object art can serve to increase quality of life and stimulate a variety of uses, such as places to meet.

Art and Money

The financial foundation of all the projects is the budget of the Virtual Museum Zuidas, funded by the city. It is vital that the VMZ have a sound financial foundation, for it is only on that basis that supplementary funds by outside donors can be raised. The Amsterdam Fund for the Arts (AFK) for instance, has agreed to a partnership for the Gershwinplein art project, for which the AFK and the VMZ will each assume 50 percent of the costs.

Although the VMZ regards cooperation with subsidy donors, such as SKOR and the AFK, as vitally important, it is often difficult for government institutions of this kind, in practice, to finance projects with extended preliminary and production periods. The policy objectives of donor funds are oriented to the short term and span at most two years. 'Participatory construction', on the other hand, requires patience that goes beyond the short term. In order to achieve this sort of project on a communal basis and to make longer development periods possible, the subsidy conditions of donor funds need to be expanded. Moreover, donor funds, like city governments, sometimes have to deal with the consequences of politically mandated cutbacks, which can place allocated funding at risk.

For this reason, and in keeping with current social developments whereby private and public investors are joining forces, the VMZ is looking beyond the government and donor funds and has begun to tap a third source of funding. It has set up partnerships, for the short or long term or per project, with corporations and parties located and operating at the Zuidas, such as Nuon, KPN, AKZO-NOBEL, Faircom, WTC, ABN-Amro, ING, Houthoff-Buruma, the Dutch Association of Corporate Art Collections, the Holland Festival, Gerrit Rietveld Academie, the Sandberg Institute and Platform 21.

The question remains whether all these efforts will benefit the new city, its future users and art, or simply serve the interests of the project developers. The Amsterdam alderwoman for culture, Carolien Gehrels, is convinced, like many others, that art and culture drive up land prices and increases the value of real estate. This is undoubtedly the case at the Zuidas as well. Artists and project developers have differing objectives. Artists work on an artistic development, project developers on an economic one. But there are also shared motivations. Both groups want to create a beautiful city, one that exudes liveliness, is unique and attracts people. Art's contribution is vital, for it plays a part in ensuring the success of the project developer. On the other hand, if art is to contribute to a sustainable urban environment, to the level of civilization of the city and the country and to the development of art itself, this can only be achieved, in this ambitious construct, in areas where money is and where money is made. It becomes imperative to join forces and take advantage of opportunities. Money and financial profit seeking need not be a threat to pure art and artistic freedom, as Belgian sociologist Pascal Gielen argues. The 'melting pot of artistic and economic values' also offers advantages and opportunities, Gielen says – in this case the opportunity for art to go all out, to relate to its setting and to reach a broad audience.[3] The necessarily broad base of support need not automatically result in lazy art. In fact the joint effort to create a unique work rewards the involvement of the project developer. His contribution becomes an honourable brief, a showpiece that differentiates him and shows he is not a barbarian.

Art belongs not just in a museum, but in the public space as well. That is where it does its work, creating opportunities for encounter and contributing to the city's level of civilization, affording a sense of identity and establishing itself in the collective memory, like the 'total urban planning' of Berlage's plan for Amsterdam Zuid in the nineteenth century. That area has now been included in UNESCO's list of World Heritage Sites. We nurture similar ambitions for the Zuidas, but without Berlage's didactic tendencies and detailed regulations. The goal now is to create artworks that stand for freedom and tolerance, that please the senses and stimulate the mind, that relate to society, to the art world and to people and will remain standing for many years to come.

Nicola Salvi, *Fontana di Trevi*, Rome, 1762

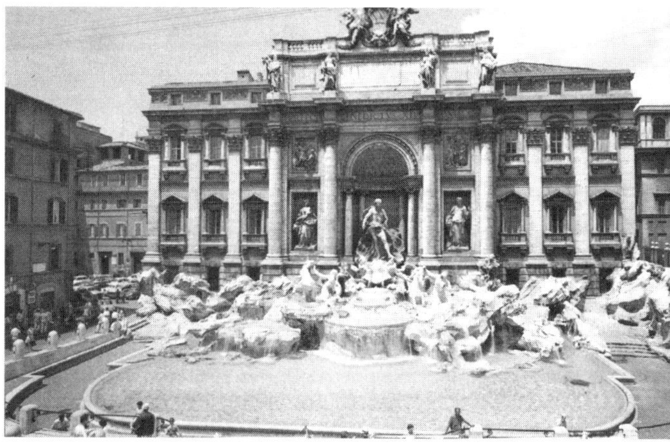

Notes
1. Nuon is a Dutch energy company.
2. Reinier Kist, 'Buitenkunst Zuidas Amsterdam', in *NRC Handelsblad*, 12 October 2007.
3. Pascal Gielen, 'Artistic Freedom and Globalization', in *Open* no. 12, *Freedom of Culture* (Amsterdam/Rotterdam: SKOR/NAi Publishers, 2007) pp. 30-38.

With thanks to Marina de Vries

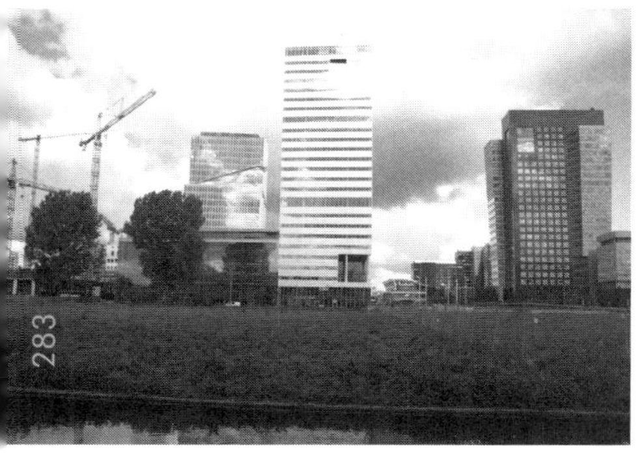
283

Renée Kool

Étonnée de se retrouver ensemble
Artist in Residence at SC Buitenveldert

Introduction

My contribution to this volume is a collage of short and highly diverse texts. It is a preliminary progress report on a period of work and a production process that runs from the summer of 2004 to the present. This collection of texts serves as a prelude to a longer and more detailed collection of texts that will be published to mark the completion of my research for the Research Group Art and Public Space.

(From a report text, 2005)
Since the beginning of 2004 I have served as artist in residence at the football club SC Buitenveldert in Amsterdam. In 2004, Free Spaces Zuidas invited artists and researchers to move in as artists in residence 'at the Zuidas' in Amsterdam for a period of several months. The idea was to produce work in and about this huge urban development project from within existing institutions such as the Vrije Universiteit, the Nicolaas Lyceum, the school gardens and the water company.

Renée Kool

Influenced by my recent teaching experiences with architects/urban designers and
'landscapers', I now see this district and its
urban development with very different eyes. I
have also found a unique guest institution in
SC Buitenveldert: like a little David on the pric-
iest land in the Netherlands – right up against
the A10 motorway – it manages to manoeuvre
amazing well in the interplay of forces among
the various Goliaths.

336

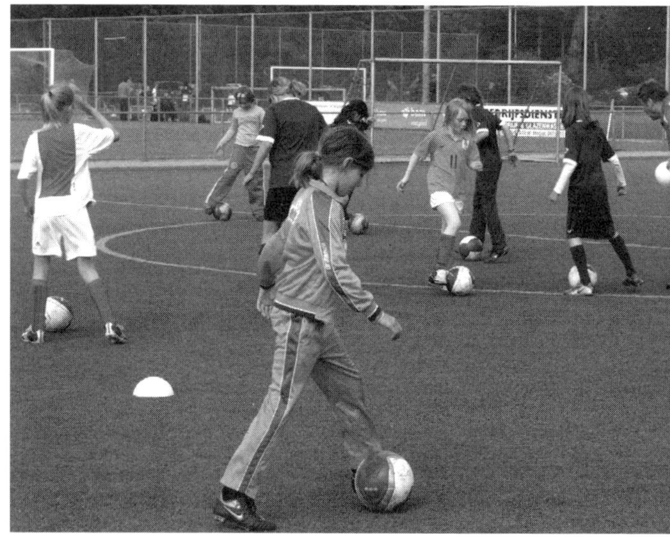

The landscape of my childhood

(written in 2004 as a 'voice over' for the short film *Tijdens
de vooruitgang* schijnt de zon ('During progress, the sun is
shining'), my contribution to the Free Spaces Zuidas. In this
film, I formulate my plan to take up residence at the football club for far longer than the planned period of six
months)

Past a moss-clad Emma on her pedestal,
I cycle through poplar cathedrals.
The Valeriusplein.
The poplars of progress and reconstruction.

Under the 'Potius Deficere Quam Desperare'
of the Amsterdam Lyceum.
Past Hildo Krop's stalwart family.
Like straight-backed gatekeepers the children
stand on the bridge,
still the prelude to Van Heutsz's Denkmal.
I cycle through gems of urban renewal.
Should I turn right or left?
French friends wax lyrical about Plan Zuid,
Plan Zu-weed, they say.
The squares,
the quays with their red brick,
they find it all equally beautiful.

Today I keep cycling past De Groot en
Compagnons
and 'spacious 2-, 3- and 4-room apartments
regularly up for sale.
Poelwijck en Zweers Makelaardij OG'.
Under Houthoff en van Buruma,
Camex

Renée Kool

the courthouse
…
after the viaduct the landscape has been dug
up.

the birth of a new city centre

proclaims a huge billboard.

*Housing - Shopping - Lunching - Working -
Strolling - Sports - Lounging - Dining*

I'm travelling inside a renewed Droste effect.
In the distance still BP green
and the *Vrije* - italics - Universiteit.

My grandma used to talk about CPN rallies
in the Olympic Stadium

Citroën C5
I can't wait to meet you

The new Citroën
The urban sports car

My father told me they used to play on the
dredged-up ground.

And I...
I'm also on my way to the landscape of my
childhood:
Breathless I would look from the back seat,
at the advances
of the big city.

At the Floriade,
the PTT tower,
the hotels,
the office buildings.

Our summer Sunday drive to a boat
that never seemed to be finished.
Along the Boelelaan.
On the left the university under construction,
on the right the playing fields.

I couldn't wait for the constructions to look
like the architectural projections that were
promised
on the billboard at the entrance of the
building site.

Actually it was always a letdown.

Further along, past the hospital, later under it.
Aunt Hilda lived on the left on the
Amstelveenseweg
and on the right was the Water Tower.
There you had to turn into a lane with reeds
on either side,
across some railroad tracks
and then you reached the marinas.

My childhood disappointment about the gap
between the grandeur of the perspective
drawings
and built reality is over.

The architectural Droste pictures are more
perfect than ever.

Renée Kool

The towering structures themselves seem
Photoshopped.
Products of the latest versions of 3-D soft-
ware.
Technological marvels.
'The sun is shining,
the sky is blue
and the grass green...

That amazed smile...
(from a project document, summer 2006)

... The relationship between the world of football and the press has always been an intimate one. Huub Wijfjes and Eric Smulders had good reason to describe the relationship between the sports world and the (audiovisual) media as a symbiosis. This might be the result of various factors. Public sports and mass media are both pastimes that began to take up an important place in everyday life once the Industrial Revolution had firmly taken hold. Attending sports events became popular in the same period as the advent of the technology of the motion picture. Both television and big-time sports have evolved into advertising vehicles for business. What's more, for the Netherlands in particular, the breakthrough of television more or less coincided with the introduction of professional football ...

I came across the above quotation, from the article 'Een lockere goed-nieuwsshow – het persbeleid van de KNVB tijdens het WK van 1974' by Jan-Willem Navis while leafing through the *Tijdschrift voor Mediageschiedenis* (a periodical on media history). It outlines the relationship between football and urbanity in a few strokes. Football as an 'urban experience' that is further reinforced by television and the inevitable adverts.

Etonnée de se retrouver ensemble

This quotation also made me realize that the territory of the Zuidas and the phenomenon of football – in more than one regard – are part of the landscape of my childhood.

We used to live near the Ajax stadium. As a child I would gape at the masses and masses of people decked out in red-and-white scarves and hats, brandishing banners and armed with 'fog horns' who streamed across the Kruislaan on their way to the De Meer stadium. Practically every week. The homeward march of the Ajax supporters could be really sinister. Lots of shouting and carrying on, and the certainty that that one tram-stop shelter would be demolished.

Similarly, I remember watching TV on Sunday nights, in the late '60s and early '70s as 'sitting through' *Studiosport* – as a family. In addition to the intense boredom, I can almost still feel the experience of great alienation: those excited, almost hysterical commentator voices, the incomprehensible rules of the game, the images of stands full of collective swaying and bellowing – what was supposed to be fun about it all?

I have to admit that I didn't figure it out until some time after I took up residence with SC Buitenveldert. Gradually we got used to each other, got closer to one another, got an insight into each other's 'tribal rituals'. And oh yes… I turned out, to our mutual astonishment, to have the proper credentials! My family, on my mother's as well as my father's side, has consisted of true 'Amsterdammers', born and bred, for generations. Once that was made clear, I was definitively accepted.

Why go into such detail here? Because I recognize the amazed smile or the grimace on the faces of my conversation partners outside football as well, and remember their attitude. Admit it: an artist, and a woman at that, in residence at a football club is ultimately a strange and abstract idea. Now that I use it as an absurd joker, when I meet fellow artists or other art or culture professionals, playing this card never fails to be effective. Guaranteed attention, here and abroad!

Something similar happens in reverse: the clichés and stopgaps about art and what it is to be an artist are legion, and often get in the way. To avoid such preconceptions and expectations, I asked not to be introduced to the club or to individual members as an artist. For a long time I was referred to as a photographer, the club photographer – much later I became 'our artist' or sometimes jokingly 'the artist on duty'. My role and my position at the club have always been kept deliberately vague, and that is actually still the case. What is clear is that I belong there. I'm one of us.

Etonnée de se retrouver ensemble

BUT WHAT DO YOU DO THERE?

First an orientation:

It turned out I'd ended up at the second-largest amateur football club in Amsterdam. Including the largest number of girls' and women's teams in the Netherlands, perhaps even in Europe.

Like all amateur football clubs, SC Buitenveldert is a volunteer organization, but one, thanks to its history and its playing venue, that can rely on an intricate and professional network.

Above all, however, 'Buitenveldert', as members call their club, is a community, so diverse in age distribution – the average age of those who produce the club newsletter is well above 70 – and so diverse in social and ethnic backgrounds that many social organizations might envy it.

Yet it is perhaps most important that SC Buitenveldert is a club with a social agenda. 'Buitenveldert' wants to be an affordable football club for young and old, for boys and girls, in a venue safely accessible to all by public transport. Not a spectacular ambition, at first glance. This changes, however, when you weigh it against the scale of the Zuidas developments and the interests involved in them. For SC Buitenveldert plays on the most expensive land in the Netherlands...

Renée Kool

'We're a club for regular people,'
I kept being told in the beginning

At the time I was getting acquainted with the club, it was not at all certain that they would be able to keep their venue, a stone's throw away from the VU, the university medical centre. Planning development up to that point (2003/04) provided space for one football club, AFC, the prestigious Amsterdam Football Club. In keeping with the principle of dual land use, they will be playing in their sports complex on a motorway overpass.

When I arrived at SC Buitenveldert I found a self-assured organization that eschews victimhood and instead acts proactively and tries to influence decision making on as many fronts as possible simultaneously. Including submitting proposals focused on the essential integration of the club as a facility in the 'new urban fabric – to be'. One example is the commission the club, along with their main sponsor, has given to NL Architects for several sketch designs in which the club can continue to play at their own location, on the overpass spanning the A10 motorway.

This same thinking led the club to agree to host an artist as part of a project of the Virtual Museum Zuidas. I was inducted into the ranks as part of their strategy. And they were open and honest about that.

It quickly became clear to me that I found myself at a focal point of 'urban history in the making'... which I would not be done with in six months.

A question of endurance:
(from a report text, 2005)

In my short film *Tijdens de vooruitgang schijnt de zon* (2004), made for the Free Spaces of the Virtual Museum Zuidas, I formulate a question: How is the evolution of the city of the twenty-first century being put into effect and who has the wherewithal to influence these processes? And I announce my intention to follow the club for at least two years and adopt their dance as a sight to track this future development of urban history.

. . .

In working with architects and urban designers, I have learned that in urban development processes such as these, entirely different chronologies apply. In comparison, the development time of art projects, even those for public space, is extremely short-winded. The chronologies may be slow, but hundreds of details change every day, as does the social dynamic, which I want to track closely. Since I live 10 minutes by bike from the Zuidas, I want to seize the opportunity to operate ad hoc: to be discreetly present with

Renée Kool

the minimum logistics necessary to produce high-quality shots.

With the ambition, and the question of whether a process of such magnitude can be recorded in its 'everydayness'. And with as an expected by-product a form different from documentary film. My 'toolbox' remains of course differently oriented from that of a documentary maker. The label 'documentary' is meaningful, however: it now serves as a pass key that makes possible contacts and exchanges that were previously difficult to come by . . .

I presented my proposal to the club to stay on board, and I still am

Gradually we have found and formed my role at the club together.

Visibly, for most club members, I have documented parties and events. Within a smaller circle I have been increasingly involved in the strategy and representation of the club.

I have produced a booklet about the club's identity, outlining its history, its demographics and its ideals, as well as the value and the importance of the club facilities for physical education classes, other school activities and after-school activities in their metropolitan region.

With my sparring partner at SC Buitenveldert, Tjarda Gerlof, I have also developed several pictorial narratives for club presentations to the authorities and other decision makers involved in the planning of the Zuidas.

In part I have become the chronicler of celebrations and special events: I have recorded the Saint Nicolas festivities and the annual girls' football day. Or, very aptly, I have filmed the annual Zuidas Tournament, in which the football teams of the organizations and businesses involved in the Zuidas development face one another on the turf. One year at host SC Buitenveldert and the other year at competitor AFC, the other football club in the Zuidas. But I have also produced the commemorative book for Mr Henk Voskuilen's 25 years as club chairman.

Over time I have thus compiled a pictorial archive (in photos and video) of life at the club as well as of the daily changes in the Zuidas landscape that surrounds it.

Another angle:

Because I am in residence with one of the stake-holders, I have a different perspective; I can look at the development process of the Zuidas from another position. To put it in organizational terms, the football club works from the bottom up (and working with or from within the football club is from the bottom up). The other possible positions of the designer (for the sake of the argument I count myself as one as well) are from the top down, or alternatively that of the cultural critic or the (cultural) critical commentator. I am not comfortable in either position! In the end, of my own volition, without commission (and without pay) I decided to stick with the club. In football association terms I have become – for this project – a volunteer.

The future is not what it used to be either!

'What is this place,' Turner asked the cabby, leaning forward to thumb the SPEAK button beside the steel speaker grid, 'the address we gave you?'

There was a crackle of static. 'Hypermart. Not much open there this time of night. Looking for anything in particular?' 'No,' Turner said. He didn't know the place. He tried to remember that stretch of Madison, Residential, mostly. Uncounted living spaces carved out of the shells of commercial buildings that dated from a day when commerce had required clerical workers to be present physically at a central location.

Some of the buildings were tall enough to pene-trate a dome.

'Where are we going?' Angie asked, her hand on his arm. 'It's okay,' he said.

'Don't worry.' 'God,' she said, leaning against his shoulder, looking up at the pink neon HYPERMART sign that slashed the granite face of the old building, 'I used to dream about New York, back on the mesa. I had a graphics program that would take me through all the streets, into museums and things. I wanted to come here more than anything in the world.' 'Well, you made it. You're here.'...

From *Count Zero* (1986)
Author: William Gibson

Gibson describes a view of the future I subscribe to in part, although I only became aware of this when I recently came across the above quotation again. Considering the current level of information and communication technology, you would expect that the new urbanity being proclaimed, or at any rate its business/commercial component, would be able to adopt different architectural forms.

What intrigues me is that the edifices being built at the Zuidas up to now seem to differ so little from the edifices of the modern city. The dimensions and the scale of the business build-ings, including their pedestals still easily satisfy

the iconography of Modernism ... although...
There are also edifices that you might more
readily described as Nouveau Corporate
Kitsch.

I thought of this label when I was making a
tour of the United States with fellow artist Erik
Weeda. A visit to Atlanta had long been high
on my wish list, because it is one of the few
American and perhaps Western cities with a
large black middle class. I was curious to see
whether this fairly unique demographic feature
had an impact on how its urbanity had
evolved.

From highways and turnpikes we saw the
skylines of many cities rise up and vanish
behind us. Most displayed a more or less identical composition: clusters of new, not so new
(and 'old') high-rises, skyscrapers, large-scale
industrial edifices, residential complexes and,
last but not least, shopping and entertainment
malls, the new typology of which seems to
consist of large, blank (light comes from
above!), linked boxes of dark-brown ceramic
blocks with verdigris tapered gabled roofs.

Atlanta was different: We drove toward a
skyline that was booming. Mega-sized projects
were under construction in various locations.
The majority of the existing buildings had been
built in roughly the last 10 years. Huge office
buildings and other structures. What stood out,
however, was that these high-rise complexes,

without exception, featured 'classical' ornamentation, glittering in the sunlight.

On closer examination the buildings turned out to be fusions of different architectural periods, styles and concepts. I realised that this blending of visual idioms, in every instance, was intended to suppress the image of 'the office building' and evoke the image of the 'prestigious edifice', of the 'headquarters' and of 'landmark architecture', as a sign of corporate success and to be broadcast as a brand.

Much of the information being disseminated about the development of the Zuidas – take for instance the public information published by the Zuidas Project Bureau – focuses on what is being constructed on as well as under the ground to accommodate this city centre of the future.

Large billboards show artist's impressions featuring cross-sections of underground strata containing great conduits, tunnel systems almost, in which all basic utilities are housed: high-voltage wires, fibre-optics and every other technological hardware imaginable, to facilitate high-speed data transfer, for instance. In other words, this new city is indeed being built, but we can't see it! See, THAT is what interests me.

I want to know WHAT it is we can't see… and then I wonder whether there really are things

Renée Kool

we can't see... perhaps we can't identify their forms yet... could this be an instance of steam-punk aesthetics?* Or perhaps of a horseless-carriage problem ... or...

*see en.wikipedia.org/wiki/Steampunk

Count Zero is a science fiction novel written by William Gibson, originally published in 1986. It is the middle volume of the Sprawl trilogy, which includes *Neuromancer*, *Count Zero* and *Mona Lisa Overdrive* and is a prime example of the cyberpunk sub-genre: en.wikipedia.org/wiki/Count_Zero 17.09.07

352

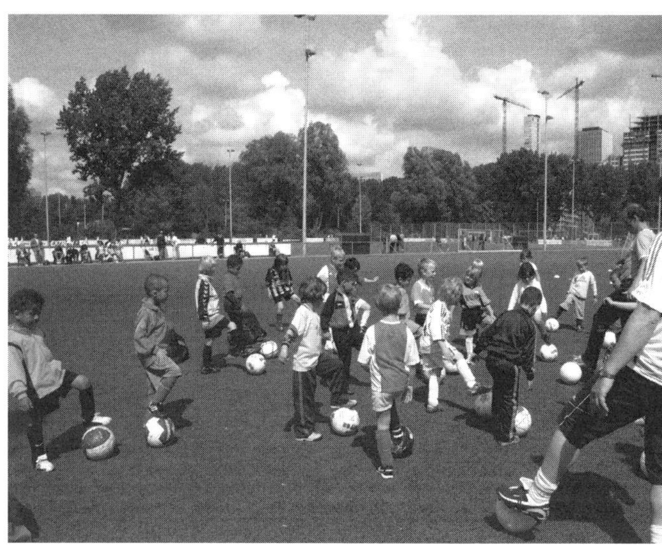

The new city as poster fence

– on the proclaimed new urbanity and the new urbanite

(from a lecture for the Studium Generale programme 'Het verlangen naar de werkelijkheid' ('Yearning for reality') at the AKV/St. Joost, Avans Hogeschool, 's-Hertogenbosch, February 2006)

. . .

When we direct our gaze toward the representations of the future, the new urbanity in the public space in the Zuidas, what do we 'read'? What do these visual and textual scenarios of the future tell us?

What do these images and texts, generated by businesses, authorities and other stakeholders, say about their perceptions of this future city? Or how can we explain the simple fact that the billboard advertisements in this part of the city are clearly aimed at a particular audience – often an audience in transit, no less.

. . .

I am also interested in the demographic forecasts, perhaps rather the demographic fantasies expressed by these images.

And I insist in posing the obvious question: Why does the proverbial 'other' remain underrepresented in these images – non-white people, the elderly, children, the disabled, for instance? Bringing this up may seem a gratuitous exercise in political correctness, but believe me, it must be done.

...

On the many billboards, temporary poster façades and other advertising constructions, you mostly see lots of good-looking – not extremely beautiful, mind you, but realistically attractive – professional women between about 28 and 38 years of age. White, focused... well, you can fill in the rest. A remarkably high number of multi-racial feminine beauties, too.

What concerns me as an artist/researcher, as the resident of a football club, and what I also try to portray in my work, is the complexity, the juxtaposition and interaction of different worlds and 'worldviews' – within a single area. On the one hand there seems to be a world ruled by an enormous faith in technology, by self-evident mobility and in continuous connectivity > technophile, hardware- and progress-oriented. In this worldview, it is more or less assumed that this 'technology' naturally generates interpersonal communication. On the other hand, there seems to exist a day-to-day life of people who have not explicitly chosen one another but have nonetheless decided to band together – after all they are playing a team sport – and that form a community, sometimes in spite of themselves. In which it is precisely the dynamic that is of paramount importance, in which details count in communication and in which you must repeatedly 're-attune' yourself to the other.

I'M NOT HERE TO BRING ANYTHING, I'M HERE TO PICK UP SOMETHING
prelude to a research project

The relationship between art and the Zuidas is a difficult one.

In the recent past, statements have been made, declarations of intent have even been issued about the active contributions of artists to the development process of the Zuidas district (see the Vision for the Virtual Museum Zuidas).

Perhaps this is the origin of the yearning, the expectation or the faith I detect in the attitude of my art-professional conversation partners when we happen to talk about my residency at the Zuidas.

Have I found 'something' yet, have I figured it out? Have I discovered a way or a form to cope with this complex problem?

What I am going to bring, what can I contribute to the Zuidas with my artist's alchemy? What am I going to DO?

After a long period of time, I have decided that I am not going to bring anything; instead I am there to pick up something… and that I am going to turn this – which has not yet been specified – into the focus of my investigation for the Research Group.

As time has gone by I have come to realize that 'the Zuidas project' is a research subject par excellence, particularly at this moment in my practice and my career.

The complexity of the project: the simultaneity of countless processes coming under equally countless domains, disciplines and interests. The very scale and chronology of the Zuidas project make it an optimally multi-faceted and effective research subject for me as an 'author'. Not to investigate it as a whole, but to scrutinize elements that, however divergent, nonetheless relate to a single greater subject area.

For some time, I have been looking for ways to form an art practice situated more between a design practice and a scientific practice in terms of research and authorship.

This is not, incidentally, a 'manifesto-like' attempt to redefine what it means to be an artist today. It can best be described as a process of emancipation of my identity as an artist. I may call myself a visual artist, but because of my personal qualities and shortcomings, accumulation of knowledge, hang-ups and fascinations, my range of action has long extended beyond the domain of visual art. Even more significantly, the audiences I address are often not specifically art-oriented.

The results of my works, research projects, therefore require a different 'dramaturgical approach' as well… At the same time, for me, this research project is a search for sparring partners and a search for conceptual and work models.

The assumptions and presuppositions upon which the processes of the Zuidas development are based, the adjustments to these, etc. – THAT is what it's about for me.

I admit it: I want to have my cake and eat it too…

Post-script

At the end of the construction of the textual structure for this volume, I realize that I actually just keep coming back to the notion of 'new' (or 'the new'): the new city centre, the new urbanity, the new urbanite, a new concept of art, a new approach to art and public space . . . een nieuwe lente, een nieuw geluid…[1]

It's not so much the urge to demonstrate that what is called 'new' is not new… that the designated methods, concepts or approaches have been used before. Nor do I seek to unmask or dethrone the proclaimed new urbanity in all its potential aspects, or qualities. Nor do I want to reveal the 'true' face or the genuine provenance of this sloganeering as, for instance, the product of integrated communication strategies and neo-liberal power plays among various stake-holders.

I am far more preoccupied by what 'the new', the different might be… might become. What are the strategies and concepts to develop substantive new forms and conditions of urbanity, that deliver substantive surplus value? Why else, after all, would you bother?

What elements are part of the witch's brew that is being cooked up into urbanity anyway – and must therefore be part of this proclaimed new urbanity in every case? An urbanity and an urban area that resist demographic, cultural, economic and functional monotony and monomania. An urban area – a New City Centre – that operates in a truly metropolitan way. Including neighbourhoods where 'like knows like' still applies, as well as major transit zones for people, goods and information. With a turntable function for the Randstad Metro-politan Region as well as for international travel. A public domain in which all permanent and temporary residents and users must relate to that which is other than themselves, with all the positive and negative aspects this entails.

Etonnée de se retrouver ensemble

1. ... a new spring, a new sound... (from the poem Mei (May) by Herman Gorter)

With thanks to Tjarda Gerlof, initially my contact and later my sparring partner at SC Buitenveldert and to my colleague Karin Arink, for her always critical yet perceptive feedback on my texts.
And last but not least with many thanks to my young colleague Pieter Wackers who has been assisting me on countless filming sessions at the football club, and who has become a member of SC Buitenveldert along the way!

359

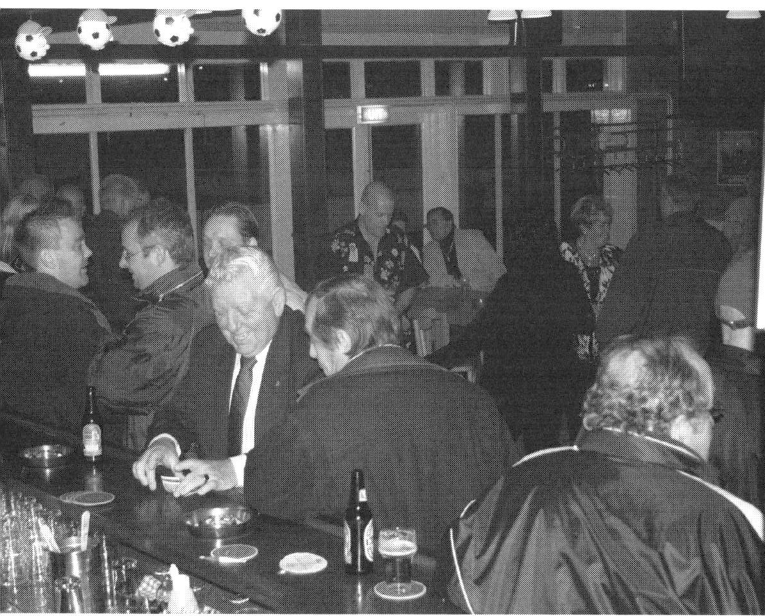

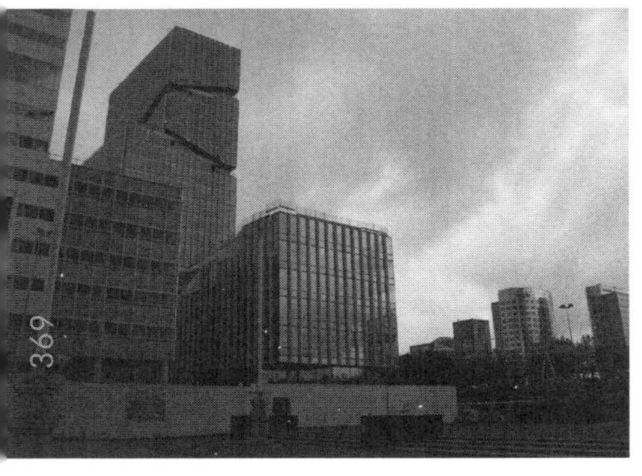
369

Jeroen Boomgaard

Radical Autonomy
Art in the Era of Process

At first sight, art seems to be doing quite well for itself, particularly outside its traditional spheres of action. There are plenty of commissions for work in the public domain and for the enhancement of new buildings, and artists regularly play a part in landscape and urban redevelopment projects. This erosion of boundaries between art, architecture and design seems like the accomplishment of a long-standing dream. Many avant-garde ideals are fulfilled in the progressive integration of art with society. But this goes along with new obligations and duties, and these tend to be projected almost blindly onto the whole field of the visual arts. The reduced autonomy of the artist in the field of publicly commissioned art results in problematizing the autonomy of art in general. Autonomous art is out of favour, and with it the widely held view that art, if quite important, is on the whole a dispensable frill.[1] This idea of mandatory inutility is an outworn idea. Art is now supposed to serve a purpose, to achieve an effect, to 'do something', much more than in the past.

A salient illustration of the new tendency is the demand for interactive art. Visual art that explicitly seeks interaction exists in many kinds and on many scales. They range from works of art that raise their roguish caps on command like pathetic circus chimps, to substantial projects that elicit public participation in various forms and at multiple levels. A much-favoured medium is currently the website, embodying as it does the ideal of endless and unbridled interactivity. What these forms of expression have in common is the intention to elicit an active interchange between the work of art or the artist on the one hand, and the spectator, target group or general public on the other. The work of art is no longer permitted simply to exist and be viewed or experienced; it demands a reaction and reacts in its own right. The significance of the work is placed more than ever within the spectator's sphere of responsibility. Without his presence or participation, there would seem to be no point in the work's existence.

Interactivity is nothing new. Twentieth-century avant-gardes, particularly those of the nineteen-twenties and of the sixties and seventies, sought to achieve direct contact with the spectator as a way of overcoming the existing boundaries of art. It was a form of interactivity that required patience on the part of the viewer, who often seemed more like a victim of the artist's imaginative whims than a participant with something of his own to contribute. A good illustration of this passive kind of interactivity is provided by Tinguely's mechanical objects. These typically consist of a big red button connected to a monstrous machine which flails wildly and makes a terrifying din. The public in this case serves as no more than an agent to activate the mechanism which then proceeds entirely in accordance with its own built-in logic. The work celebrates interactivity while at the same time taking it to the absurd. Yet more complex forms of interaction, such the Happening, similarly roped the spectator into their own artistic scenario, rather than attempting to scan the wavelength of the audience. In the sixties and seventies, autonomy was more important than interaction.

The Equivocality of Autonomy

That rather half-hearted interactivity illustrates the ambiguity of the avant-gardes of those years. The autonomous status of art was upheld, although the goal was the transgression of both artistic and social frontiers. But this duality is inherent to autonomy itself. The belief in artistic independence arose in a period when it was seen as art's constant duty to draw attention to the prevailing shortcomings, to proclaim truth and beauty in a world that did not want to hear. Surrounded by a dishonest, unjust society, art stood for the Utopia of universal and total communication, although without being understood by more

Jeroen Boomgaard

than a handful of insiders.[2] Art bore a heavy burden – or pretended to – and paid the price with poverty and isolation. Although the contemporary critique of autonomy might lead us to think otherwise, autonomy did not mean that art was supposed not to be about anything, or that its only subject matter could be the artist's own inner life. Autonomy meant above all that visual art tried to unify its form and content in such a way that it could no longer be treated as a handy means for illustrating a moral or a story. Autonomous art does not withdraw from the world but tries to comprehend it by artistic means. The communicative or even democratic ideal implicit in this aim is the notion that art's visual language not only touches on the essence of life, but is, precisely for that reason, universally understandable. However, since its reach and the comprehension it received fell short of expectations, the impression arose that art existed solely for art's sake. Autonomy changed from being the promise that art held out into the proof of its unwillingness or incapacity to fulfil that promise.

Autonomy was, and still is, seen by many artists as a self-imposed destiny, but like most things in life it is more a matter of fate than of free will. In bourgeois and generally democratic societies, art, as explained, fulfils the role of a conscience and a contemplative response, of a representative of those higher things which risk getting lost in an existence gauged to functionality. That role is the function of art, and the independence to which art lays claim is an essential component of Western society's self-legitimization. The bourgeois society can see itself in art's mirror as good and caring, because it fosters a highly appreciated area within itself (even while not spending a penny on it) where higher values are professed and where dependency on the market does not hold its normal sway. By placing an emphasis on individual choice, however, this ideology simultaneously underwrites the basic principle of market forces. This double illusion, of the freedom of the individual and of unimpeded universal communication, was the point on which the avant-gardes concentrated their attack. But because personal, autonomous freedom of choice remained uppermost for many artists, the duality was perpetuated and the avant-gardist output could still be unproblematically absorbed by the market. This tractable compliance meant, however, that the autonomous position of art still played an important ideological role.

Happiness – Right Now

Patience with autonomy seems to have run out. Autonomy has become a reproach and is considered one of the foremost reasons for art not functioning properly. Some people have placed it on a line with incomprehensibility, egocentricity and navel-gazing. Art is now called upon to make good its communicative pretensions, to fulfil its promise immediately and to cease hiding in a domain where it responds and is responsible only to itself. It must give up its aloofness and show genuine commitment in the form of reaction and inter-action. Art, in other words, must play along.[3] This new brief would at first sight seem to liberate art from the ideological shackles the bourgeois society has held it captive in. Art is no longer expected to proclaim higher values or hold out the promise of future happiness, but to pursue direct involvement in the realiza-tion of a better world here and now. The ideal of the avant-gardes of the past has at last some prospect of success, in a way that over-shadows the achievements of those avant-gardes.

It is not immediately clear where this aver-sion to autonomy and explicit desire for inter-action come from, or what their further impli-cations are. One could after all argue that, as a symbolic system, art is always interactive, that it always communicates.[4] And precisely because art's role is not an entirely self-chosen one and because it has a clear relevance to society, there is an existing framework within which it can be interpreted and it can enter into a dialogue with us. When we come across a work of art, we do not know exactly what to expect of it, but we do realize that it is something that demands a special effort of attention. The act of interpretation is part of the work itself, which is even changed as a result, for our interpretation is passed on within the institution of art quite independently of anything the artist wanted or intended. The rejection of this form of interaction and the demand for a more emphatic way of reacting implies that the symbolic meaning that art clearly used to have is no longer understood or no longer recognized. This gives rise to ironic situations, for example that the desire for art which proffers clearly unifying symbols proves the decline of art's symbolic value; or that this expectation hence fits seamlessly into the tendency discussed here to require art to have a definite repercussion or effect.

The confusion there has been about the nature of the new symbols art is required to provide, typifies the vagueness surrounding the desired interactivity. Despite a requirement of relevance, art still stands for the unconventional, the unexpected, the indefinable and the creative; in short, for everything we do not presume to encounter in everyday life. But the purpose is no longer an acute analysis of today's deficiencies or the promise of happiness in a future world. The deficiency must be compensated, and the promise must be fulfilled immediately. A wholly improved world is no longer the objective: a small contribution to local satisfaction is sufficient. But the modesty of the expectation should not be allowed to obscure the arduous character of the task. The dualism which art so long suffered and which it formerly tried to justify to itself in the form of autonomy, is, especially now that autonomy is no longer available as a buffer, more than ever a hallmark of art. The artist is required to provide originality and surprise, something that is not on the programme; but it must still meet our expectations, take account of our wishes and be grist to the mill of today's amusement economy – without appealing to autonomy or serving an agenda of its own. This has not made the artist's task any easier.

Two Birds with One Stone

The impact of the changed job description for art is conspicuous – not only in the upsurge of socially-involved, well-meaning projects 'for the people', but at a more fundamental level, in its relation to time. Scarcely any work is still made in which the temporal dimension does not play some part or other. If the work does not simply move, then something inevitably grows or rots away; and if the spectator is not required to sit through it he must at least play along with it. Time, in the sense of a shared moment, is included in art's brief as an opportunity to connect with the public. Shared time is less permissive than a shared place. By engaging with the spectator for a little while, the work of art declares its solidarity: it can no longer be indifferent to the presence of the Other. The preference for a shared moment rather than a shared place not only enables art to offer its public an altered temporal experience, but subjects art to a regime of movement and change – a regime that may be considered revealing about our society.[5]

The crucial political trend of recent decades is the government's systematic withdrawal from the guiding and shaping of society. This has not only resulted in a new social model but in an entirely different dynamic. The discipline of process management which has laid claim to the relinquished territory places advancement of the process before all else. Principles and points of departure are seen as barriers to progress, and specific interests are the only thing that counts. The old participation model seems to have been radicalized, in the sense that everyone is now able to become involved. There is no longer a clear central authority which sets itself up as the mouthpiece and custodian of the public interest; rather, there is a non-centrally governed process in which each player is free to stand up for his own rights. This ostensible consummation of democracy has side effects that achieve the exact opposite of what the model suggests. All

Jeroen Boomgaard

the disparate interests are taken into account, but the linchpin on which the process turns is The Market. That linchpin is primary in controlling the continuing motion but is itself never at issue; it is the obscure point whose influence prevails at all levels but which never comes up for discussion as an interest to be defended. The consequence of this implicit dynamic is that the process tends to steer in the direction of those parties with the greatest market share; but, since everyone is implicated, the result may be portrayed as a natural outcome.[6]

The government's role nowadays seems reduced to the launching of absurd, impractical, electorate-serving efforts at palliating the symptoms, while major infrastructural decisions are left almost entirely at the mercy of market forces.[7] But that is not the whole truth: the government also explicitly concerns itself with the progression and legitimization of the model. The demand, backed by subsidies, for interactive and often participatory art projects is a consequence of official concern about malfunctioning of the process model. Not participating in society has become more than ever a social sin. Here, too, it is not so much the outcome of taking part that matters as the participation itself; and reaction or interaction is considered proof of participation. By officially declaring everyone to be a participant and by condemning or even punishing nonparticipation in the name of public interest, the government manages to mask its abandonment of that public interest. Involving artists in this undertaking kills two birds with one stone. They are able to breathe new life into the exhausted participation models, and at the same time artists are stripped of their role as official outsiders and hence of their symbolic payload that once held out the promise of a better world.

It all seems so neat: art with a function, and artists included in the planning process. But this development robs art of much of its dissident potential. In the best case it may introduce an artistic dimension, although art will be the first to fall by the wayside in the drive towards the completion and budgetary discipline of the project under which it falls.[8] In the worst case, art will form part of the end result, and will rightly be condemned for trading in the promise of a better world for a pragmatism that accepts the misery as the natural state of affairs.

Radical Autonomy

The requirement of effect and the impatience with autonomy may be seen as symptoms of the decline of a traditional bourgeois society. Not much can be done about it, nor is it something we would wish to go back to. That does not mean that we must unthinkingly

Jeroen Boomgaard

embrace all the phenomena that go along with this change. In a society that seems to have abandoned most of its values in favor of untrammelled market action, returning to artistic autonomy could have its merits. Especially now that the ideological implications of autonomy are fading, revival could bring its inherent contribution into play. The role imposed on art by the bourgeois ideology was, after all, more than a product of that society. Defining autonomy as the mere legitimization of a defective system would not only strip works of art of some of their critical potential, but would eliminate any prospect of changing the system from within. Autonomy allowed art to make the idea of a different and possibly better society seem credible. It also became possible for the avant-gardes to test the limits of that autonomy, and hence of the dominant system, by putting interactivity and direct involvement on the agenda.

The special position art once claimed is nowadays translated into the requirement for the amenable alternative. The indefinable and the unconventional, the surprising and the tongue-in-cheek, and even the critical and the subversive are all usable, because they do not stand in the way of the fundamental law of movement and progress. Indeed, the artistic alternative may succeed in furnishing the current state of affairs with a conscience, or in making it seem more light-hearted, without actually changing anything about it. Society proclaims its tolerance by allowing even the most dissonant expressions to thrive. The participation of the artist who has relinquished his autonomous position shifts the spotlight onto process management as a natural, unassailable process. In this situation art loses its visibility and its legitimacy. The huge artificial structures that define social life are not only capable of incorporating or even rewarding any form of rejection, but they leave no room for art, which is simply no match for the experience of economy's lavish excesses of artificiality.[9] All art can do is counter these with something which is not born of our longings or which is not explicitly calculated to satisfy our wishes. When interactivity threatens to become obligatory, autonomy becomes useful again for probing the limits of the system. Only an autonomous work that relates to its context, but which chooses its own time and place within that context, is capable of leaving the world of artificiality and of revealing something that lies beyond the limits of our expectations.

Opting for autonomy may have another benefit. The requirement of effect and interaction which is placed on art conceals the facts that the effectiveness of process management primarily benefits the market, and that interaction with all the individual interests is little more than a diversionary tactic. The public interest that it claims to serve is nothing but shameless self-interest and a case of the right of the strongest prevailing. An autonomous work of art can, in this context, not only succeed in unmasking self-interest as the dominant principle, but can impart new authority to the symbolic freedom that was formerly the hallmark of autonomy. Because the artist chooses of his own free will to create an entirely personal world, he shows that it is possible to choose radically. And because he places that out of self-interest-created world in the real world as a symbol of the possible, he succeeds in charging the idea of public interest with new energy.[10] The power of that gesture lies in its real presence. Even if the work is ephemeral, even if it is little more than the brief pleasure of a shared meal, it differs fundamentally from the world of self-indulgence we create for ourselves because it adds something new. The work of art produces presence instead of consuming it.

Interactivity, process art, social involvement: all these things are possible. They only become truly effective, however, when they depend not on the calculated effect of process management but on a radicalized autonomy. The autonomous work of art meets the demand for the abnormal, for the different, which is capable of feeding the imagination once more while doing so in a way that contradicts expectations. Radical autonomy can play along with every process; the place, the public and the discourse are all factors that can be a part of it. But the radically autonomous work of art will always add something which transgresses the borders of the context and adds a value that cannot simply be classified as a pragmatic benefit. The artist's symbolic act can consequently propagate the idea of freedom even more strongly than it could in the days when autonomy was still the hallmark of art – if only because that autonomy no longer has an ideological background. The autonomous action of the artist depicts the world as we do not yet know it. Interaction can only follow panting in its footsteps.

Jeroen Boomgaard

Notes

1. An idea recently expressed once more by the departing head of the Council for Culture, Winnie Sorgdrager, in *de Volkskrant*, 29-12-2005.

2. Yves Michaud uses the term 'communicative Utopia' in connection with the history of autonomy in: 'Het einde van kunstutopie', *Yang*, volume 39, no. 3 (Ghent, November 2003), pp. 259-381. Other primary texts on artistic autonomy and the attempts of the avant-garde to break away from it are Martin Damus, *Funktionen der Bildenden Kunst im Spätkapitalismus* (Frankfurt am Main: Fischer, 1973); Peter Bürger, *Theorie der Avantgarde* (Frankfurt am Main: Suhrkamp, 1974); Hal Foster, *The Return of the Real: Art and Theory at the End of the Century* (Cambridge, Mass./London: The MIT Press, 1996).

3. There are far too many instances to name. Suffice it to note the appeal rising from the publication Rutger Wolfson (ed.), *Nieuwe symbolen voor Nederland* (Amsterdam: Valiz, 2005).

4. I am not concerned here with claiming, in analogy with Bourriaud, a certain capacity for art. It is rather a fundamental aspect of symbolic systems, of which art, like language, is one. That the interpretation is sometimes extremely limited, understood by few, and possibly serves as a distinguishing feature in Bourdieu's sense, is another matter altogether.

5. See for instance 'Kunstenplan Openbare Ruimte Tilburg 2002-2010' (Tilburg Plan for Arts in the Public Domain), published under the title *Kort* (Tilburg, 2001).

6. See also BAVO (Gideon Boie and Matthias Pauwels), *De metropool of je leven!* (The Metropolis or Your Life!), private publication, undated.

7. At the time of writing, the Dutch Minister for Integration and Immigration Rita Verdonk had just uttered the ridiculous proposal to make the Dutch language mandatory in the streets of the Netherlands. Presumably this idea will be long forgotten by publication time, but it is nonetheless typical of the present government.
8. This aspect comes out clearly in a dialogue among several leading players in the public-private collaborations. See Jaap Huisman, 'Kansen en risico's zijn getrouwd met elkaar', *Smaak*, vol. 5, no. 24 (December 2005), pp. 6-11. It appears from this article that artistic (or 'soft', as the article calls them) values have little prospect of survival in collaborations of this kind.
9. See also Peter Sloterdijk, *Sphären III. Schäume* (Frankfurt am Main: Suhrkamp, 2004), pp. 812-813.
10. A good example of this is presented by the work of Thomas Hirschhorn, who rejects the notion of interactivity and instead emphasizes activity. His work never complies with external expectations or wishes. On this, see Claire Bishop, 'Antagonism and Relational Aesthetics', *October* 110 (Fall 2004), pp. 51-80.

This article was first published in: *Open* no. 10, *(In)tolerance* (Amsterdam/Rotterdam: SKOR/NAi Publishers, 2006) pp. 30-38.

BAVO
is an independent research collective focused on the political dimension of art, architecture and planning founded by architect-philosophers Gideon Boie and Matthias Pauwels.

Jeroen Boomgaard
has been teaching art history of the modern era at the Universiteit van Amsterdam since 1983. He has been Professor for Art and Public Space at the Gerrit Rietveld Academie in Amsterdam since January 2003, and holds a position in the Faculty of Building and Architecture at Eindhoven University of Technology.

Gerard Drosterij
is a political scientist and is currently finishing his thesis (Politics as Juris-diction), which centers on the public/private distinction in political theory. He is co-editor (with Toine Ooms and Ken Vos) of *Intruders: Reflections on Art and the Ethnological Museum* (Zwolle: Waanders, 2004).

Katja Gretzinger (Logo Parc)
is a graphic designer, based in Zürich and Berlin.

Renée Kool
is or has been affiliated with a number of academic programmes for art and design in the Netherlands and in France. Since September 2005, she has been teaching Film & Media Literacy as part of the CMD (Communi-cation & Multimedia Design) programme at the Academy for ICT and Media in Breda. Her work is regularly exhibited in museums and other art institutions in the Netherlands and abroad.

Matthijs van Leeuwen (Logo Parc)
is a graphic designer based in Arnhem.

Stan Majoor
works at the Amsterdam Institute for Metropolitan and International Devel-opment Studies of the Universiteit van Amsterdam. Currently he is a visiting assistant professor at the Centre of Urban Planning and Environ-mental Management – CUPEM, University of Hong Kong.

Quintus Masius
teaches Law Theory and Alternative Dispute Resolution at the Universiteit van Amsterdam. He's also a design student at the Gerrit Rietveld Academie and is furthermore working on a master thesis for Philosophy.

Chantal Mouffe
is Professor of Political Theory at the Centre for the Study of Democracy at the University of Westminster in London.

Contributors

Orgacom

consists of Teike Asselbergs and Elias Tieleman, who are graduate artists (Gerrit Rietveld Academie and Sandberg Institute, Amsterdam). They have been working together on their initiative Orgacom (www.orgacom.nl) since 1997. Orgacom focusses on visualizing the culture inside organizations.

Matteo Poli (Logo Parc)

is an architect in Milan.

Jelle Post

studied architecture at the Delft University of Technology. He has developed virtual environments for (day)light research and simulation, virtual sets and animations for feature films, commercials and exhibitions.

Anette Tibud

graduated in graphic design from the Gerrit Rietveld Academie in 2007. The design concept and layout of this book is her graduation project. The map-like structure that forms the basis of the layout is related to urban design – a city on paper that becomes a city of itself again.

Roemer van Toorn

is an architect, culture critic, photographer, curator and teacher of architecture theory. As Professor, he runs and coordinates the Projective Theory Programme at the Berlage Institute, and he is a staff member of the Delft School of Design (DSD) at Delft University of Technology, while at the same time pursuing a career as an international lecturer.

Paul Toornend

studied architecture at Delft University of Technology. Since 1993 he has worked under the moniker IR. PRJ TOORNEND on various projects in the field of architecture and urbanism.

Daniel van der Velden

is a graphic designer based in Amsterdam. He is a partner in the design research think tank Metahaven, based in Amsterdam and Brussels, that focuses on the role of the political in visual identity. His work deals with research informing design practice, especially when creating logos, icons, symbols and maps. Daniel van der Velden is currently an advising researcher at the Jan van Eyck Academie in Maastricht, where he headed the Logo Parc research project. He is also a tutor at the Sandberg Institute in Amsterdam and a critic in graphic design at Yale University, New Haven.

Barbara Visser

is a visual artist. She works with a diversity of media, such as photography, film, video, text, printed matter and performance. In her work she analyzes the authenticity and ambiguity of the image as well as the view of the spectator.

Henk de Vroom

is a visual artist who has worked as an adviser in the field of visual art in public space since 1987. In his capacity as consultant to the IJ-As project group (Werkverband Kunst IJ-as), he has organized art projects, for example in the Amsterdam eastern dock area, and is currently member of the programme board (Art and Public Space) for the Virtual Museum Zuidas. Henk de Vroom also works for the Research Group Art and Public Space of the Gerrit Rietveld Academie as coordinator of education projects.

Gon Zifroni (Logo Parc)

is a spatial designer, based in Brussels.

Joost Zonneveld

is an anthropologist and an independent journalist and researcher. The built environment and urban renewal projects are major themes in his publications.

Colophon

Editor: Jeroen Boomgaard, Professor of Art and Public Space / Gerrit Rietveld Academie
Contributors: BAVO, Jeroen Boomgaard, Gerard Drosterij, Renée Kool, Stan Majoor, Chantal Mouffe, Orgacom/Quintus Masius, Roemer van Toorn, Paul Toornend/Jelle Post, Daniel van der Velden, Barbara Visser, Henk de Vroom, Joost Zonneveld
Graphic design: Anette Tibud, Amsterdam
Copy editing: Pierre Bouvier, Marieke van Giersbergen, Lynne and Paul Richards
Translation Dutch-English: Pierre Bouvier, Amsterdam (texts by BAVO, Jeroen Boomgaard 'Highrise *and* Common Ground', Renée Kool, Orgacom, Barbara Visser, Henk de Vroom, Joost Zonneveld)
Production: Alexandra Landré, Astrid Vorstermans
Paper folded cover: hvo offset 70 grams
Paper inside: hvo offset 100 grams
Typeface: Futura
Printing: Krips, Meppel
Publisher: Valiz Publishers, Amsterdam
with Research Group Art and Public Space / Gerrit Rietveld Academie

www.valiz.nl
www.lkpr.nl
www.gerritrietveldacademie.nl

This publication was made possible by the generous support of:
Universiteit van Amsterdam www.uva.nl
SKOR www.skor.nl
Virtueel Museum Zuidas www.virtueel-museum.nl

Photography / Images

Deror Avi, p. 328 (bottom); Leonardo Bezzola, p. 326; Bik
Van der Pol, p. 313; Casa Editrice Lozzi Roma, p. 332;
CIIID, pp. 319, 320; Forum Barcelona, pp. 68, 75, 81;
Andrea Friedli, p. 302; Renée Kool, pp. 6, 10, 28, 50, 64,
92, 134, 158, 182, 200, 218, 256, 300, 334, 336, 352,
359, 360; Logoparc, pp. 267-281; 284-287; 290-291;
Stan Majoor, pp. 69, 73, 85, 87; Richard Niessen/TM, pp.
23, 334; Sjoerd van Oevelen, p. 312; Paul Toornend and
Jelle Post, pp. 98-103, 106-111, 114-119, 122-127, 131;
Barbara Visser, pp. 30, 32, 33, 35, 37, 39, 40, 43, 49;
Henk de Vroom, pp. 213, 319, 321, 328 (top).

It was not possible to find all the copyright holders of the
illustrations used. Interested parties are requested to
contact the Research Group Art and Public Space, Gerrit
Rietveld Academie, Amsterdam, www.lkpr.nl

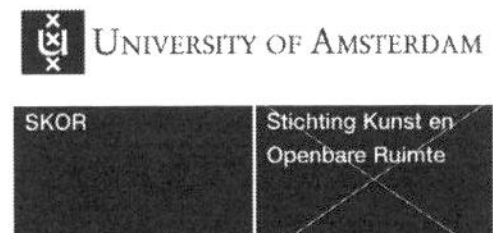

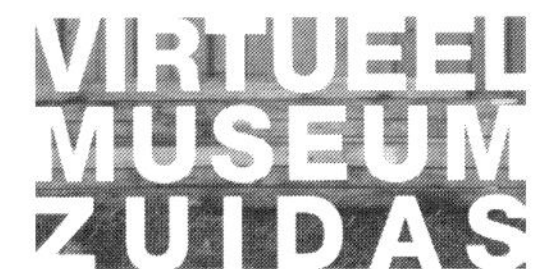

Available in the Netherlands, Belgium and Luxemburg through Centraal Boekhuis, Culemborg; Scholtens, Sittard and Coen Sligting Bookimport, Amsterdam, NL, sligting@xs4all.nl, fax +31-(0)20-6640047
Available in Europe (except Benelux, UK and Ireland), Asia and Australia through Idea Books, Amsterdam, NL, idea@ideabooks.nl, fax +31-20-6209299, www.ideabooks.nl
Available in the United Kingdom and Ireland through Art Data, London, UK, orders@artdata.co.uk, fax +44-208-742 2319, www.artdata.co.uk
Available in the USA: DAP, New York, dap@dapinc.com, fax (+1) 212-6279484, www.artbook.com

NUR 646, 648
ISBN 978-90-78088-18-9

Printed and bound in the Netherlands

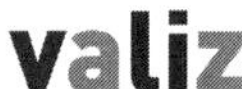

The Amsterdam Zuidas area aims to become a new city centre for Amsterdam, with offices, residential areas and cultural amenities. The development of the Zuidas is defined by these high ambitions, and it is taking place within a 'state of exception'. However, the key issue remains the possible effect and significance for the position of culture and art in the public domain that emerges from this particularity. *Highrise — Common Ground* offers a critical reflection on a variety of issues concerning the relationship between art and the urban development of the Zuidas.
The book features theoretical contemplation as well as unique contributions by artists in an examination of the Zuidas phenomenon. This qualifies *Highrise — Common Ground* as a cultural intervention in its own right.

Research Group Art and Public Space / Gerrit Rietveld Academie

Valiz, Amsterdam

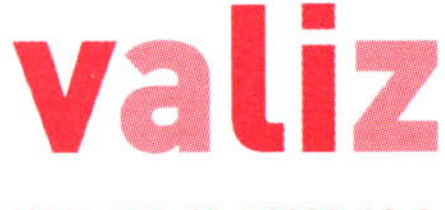

ISBN 978-90-78088-18-9